MadScam

Kick-Ass Advertising Without the Madison Avenue Price Tag

George Parker

EP
Entrepreneur Press

Editorial director: Jere L. Calmes
Cover design: Barry T. Kerrigan
Composition and production: Eliot House Productions

This publication is designed to provide accurate and authoritative information in regard to the subject matter covered. It is sold with the understanding that the publisher is not engaged in rendering legal, accounting, or other professional services. If legal advice or other expert assistance is required, the services of a competent professional person should be sought.

Library of Congress Cataloging-in-Publication Data
Parker, George, 1937–
   MadScam: kick ass advertising without the Madison Avenue price tag/by George Parker.
      p.   cm.
   ISBN 1-59918-042-1 (alk. paper)
   1. Advertising. 2. Small business—Marketing. I. Title.
HF5823.P29 2006
659.1—dc22   2006020656

Printed in Canada

11 10 09 08 07 06   10 9 8 7 6 5 4 3 2 1

Contents

CHAPTER THREE

The communications plan: how it can build your business, straighten out your mind, and drive your competition nuts 35

CHAPTER FOUR

Do I really have to spend an arm and a leg on advertising? Or can I do it on the cheap? 63

CHAPTER FIVE

Where should you spend your advertising budget? So many bad choices, so few places to hide! 81

CHAPTER SIX

Creating print ads the old fashioned, excruciatingly painful, yet strangely rewarding way *97*

CHAPTER SEVEN

Creating TV ads: welcome to the wonderful world of showbiz, excitement, glamour, and acid reflux. *131*

Foreword

In the ruins of ancient Pompeii, archaeologists discovered a Greek character pressed into the now-frozen dust of the city's streets and byways. After much study, they determined that it was a logo embossed on the soles of prostitutes' sandals, so wherever they walked, they left a trail of footsteps that said, "Follow me!" Thus proving, once and for all, that advertising is the world's second oldest profession.

To celebrate this discovery, I am proud to present one of the maddest rants about the depredations, machinations, and general skullduggery of my chosen career ever penned to paper.

Now it may seem somewhat contradictory that a senior executive at a major Madison Avenue advertising agency should be writing the foreword to a book whose primary purpose is to show small- and medium-sized businesses how to avoid using the services of major Madison Avenue advertising agencies.

But my fond hope is that by following George's advice, your business will become very, very large. Perhaps global. Then, in gratitude for all the trouble, pain and lucre George's wise counsel has spared you and your company, you'll give your account to me.

Without a review.

Because while everything George says about the evils of ad agencies is absolutely and incontrovertibly true, my agency is the one exception. On this continent. In this city. (This may not save my job, but it was worth the shot.)

Having worked with George on numerous occasions in our equally checkered careers, I can assure you that what George doesn't know about the insanity and paranoia of this business isn't worth knowing. And he knows something more: how to avoid becoming part of it.

You'll find tales of crooks, fakirs, politicians, bozos, and boozers galore. Stories to raise your hackles and the hair on the back of your neck.

But you'll also learn how to sort the wheat from the chaff. How to cherish and nurture talent when you do find it. And how to blaze your very own trail through the maze of marketing muzz muzz.

Because, above all else, I agree with George's opinion that in the current rush to exploit the ever-expanding choices of new media, there is an increasing tendency amongst those who should know better to give short shrift to the actual content of their communications. Or, to paraphrase on old advertising homily, "Before you can begin selling the sizzle, you have to start off with a steak."

MadScam concentrates on creating the highest quality, top grade, Angus beef, in the belief that if you do, everything else, including the sizzle, will follow.

I couldn't agree more.

—*Steve Hayden, Vice Chairman,*
Global Creative Director, Ogilvy & Mather, Worldwide

Preface

The purpose of this book is to show you how, as the owner or founder of a small- to medium-sized business, you can go about developing and implementing a kick-ass advertising program capable of returning immediate benefits to your bottom line, while building a long-term and highly profitable brand image for your company.

Let's get one thing straight right away. The purpose of this book is not to help you invent "The Next Big Thing," develop a killer business plan, raise venture capital, create a bomb-proof manufacturing schedule, a blockbuster sales strategy, or a corporate identity and logo program to die for. It won't even tell you if your conference room table should be made of baize-covered particleboard or refurbished 18th century ship's timbers. (Of course, the odds are that at this stage of your development you probably don't have a conference room, let alone a table to put in it.) And the best news of all? To do it you don't have to rely on the Armani-suited charlatans of Madison Avenue whose major concern is liposuctioning away your cash.

I have to assume that as an entrepreneur with the ambition and drive to build your own business, you've taken care of all the essential spadework itemized above. If you haven't, it's far too early to be thinking about advertising. But, if you've done all the housekeeping stuff, then this is the only book about advertising you'll ever need (or at least until you grow to become a corporate leviathan such as Procter & Gamble or General Electric). It will show you how you can successfully use advertising to build your business at this crucial stage when a relatively small amount of money, craftily spent, can generate tremendous awareness, goodwill, and most important of all, that Holy Grail of any business—sales.

For over 30 years I've created advertising for many kinds of clients, big and small. Some I've worked with directly. For many others, I've worked in conjunction with their advertising agencies. In every case, the primary aim of what I've done is to communicate to their respective target audiences that the client is someone they should initially buy products and services from and then continue to do business with. And this, if you think about it, is all you can ask your advertising to do. Or as the famous, long-dead ad man, David Ogilvy, so succinctly put it, "Advertising is about selling."

As an entrepreneur (and why else would you be reading a book published by Entrepreneur Press?), you obviously understand the critical importance of making sure your company becomes known and recognized as one offering intrinsically unique products or services to existing and prospective customers. The issue is how you can best do this if you're operating in a start-up mode or scrambling through the first few years of building your business. These are the years when your company resources and funds are stretched to the limit, and your attention is needed for the 101 other things necessary to ensure the success, even the survival, of your venture.

Quite simply, the answer is through a well-thought-out and well-implemented advertising program that you must recognize as a worthwhile investment in your company's future, rather than, as happens far too often, a much begrudged, current expense. Contrary to the innumerable slings and arrows the ad business has suffered over the years, and in spite of the explosive and increasingly confusing growth of new media vehicles and communication tools available to anyone wishing to promote his company, it's still widely accepted that advertising is an effective and, if done smartly, cost-efficient way to achieve customer recognition and appreciation.

Webster's Dictionary defines an entrepreneur as, "One, who organizes, owns, manages and assumes the risks of business." Encarta nails it with, "A risk-taking business person who sets up and finances commercial enterprises in order to make a profit." But if entrepreneurs are in business to make money, why over the years have so many blown boatloads of cash on useless advertising programs?

Could it be that even the smartest amongst us lose all sense of judgment and rationality when they deal with their advertising? Or is it simply, as a great many people suspect, that the advertising business, particularly as practiced by the multi-national goliaths of Madison Avenue, is a giant scam run by a bunch of snake oil merchants and charlatans? Or perhaps, it's simply because the consuming public is acquiring a thick shell of indifference and becoming increasingly less influenced by the ever-growing tsunami of nonstop advertising everyone is exposed to?

Maybe it's because everyone spending money on an advertising program, whether it be small, medium, or the size of the national debt, is faced with the constant dilemma so elegantly expressed by such well-known captains of industry as John Wannamaker, Henry Ford, Genghis Khan, and Adolph Hitler:

I know that 50 percent of the money I spend on advertising is wasted: Unfortunately, I don't know which 50 percent.

The problem is that John, Henry, Genghis, and Adolph were only partially correct in their anxiety; in reality, it's often more than 90 percent of the money companies spend on their advertising that's wasted. Unfortunately, this state of affairs is getting worse by the day.

So, how can a small- or medium-sized business run by a smart entrepreneur like you avoid the excesses, excuses, and futile expenditures on ineffectual advertising programs the rest of corporate America seems happy to put up with year in and year out? The answer is straightforward; you must apply the same common sense and logic to your advertising program that you apply to all your other business processes. Whether you manufacture and sell a product, or provide a service, isn't it appropriate that you should expect the same value for money and healthy return on investment (ROI) from your advertising and promotional expenditures as you do when you invest your capital in other business services?

Even though I've spent my entire career in the advertising business, I find it strange that advertising agencies have never been held to the same standards of effectiveness and accountability as the suppliers of such mundane commodities as personnel, raw materials, infrastructure essentials, and financial and legal services, that is, just about everything you need to run a business. Could it be that in common with John, Henry, Genghis, and Adolph, purchasers of advertising have been browbeaten and bamboozled over the years by their respective ad agencies into believing that the value of what they provide is immeasurable?

Fortunately, today this argument is no longer sustainable. (Not that, in reality, it ever was.) Now there are much better, more affordable, and certainly more effective ways to reach and influence a target audience than the outrageously expensive and very often ineffectual ones advertising agencies have been able to dragoon their clients into paying for over so many years.

There are ways of creating advertising that entrepreneurs running small and medium businesses with limited advertising and marketing budgets can use to their benefit. It's simply a matter of knowing where to go, what to look for, what results to expect, and most importantly, what you should pay to get these results.

This book will show you how to create worthwhile and effective advertising as good as any produced on Madison Avenue, either on your own or with the help of others. It will also show you how you can work successfully with an ad agency when you think you've grown to a size big enough to benefit from such a relationship. It will even show you how to avoid the insanity and paranoia that far too often seem to be an integral part of many client/agency relationships.

One thing this book will not do is insult your intelligence by providing a series of simplistic checklists, templates, mnemonics, annotations, cheat sheets, acronyms, and all those things that seem to be the hallmark of many how-to-do-your-own-advertising books and make them look like plumbing supply catalogs written for an audience of 12-year-olds.

Even though it will cover methodology and process, this book, above all else, concerns itself with content. In other words, what you must say and how you must say it to convince prospective customers why they must do business with you rather than with your competition.

I hope you are not looking for simplistic "Twelve incontrovertible rules for advertising greatness" or "Advertising effectiveness for a dollar a day" solutions. Other than on the shelves of the business section of bookstores, these instant panaceas don't exist. What you will find within the pages of *MadScam* is a better methodology for producing great advertising at a fraction of what it would cost you if you attempted to do it the Madison Avenue way.

Rather than lard each chapter with various sources for information and data, most of which are increasingly available online, I have put resources that might be helpful at the end of the book in Resources. This way you can refer to them on a chapter-by-chapter basis, as and when you feel the need to get specific information to help you develop a particular part of your advertising program.

This book will help you create effective and impactful advertising that can grow your business without it being necessary for you to devote an excessive amount of time and money to achieve that goal. It's not about the size of your budget; it's about the scope of your imagination.

CHAPTER ONE

Are you absolutely, positively, cross your heart and hope to die sure you need to advertise?

ar too many people assume that because they have arrived at a certain stage in the growth of their company, it's now time to start advertising. In some cases, this may very well be true. In a great many others, the time, effort, and expense wasted on an ineffectual ad program would perhaps have returned far higher dividends if invested in some other part of the company.

STARTING OFF ON THE RIGHT FOOT

Let me illustrate with a couple of examples. The first was a few years back when I was the creative director of a London ad agency specializing in business-to-business (B2B) advertising, we were invited to pitch for the account of a large communications equipment company doing business throughout Europe, the Middle East, and Far East. Because we were so good at what we did, with virtually all of our new business referrals coming from very satisfied customers (modesty, as you may well know is not a common trait in the ad biz), we had a policy of not doing speculative presentations. If someone wanted us to pitch for an advertising account, we expected a fee of several thousand pounds (not an inconsiderable amount of money in those days), plus expenses and eight weeks to get our act together.

We used the money, and the time, to go out and talk to the potential client's present, past, and hopefully, future customers. We went on the road with its sales force. We talked to industry consultants. We talked to the trade press. We talked to the potential client's competition (without giving away who we were). Then we went to the pub, sat around talking about last night's Manchester United game, had a few beers and smokes (it was England, remember), and got down to work.

After eight weeks and lots more beer and smokes, we presented our recommendations to the client. This was in the form of a comprehensive communications plan that outlined the current market situation, the state of the competition, the target groups the advertising should impact, the objectives to be achieved against these target groups, the communications components that would be necessary to achieve these objectives, the creative strategies to implement the objectives, the advertising we would create to execute the creative strategy, and finally, the research we would use to measure the effectiveness of the communications program after an agreed period of time.

The presentation was structured in such a way that we and the prospective client had to agree on each of the component parts of the plan before we moved on to the next. This way, we could jointly travel down the inexorable path that culminated in the showing of the creative materials. And because the client had signed off on everything that had preceded it, we could be 99.9 percent sure that it would sign off on the creative. (I shall deal with this fool-proof methodology for the creation and implementation of the communications plan as the only sensible and worth-while way to approach any advertising program in greater depth in Chapter 3.)

The point of this story is that based on the research we had done with customers, consultants, and the trade press, it was patently obvious that the company had an appalling reputation for after-sales service, even with customers who had invested substantial amounts in its systems. Everyone loved its products, but if anything went wrong and the client needed immediate help and assistance to get part or all of its network back up and running, forget it. As a consequence, the company's repeat sales were taking a beating and its overall reputation was starting to smell like last week's fish.

So when kicking off the presentation, I diplomatically pointed out that the best ad campaign in the world wasn't going to help the company if it didn't address its internal problems. Namely, it had to get its service act together. The CEO of the company was, to put it mildly, extremely pissed. He told

> In a recent study conducted by the American Advertising Federation among senior corporate executives, after legal services, advertising was listed as the second least important function in their respective businesses.

me in no uncertain terms that I was full of crap, as he knew for a fact their after-sales service was second to none. Then, taking an extra deep puff on his gold-tipped Balkan Sobranie cigarette (England, remember?), he sneeringly announced that my information was obviously faulty. The brown-nosing, Moroccan-leather-organizer toting, Armani suited, tasseled loafer wearing, company senior executives surrounding him at the conference table vigorously nodded in agreement.

Pressing on, I offered to put him in touch with the many dozens of sources on which we had based this conclusion. He replied that my function was to produce advertising, not get involved in things I obviously didn't understand about his business, even though one of the initial requirements necessary for us to present for the account in the first place was to demonstrate a thorough understanding of his business.

After a couple more attempts to convince him that his company had a major problem, I realized the futility of continuing with this charade, so we packed our bags and departed. I subsequently discovered the not altogether surprising fact that the Director of after-sales service was married to the CEO's only daughter. The company no longer exists.

The second example took place much more recently and involved a major US high tech company who for years had been the leader in printers but was starting to lose market share to a large direct sales computer company that was offering comparable products at significantly lower prices. Because of my experience in this market with IBM, Apple, Compaq, and particularly Dell, the printer company brought me in to create advertising that would slow down and hopefully reverse the loss of sales that was taking place. They wanted me to do a campaign talking about their years of leadership and innovation, the quality of their products, and their extensive dealer network.

I told them that with their current product range and pricing, this approach wasn't going to work and what they needed to do was reduce the prices of their low-end products (which were very low margin anyway) and concentrate the advertising on their high end, big system, networked products that not only had substantially higher margins, but also lent themselves to a much more believable (and provable) quality/value story.

They didn't want to hear that. They had this fear of giving up market share in any of their traditional markets. Consequently they poured millions into a campaign that did very little for them, and now a couple of years later their share of the low-end printer market has declined by 30 percent.

The Moral of These Two Stories

In fact, there are several, one of which is not marrying your daughter off to some company nebbish. But the single most important one is that advertising cannot solve the problems inherent in a company that delivers bad products and services, or isn't prepared to acknowledge that as their markets are changing, so should they. You can spend money ad nauseam on an ad program that might convince the great unwashed masses out there to buy your stuff once. But if what they've shelled out good money for doesn't live up to the promises you made in the advertising, not only will they never buy it again, they'll also unhesitatingly tell everyone they come in contact with to avoid you and your lousy products like the plague.

And if you offer a "me-too" product at a higher price than all your competition, don't continue to pour money down the drain of futility.

Therefore, be sure before you consider blowing a ton of cash on an ad campaign that everything is in order back at the ranch. And the only way you can truly be aware if this is so is not by asking the sycophants on your payroll, but by getting out there in the trenches and doing a bit of incognito digging for yourself. It's amazing how many companies commit

> Your advertising is the face of your company. In most instances it's the first contact potential customers will have with you. Shouldn't that first impression be the most favorable you can possibly make it?

to an expensive ad program when they could be spending that money more usefully getting their act together in terms of better product quality, improved distribution, enhanced customer relations, beefing up the sales force, or even putting a new coat of paint on their beat-to-crap delivery trucks.

AN IDEA

Sit down. Pour yourself a stiff drink. Then, on one side of one sheet of paper write down all the reasons why you think you should be advertising. After you've done that, refill your glass, turn over that same sheet of paper, and write down all the reasons why you shouldn't be advertising. Only if the reasons on the first side of the sheet outweigh those on the reverse should you consider committing a portion of your hard-earned revenues to an ongoing ad program.

Let's consider what some of those reasons might be. The pros could be:

- You're in a start-up mode; you need to let people know you exist.
- You've been around a while, and people still don't know you from a hole in the wall.
- Your competition advertises.
- Your competition is killing you.
- You have a deep-seated desire to kill your competition.
- You think you have a unique product/service.
- You are convinced you have a unique product/service.
- You want to be the next GE/IBM/Nike/P&G.

- Everyone else seems to advertise.
- Your wife/husband/partner/dog thinks it's a good idea.

The cons could be:

- You have no idea where to begin.
- You don't think you have enough money to do it properly.
- You know your competition will probably outspend you.
- You're not sure if you have a unique product/service.
- You are absolutely sure you don't have a unique product/service.
- You're not ready to commit to a long-term program.
- You see advertising as an ill-begrudged expense, not an investment.
- Your best friend once got ripped off by an ad agency.
- You're quite sure you've never been influenced by an ad in your life.
- Your wife/husband/partner/dog thinks it's a dumb idea.

I'm sure you can come up with a lot more reasons, both pro and con, but the point of the exercise is to get you to start thinking about whether or not you really need to advertise in the traditional sense. Maybe there's a better way, a nontraditional way. And guess what? There is.

HOW MUCH IS ENOUGH?

One thing I learned many years ago was that when making a presentation to a potential or existing client, never give him the unborn yak skin, custom-bound, leave-behind piece up front. Far better to do the full-blown dog and pony presentation in its entirety, then give him the summation document at the end.

Why? Because if you don't, before you're two minutes into your best impersonation of Winston Churchill giving his "We shall fight them on the beaches" speech, you won't be able to ignore the fact that everyone in the audience is sneaking a peek at the last few pages of the document—because that's where the budget is.

It doesn't matter if your presentation has the depth and sincerity of a Marcus Aurelius meditation delivered with the passion of a Shakespeare sonnet, you have lost your audience. For the rest of the presentation everyone is thinking, "Omygawd, do we have to spend this much bloody money with these clowns?" It also doesn't matter whether you're selling sausages or safety belts; it always comes down to the bottom line: What is this fiasco going to cost me?

This is particularly true when it comes to advertising because then money overrides every other consideration. For the advertiser, it is the reluctance to spend hard-earned cash on something as intangible and in many ways as unaccountable as an ad program. For the ad agency and the various media who are on the receiving end of the client's largess, the impetus is always to get the client to spend more. After all, when you consider the origins of ad agencies, once their sole income was from the rebated commissions (for many years a standard 15 percent the media paid them when they persuaded clients to place ads in their publications). This rebate of commissions practiced by the print media was later followed by the radio and TV networks. In other words, you have to recognize that historically, the whole advertising agency business has been based on kickbacks—which, in any other line of work would get you serious jail time.

OK, most ad agencies now work on a fee basis. But these fees are generally based on a percentage of the money the client is expected to spend on media and ancillary activities. Ergo, the more money the agency can persuade its clients to spend, the bigger the fees it can negotiate.

What has this to do with you arriving at a decision as to whether you should advertise or not? Simply this. Don't let that decision be dictated solely by whether you can afford to advertise because there are so many situations facing small- to medium-businesses where in reality, they may not be able to afford *not* to advertise. The landscape is littered with countless examples of companies, big and small, that have stopped or drastically cut down on their advertising expenditures during a temporary slowdown in the economy, only to be left playing catch-up with their competitors (who wisely continued to invest in an ad program during the bad times) for years afterwards.

Studies have shown that the companies who stopped advertising in order to catch up with their competitors very often have to spend a significantly higher rate than they would have done if they had the fortitude and perseverance to stick with their original advertising program.

> A Gallup poll surveyed over 30 different professions in terms of the public's perception of their trustworthiness. At the bottom of the barrel were car salesmen. A mere one percentage point higher were advertising people.

GET YOUR PRIORITIES STRAIGHT

Advertising is a branch of communications. And yes, there's no question that in the final analysis, it's all about selling. If you're smart and do everything right, your advertising will help you move a ton of stuff that otherwise would be collecting dust on your warehouse shelves. But first you have to get the attention of the people who might be in need of whatever tchotchkes you're peddling this week. Another famous, long-dead ad man by the name of Howard Gossage put it best when he said, "People don't read advertising; they read what they're interested in, and sometimes that's advertising." What this implies is that you don't have to beat people over the head with the kind of abysmal pap the drug/toiletries/auto companies currently inflict upon those unfortunates forced to suffer through their TV spots as the price they must pay for watching *World News Tonight*, while eating their microwaved macaroni and cheese. The big advertisers can get away with mind-insulting stuff like this because they have buckets, nay dumpsters, full of money to throw at the problem. I am assuming you don't, otherwise you wouldn't be reading this book.

So, you have to come at it from a different perspective. A key, for instance—and believe me, this is something rarely tried by most large advertisers and their agencies—is treating your audience in the same way you would wish to be treated—with respect. To quote David Ogilvy one more time, "The consumer isn't stupid, she's your wife."

It's all about talking to people in an intelligent fashion so they may actually be interested in what it is you have to say. If you're not prepared to make the effort necessary to do this, you'd be well advised to save your money. Better yet, take all your employees on a cruise for Christmas. The goodwill you create will do you far more good than a badly planned and executed ad campaign.

TIME, INFORMATION, AND MONEY

Believe it or not, these three things are the only ingredients you need to create great advertising. And if you go back to the question at the very beginning of this chapter on whether you should advertise and you think it isn't important enough to devote sufficient time, information, and money needed to create a properly thought out, well-structured and well-managed advertising program, don't even consider starting.

Speaking of Time

Realize and accept this: A successful advertising program is only possible if you've devoted sufficient time to both the development of your communications plan, as I will get into in Chapter 3, and its execution, as covered in later chapters. That's what I call up-front *thinking time.* The flip side of the coin is realizing that if you planned your program right, your advertising will be flexible enough to be quickly modified for those unavoidable times when it's necessary to meet changing circumstances and opportunities in the marketplace. This can often mean creating and producing ads overnight, particularly if your business is retail. This is what I call *panic time.* It's the stuff you cannot possibly preprogram into your schedule because you will never know when you need to execute it.

That's one of the drawbacks of being an entrepreneur running a small- to medium-sized company. You will either have to run the advertising program yourself or delegate to another person. And unless you have reached a certain critical mass, it's very doubtful you will have anyone with any advertising experience to delegate to, in spite of the fact that everyone claims to do three things better than anyone else—make love, drive a car, and create advertising. (However, I'm the only person in the world who can do all three at the same time.) Most people wouldn't recognize a good ad if it hit them on the head from 20,000 feet. Subsequent chapters will deal with the various options available to you to solve this problem. But for now, the question you have to ask yourself is: Are you prepared to take the time and make the right level of investment to make a worthwhile ad program pay off?

If you are, then consider this: It delivers one big plus, albeit, a frightening one. In big companies with multiple layers of advertising and marketing management, the primary concern is to avoid risk.

> The average American is exposed to nearly 250 TV commercials a day. That's just over two hours a day. They watch while eating breakfast, they watch while eating dinner, they watch in bed. Some people even have TVs in the bathroom! What chance do you think a single 30-second commercial aired one time has of being effective?

Legions of middle management, all looking to save their rear ends, will not commit to anything remotely different, let alone edgy, so the resulting advertising is often wishy-washy and mostly ineffectual. In your company, you alone will be responsible for making the decisions about your own advertising. So you can make it as kick-ass great as you want it to be. But remember, there'll be no one else to blame if it sucks. Scary, right?

Information

When it comes to producing great advertising, the single most important resource you can work with is information. In fact, you can never have too much of it. All the truly great campaigns of the last 50 years have been based on solid information, rather than bullshit. One example of this prerequisite virtue is the classic David Ogilvy ad for Rolls Royce with the headline, "At 50 miles an hour, the loudest noise you can hear is the ticking of the dashboard clock." Ogilvy didn't spout pseudo engineering, "Power Glide Auto Gismo smoothes the ride and puts you in charge." Or snob appeal, "When you arrive in your pink Château La Grande, the girls at the country club will die with envy." Instead he featured the unmatched craftsmanship, quality, and design of the car via the least talked about piece of equipment in it—the clock!

This is using information as a solid selling tool in a way that allows you to zig when everyone else is zagging! Figure 1.1, an ad I did for Armenter cigars a few years ago, is a perfect example of what I mean.

When the cigar craze hit America in the late '90s and humidors and smoking rooms were sprouting up all over the place, fortunes were being spent on ad campaigns for both established and new brands. All the ads fell into two general categories. Sleek looking guys wearing $5,000 suits while sitting in opulent surroundings, such as board rooms and country clubs with lots of mahogany and sporting prints on the walls. In one hand was a sparkling Waterford crystal brandy snifter the size of a goldfish bowl, in the other was a King Carlos Fantasia stogie the size of a nuclear missile. The single line of copy was usually something like "Men of distinction choose a distinctive cigar!" The second category visualized a hot chick falling out of a very low cut dress, sitting in a lush interior clutching the same gold

FIGURE 1.1: *This ad has more words in it (1,438) than the Declaration of Independence (1,322!). And all it does is talk about a single cigar. It sold a hell of a lot of them too!*

fish bowl-sized snifter and missile-sized cigar. In this case the headline usually went something like "My men of distinction choose distinctive cigars!" Every one a zig.

My zag was the Armenter ad. As all these cigar aficionados were paying a small fortune for these things, or in the case of smuggled Cubans, a big fortune, it seemed to me they might want some real information about the brand before they coughed up (coughed up… get it?) their money. So, in nearly 1,500 words I went into painstaking detail on what makes a good cigar in general, and what makes an Armenter a great cigar in particular. The ad was received enthusiastically by cigar stores, as it helped the owners explain to cigar novices what they should be looking for in a good cigar. It was reprinted as an instore display piece, and was even included in every box of Armenters.

It sold a heck of a lot of cigars. Particularly to people who wanted to jump in on the craze, yet had no prior experience with cigars and needed the reassurance that they were paying out money for a reputable product. Which reinforces my point that you cannot create good advertising in a vacuum. If you try, you end up with the zig stuff I described above, which gives no one a solid reason why they should contemplate doing business with you. Start off with as much information as you can. It doesn't matter if you discard or fail to use 90 percent of it, the remaining 10 percent will contain that one nugget that will separate you from everyone else in the market. I'll also be talking about how you go about doing this in later chapters.

Interestingly enough, some of the best advertising around is produced by those companies small enough for the founder and initial management team to be involved in every aspect of their advertising and marketing. The same people who had the guts and vision to take the risks required when starting their business in the first place are people who still believe passionately in what they are doing. That's why it shows in the advertising they produce. As I mentioned earlier, it's only years later when layers of ossified second-tier management start to spread through the company like kudzu climbing a Georgia telegraph pole that the advertising function is taken over by the so-called advertising specialists. Unfortunately, these are people more concerned with protecting their position than with growing the business through exciting and impactful advertising. And as so often happens at this stage of a company's growth, the unquestionably "safe," but highly ineffectual advertising starts to happen.

> The amount of useful information in an ad is proportional to the amount of interest the reader has in the subject. It doesn't matter what you say or how you say it. If it's of no interest to the reader, it won't make an impression.

At this early stage of your company's development, this should not be something you have to worry about. But when you do grow, never forget that it was your advertising that helped to get you there. So don't hand off complete responsibility to some churl who will never look at it in the same way you did when you were starting out.

Money

I'll be going into budgets and how to develop and apply them in Chapter 4. For now, be aware that you don't necessarily have to spend a fortune to create effective advertising. If you prepare the groundwork in the way I'll be laying out in the next chapters and then execute with style and intelligence, you can have an ongoing ad program that will help build your business.

Concentrate on spending money where it will do you the most good, researching your market, developing your communications plan, and then executing well by investing in the high-quality production of artwork, photography, etc. Do not skimp on costs at this stage in the belief that you can use the money saved to buy more media, which in turn will get you more exposure. Always remember that every element of your company's advertising and communications, and sometimes the media you choose to run it in, are a reflection of your company's character. If your advertising is schlocky and the publications you run it in are schlocky, you'll come across as a schlocky company, not the kind of business that people want to do business with.

Some companies have started in a small, very limited fashion, but have invested their money into the highest quality presentation of their image. J. Peterman built a hugely successful mail order company on the basis of a single small-space ad in the back pages of the *New Yorker* magazine. (See Figure 1.2 for a sample J. Peterman ad.)

He followed up enquires to the ad with an amazingly well-written and beautifully art-directed catalogue which became a collector's piece. (See Figure 1.3 for a sample catalog.) At first, he actually wrote all the copy himself, later developing a staff of writers and artists. After becoming a long-running character on *Seinfeld*, he expanded into retail and opened several stores, which became his undoing, and he was forced to file for Chapter 11. The company has now rebounded and is back running a very successful direct-mail business that even includes a line of very high-end furniture. It's also worth noting that apart from producing just a few small space ads, he also limited his media buys to a single periodical, the *New Yorker*, which was a perfect media vehicle for his target audience.

All of which reinforces my point about the quality of your advertising and the choice of your media being a definite indication to the audience you are addressing

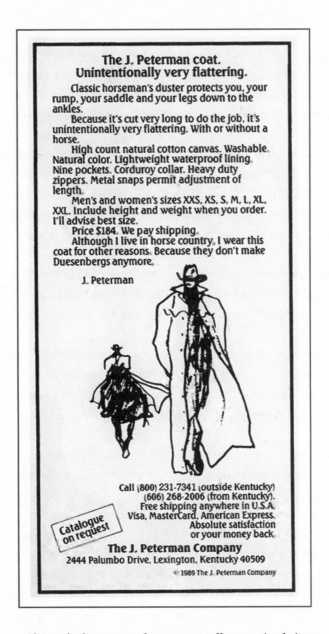

FIGURE 1.2: *The cattleman's duster coat became a well recognized signature of the Peterman brand.*

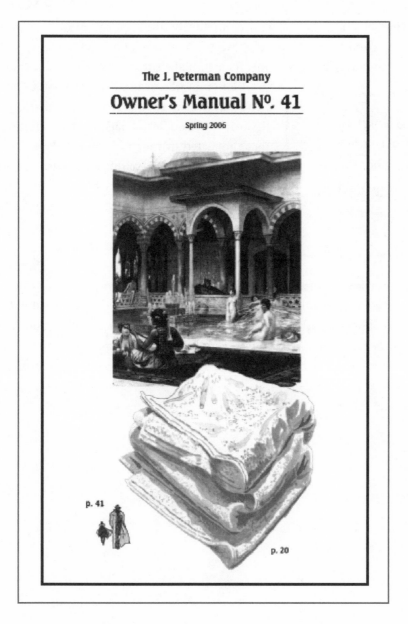

FIGURE 1.3: *Peterman's catalogs are collector's pieces and are now regularly auctioned on eBay.*

of the character and style of your company. By the application of logic and common sense, combined with tasteful execution, it won't be necessary to spend a fortune on your advertising; you just have to make sure that you spend it smartly.

Proctor & Gamble spend several billion dollars a year on its advertising. J. Peterman probably spent less than $50,000 a year in the *New Yorker*. But he did spend a great deal of money on his catalog, which paid off handsomely.

Remember Encarta's definition of an entrepreneur, "a risk-taker." That is not what the great majority of middle-management is all about, and that's reflected in much of today's appalling advertising. So why not grasp this wonderful opportunity by the scruff of the neck while you still can. Once you're a trillionaire browsing through all those ocean-going yacht brochures, it'll be too late, and you'll have missed out on all the fun.

I've tried to rein in your initial chomping-at-the-bit enthusiasm for starting to advertise the minute you open your doors—or maybe before you even have a door to open. I'll assume you've got all your other business building ducks in a row and because you're adamant about doing it, you can't wait to get started. So in the rest of the book, I'm going to explore the many options open to you as the best and the most cost-effective ways to promote your business.

Let's get started.

CHAPTER TWO

What do you expect from your advertising: fame, fortune, fast cars, peace of mind, or all of the above?

A few years ago during the heyday of the dotcom revolution, companies were persuaded to spend dumpster loads of money on massive advertising campaigns featuring their respective CEOs standing, legs spread wide and arms akimbo, atop the Great Wall of China, or enjoying the passing parade as they sipped glasses of 1945 Chateau Lafitte Rothschild at a sidewalk cafe on the Champs Elysee, or wrapped in a fur-lined Gucci parka, silhouetted against vast Arctic wastes, pontificating about how the world would never be the same again thanks to the wonders their company was about to unleash on the unsuspecting public. Others took a more vaudevillian, slapstick humor route with dancing chimps doing their thing atop an upturned pail somewhere in the Ozarks or, to the dismay of the world's animal lovers, with curmudgeonly old gentlemen firing baby gerbils out of cannons. The purported aim of all this outrageously expensive activity was to promote the "on-demand" benefits of the latest dotcom employment agency, virtual pet food emporium, or personalized greeting cards web site.

Ahhh, the glory days of the1990s, when advertising was considered by every Ermenegildo Zegna-attired venture capitalist on Palo Alto's sun-kissed Page Mill Road as the *de rigueur* tool necessary to build that orgasmic benchmark of "New Economy business success, share of market."

Then, in the middle of this profligate excess and outright lunacy, there appeared what I consider to be one of the truly great TV commercials of the last dozen or so years. It not only pricked the balloon of self-righteous bullshit that had until then been endorsed for so long by much of the business press of America, that is, that in the New Economy it was no longer necessary for a successful business to *actually make a profit.* Apart from what it actually said, an equally important aspect of this admirable TV spot was its timing, because it ran when a few of the more sober minds in the financial community were finally beginning to express doubts about this new business model.

Bucking the trend, this TV spot on behalf of IBM featured a very nervous, geeky guy facing his domineering CEO who is barking at him, "So, what exactly is this so-called e-business marketing strategy of yours?" Taking a deep breath, the obviously terrified employee gulps and answers, "For every dollar we spend, we get two dollars back." The CEO glares at the trembling churl, blinks, and you can almost see the gears grinding in his gnarly old head. Then he gets it! And so did anyone with half a brain who happened to watch the spot, because this simple, easy to understand, and direct message (and I'll be talking a great deal more about this kind of straightforward communication later) immediately cut through the clouds of acrid smoke the venture capitalists, consultants, and armies of MBAs had been blowing out of their rear ends throughout most of the '90s.

For years, companies large and small, maybe even one or two you've worked for in a previous life, got suckered into the insanity of "forget about revenues and profit for now, spend like there's no tomorrow, and build a humungous customer base you can milk like crazy in the future." The problem was that for many of the companies that allowed themselves to be talked into this infantile approach, there was no tomorrow. Everything from Boo.com to WebVan and thousands of other "companies of the future" quickly hit the wall of bankruptcy before they were even close to making enough money to cover the phone bill.

> During the high-flying '90s, venture capitalists expected the start-ups they invested in to spend a substantial amount of their seed capital on marketing and advertising in pursuit of market share. They no longer display that enthusiasm.

In reality, for the vast majority of start-ups emerging during this New Economy, there wasn't a New Market, let alone a New Economy to grab the lion's share of. With the exception of eBay, not one single company managed to come up with an original business model that wasn't simply an anemic electronic extension of an existing bricks-and-mortar business. Even with the much-hyped "paradigm shift in retailing," Amazon went through nearly ten years of disastrous losses before producing a less-than-impressive EBTIA profit. And even at the time of writing, *Time's* "Man of the Year," multibillionaire Amazon founder Jeff Bezos is still light years away from making a dent in his company's billions of dollars worth of debt. He is, however, building a private rocket launching space station in the middle of Texas and will no doubt be offering "free shipping" for premium Amazon customers who place orders of more than $10 million in any calendar year.

THE BAD OLD DAYS ARE GONE FOREVER—OR ARE THEY?

Today, everyone knows, with the benefit of that great American sport Monday-morning quarterbacking, that the much ballyhooed days of the New Economy were, by and large, an incredible waste of money. Not just in terms of the vastly over-funded, venture capital, blood-in-the-water, we'll-all-get-rich-together attitude that had far too many companies committing to ridiculous advertising budgets that were immediately flushed down the rancid tubes of Super Bowl TV ad campaigns, most of which ran once and by the next morning were long forgotten. (Unless it was the Miller Lite Girls mud wrestling in a wet cement patch outside Rockefeller Plaza, which didn't sell much beer, but by God, did garner a lot of chat around the water cooler on Monday morning.)

It wasn't only the clients who got hammered; it also ended up being a complete debacle for many of Madison Avenue's biggest and dumbest ad agencies. They spent vast amounts of money chasing after the latest dotcom account, 90 percent of which went bust within months, leaving the agency liable for untold millions of dollars in unpaid media bills long before they had recouped even a fraction of what it had cost them to win the account in the first place. And don't even spare a thought for the dozens of losing agencies who spent boatloads of money in futile attempts to get on the short list to pitch knitting.com, WebToiletries.com, or any of the other dozens of dotcom accounts with seemingly unlimited advertising budgets that surfaced on a daily basis.

If you think Madison Avenue learned a lesson from all of this, just wait 'till the next paradigm shift comes along and see how high the ad agencies jump.

DONCHA JUST LOVE HOW DUMB MOST AD AGENCIES ARE?

That is why the bulk of this book is about *not* working with agencies, but doing most of what you need to do by yourself, or perhaps as you grow, with the help of a small number of freelancers and consultants. Having said that, if you should prosper (which after following the sage advice in this book, I am sure you will) and become big and successful enough that you feel that you really could benefit from the help of an ad agency, Chapter 11 will tell you how you can make even this frightening possibility work to your advantage.

Now that you've committed to advertising, it's time to think about the objectives of your program. I could take the expected route and blithely toss out

> The majority of large ad accounts are with large ad agencies. Virtually all of these belong to one of four international conglomerates. The bottom line for all of these groups is the bottom line. In spite of what they claim, the work is secondary.

any of the time worn and much abused clichés used by legions of MBAs to express what these should be. Perhaps, it might be "Establishing ascendancy over the competition" or "Becoming recognized as the number-one player in the marketplace." Why not, "Building superior brand awareness" and "Increasing market share"? Or, one of my all time favorites, "Creating awareness for best-of-breed products." And so on and so on.

Unfortunately, all of these statements are meaningless in a real business environment. They only serve as business school placeholders in the artificial world of academia, or worse yet, as part of the never ending, multislide, soporific Power-Point® presentations inflicted on long-suffering management by over-priced and usually incompetent consultants. In my experience, consultants have developed an amazing business model whereby they are paid millions to recommend putting in new systems, which very often do not work with the existing systems, so the consultants are paid even more millions to take them out.

In a way, it's similar to how the Big Dumb Agencies of Madison Avenue operate. They also get paid millions to create campaigns that often do not work, and then they get paid more millions to produce more campaigns that don't work either. Eventually the client fires the agency, undergoes a lengthy and expensive search for a new agency, and repeats the cycle at a rapidly increasing rate. In fact, in the last few years, some agencies have been fired after producing campaigns that did work. Perhaps it's a reflection of the increasing disenchantment many clients are finding with their agencies.

In the real world of your business, advertising should have a single objective: to kick your competition's ass and sell your stuff.

It's your company, your brand, your products. I mean, c'mon, it's your money. Do you really want to squander it on the same old me-too advertising and promotional programs that are having less and less effect on the buying public? Or, would you rather do it in a more effective way guaranteed to produce measurable results?

Most of the cliché objectives I've listed above have little to do with the way you should promote

> As with all your communications, your advertising is a reflection of your company's character. Why not produce advertising that puts you in a favorable light?

your business. You cannot crush your competition through the power of advertising. You don't have enough money. It's only politicians (New York Mayor Michael Bloomberg or ex-Italian Prime Minister Silvio Berlusconi are prime examples) who can crush their opposition through the sheer weight and power of massive amounts of advertising. They can do that because they are multimillionaires capable of ruthlessly outspending their opponents, or they get massively funded by special interest groups who expect payback from their protégé if he is elected. Interestingly though, even Berlusconi's millions and his stranglehold on most of Italy's media didn't help him when he was recently defeated by his opponent Prodi in the Italian elections.

You can't build brand awareness until you have a brand. If you are a start-up, you don't exist in the minds of your potential customers. Becoming the number-one player in a market depends on the size of the market and who else populates it. You can't increase market share until you've got some market share. And best-of-breed is only of interest if you're raising thoroughbred horses.

You have to set yourself attainable goals and expectations. The fame, fortune, and fast cars will come later. For right now, why not settle for reasonable revenue growth and the beginnings of awareness of your brand in the marketplace? If you plan wisely and invest modestly in a properly structured advertising program, there's no doubt you can expect these positive results without busting the bank.

> Beware the use of jargon when planning and executing your advertising. I remember a traffic report with the announcer saying, "There's an extra-heavy vehicular loading situation on the bridge." What's wrong with saying, "There's lots of traffic"?

In the next chapter, you'll develop a communications strategy that will serve as a benchmark for all your advertising and promotional activities in the future. But before you can do this, you need to consider what your marketing strategy will be. Because rest assured, there's a big difference between the two.

MARKETING STRATEGY

A marketing strategy outlines your company's future goals. You must be sure that these goals you set are realistic, sustainable, and measurable. Giving yourself impossible goals may be good for the ego initially but will ultimately lead to frustration and disaster when you fail to achieve them. It's essential that you realize a marketing strategy is strictly about what your aims are rather than the tactics you should implement to achieve them. I cannot tell you how many companies I've worked with over the years whose management at all levels has been unable to comprehend this essential difference. Your marketing strategy should have three elements:

1. The identification of achievable goals.
2. The recognition of what you have to offer customers that will make achieving these possible.
3. The establishment of a timeline and budget to achieve them.

Let's assume you set yourself the goal of increasing sales by 10 percent in the next year. This may be achievable through an effective promotional program. But it is far more likely to happen if you have first increased your product diversity/quality, gained wider distribution, put more salespeople on the road, instituted a new pricing policy, revamped your packaging, or any of a host of other factors. Advertising cannot work in a vacuum, and it can only sell a bad product once.

> You've invested a lot of time and effort into your company, but unless you sell your products or services, that hard work will have been wasted. Great advertising can help you sell, but only if you consider it an essential component of your business.

You can more easily succeed against your competition if you develop a marketing strategy that unequivocally sets you apart from your competition. This strategy will require a considerable amount of effort on your part. It isn't enough to say, "I have the best damn company in the world, and I make the best damn products." Everyone else out there is saying exactly the same thing and probably spending a great deal more money than you are to get that totally expected message across to its audience.

SET YOURSELF APART

What you have to impress on prospective customers is the *added value* they can expect when they establish a relationship with you. It may be a single specific feature so unique to your company that it can stand alone as a persuasive reason to deal with you. But the odds on finding and isolating that single 24-carat nugget of information that makes you so special are pretty small. More than likely it's a combination of less spectacular reasons that when added up give you a definitely perceived advantage over your competition.

This single feature, or combination of distinguishing features, has been given many names over the years by various marketing pundits, but the most commonly accepted and longest lived is the *unique selling proposition (USP)*, a term coined by Rosser Reeves, the CEO of Bates Advertising back in the 1950s. The interesting thing about a USP is that this *unique* attribute or feature doesn't necessarily have to be unique to you, your product, or your services; you only have to create the perception that it is unique in the mind of the audience you are addressing. And if by so doing, you become the only one in your business category talking about your product's special attribute, you end up owning its uniqueness.

Rosser Reeves did this with Gleam toothpaste. At the time, toothpaste was seen as merely a cleaning and whitening aid. (In those days most people smoked three packs a day of unfiltered cigarettes and drank gallons of diesel strength coffee, so less-than-pearly-white teeth and paint-stripper breath was a fairly common problem.)

After talking to the people who made the stuff, Rosser discovered Gleam had chlorophyll in it, which was primarily a breath freshener. Rosser immediately renamed and advertised the product as "Gleam Toothpaste with miracle ingredient GL70." This so-called miracle ingredient was vigorously hyped as the answer to effective oral hygiene for people who couldn't brush after every meal because it helped fight both tooth decay and bad breath. If you didn't want to put up with the operating-room taste of things like Listerine, this was seen as the answer to your problems. Within months, the product was selling like gangbusters to hordes of Camel-smoking, high-test coffee drinking, hamburger-munching Americans.

But the most interesting part of the story is that just about every other brand of toothpaste on the market had chlorophyll in it. It was only because Rosser took the time to find out about every single product ingredient and its attributes, recognize that one of them presented an opportunity to create a USP, develop a completely new way to position Gleam than the way toothpaste had always been marketed to the public, and then be the only one in the marketplace to talk about

FIGURE 2.1: *Part of a campaign I did for IBM's software division where the USP was the simple, easy-to-understand explanation of what "middleware" actually did. Because IBM was the only company doing this, it became their USP and they dominated the category.*

it (making it the core element of all the advertising), that he was able to turn a me-too toothpaste into a huge brand.

This concept of a USP is an important lesson to consider when putting together a marketing strategy (see Figure 2.1). Do not doubt for one minute that there will be some particular facet of your business you can promote as being unique, whether it's in the products or services you create, the way you sell them, or the second-to-none after-sales services you develop that keep customers coming back. Believe me, somewhere in that mix there will be something you can transform into a USP. All you have to do is find it, then communicate it to your potential market.

But a word of caution here, virtually all the ads that Rosser Reeves created were appalling. Yes, they worked like gangbusters and sold a lot of products, in spite of the fact that virtually everyone hated them. He was responsible for flaming stomachs, anvils in heads, and lots and lots of charts and diagrams with unremitting supers (on-screen titles) flashing product benefits over and over. He also had a fetish about dressing every actor in every commercial in a white coat to give the impression they were doctors.

Under no circumstances should you model your efforts on the Rosser Reeves school of hard sell when it comes to executing your advertising. But by all means rely on that fundamental principle of the unique selling proposition when it comes to doing the spadework necessary to develop your communications plan.

FINDING YOUR USP

If you're a start-up, finding your USP should be much easier than if you've been in business for some time. Even though you may not realize it, your USP will have been an essential part of your business plan. That's right, the one you wrote when you were trying to convince those investors to put in a chunk of the Widows & Orphans Pension Fund money they controlled.

Your business plan was aimed at giving these people the confidence that there would be some guarantee of you making a success of your new business. So think about it. What was the key argument you made which convinced them to invest in you? Had you designed a better product? Did you show them your amazing plans for creating a new market for an existing product? Had you come up with a more efficient method of distribution? Was it a business model that turned new customers into raging evangelists for your company?

There had to be something in your ideas that initially convinced you, and ultimately them, that you had a hell of a good chance for success. The problem is that since then you've been buried in the day-to-day minutia of getting the company off the ground and making enough money to meet the payroll and pay the bills, not to mention the 101 other things you need to take care of in your 25-hour day. Who knows? By now you may have even forgotten what it was you were so convinced would make your company special in the first place. Always assuming, of course, that you had an original idea and didn't merely copy or import an existing idea or business model from someone else's business. No, of course you didn't.

So, let's dig around and isolate that USP, once and for all. Whether you are B2C (business-to-consumer) or B2B (business-to-business) is really immaterial, because your USP should give the perception that only you can satisfy the specific needs of the audience you wish to reach, whether it is buying ice cream or off-shore drilling rigs. Your advertising and communication program must leave everyone exposed to it with the absolute conviction that what you have is unobtainable anywhere else.

There will always be something you do better than your competition (otherwise, you shouldn't be in business). Or perhaps you should surrender to the notion that most companies do most things in exactly the same way their competition does. In which case, what is it that makes one company successful and another one not? Maybe it's best summed up in that well-known and certainly well-worn phrase "Perception is reality." Remember, "Miracle Ingredient GL70" existed in all of Gleam's competition. The significant difference was that none of them had the gumption to recognize the marketing potential of a somewhat esoteric manufacturing additive that for years had been put in the 50,000 gallon toothpaste mixing vats by $50-a-day junior chemists at a laboratory somewhere in Middle America. (I just made up the bit about the $50-a-day junior chemists, but I think you get my drift.)

> You should instinctively know your own USP. But if you don't, someone in your company does. Make it a company project to come up with the killer USP. Besides the fact that you need it for your advertising, it will make everyone in the company start to realize what it is that makes your company special. Then, give the winner a prize.

Believe me. You have something comparable to "Miracle Ingredient GL70." All you have to do is get smart enough to recognize it; then when you do, grab it by the scruff of the neck and make it the keystone of your communications program. The next chapter deals with exactly how to go about doing this.

If, on the other hand, you've been in business for a while and you've shelled out good money for this book because you feel the need to kick your advertising program in the pants and begin some kind of reinvention program, don't despair. Without a doubt, you've still got a USP. You'll just have to dig a little harder to find it, that's all.

If you are in the latter category, consider this: you're still in business, which means you already have a brand. OK, right now, it may not be the world's greatest brand, but it exists. What an advertising and communications program needs to do for you is make your target audience aware of this brand while enhancing its value by demonstrating the tangible benefits to anyone doing business with you. This will require you to take a couple of steps back from the way you've been doing business and promoting yourself in the past and to consider a new direction. Don't panic. Very often this new direction doesn't have to be radical; sometimes it merely requires the finessing and fine tuning of an existing brand attribute.

McVitie's Biscuit Campaign

Some years ago, when I was the "Agency Fireman" (more on that in my next book, *AdScam*) at a large agency in the United Kingdom, I was asked to help revive the flagging fortunes of the McVitie Biscuit Company. (Unlike America where they cover tasteless, pasty white biscuits in tasteless, pasty white gravy while chowing down on hominy grits and corn pones, in Britain biscuits are sweet crumbly things you dip in your tea.) Anyway, for years McVitie's advertising had featured the tagline "McVitie's Bake a Better Biscuit!" In my infinite wisdom, I thought it was time to explain to the Mums of Britain why this was so. Mums were the primary target market as they invariably used biscuits as bribes to keep their howling kids quiet between meals.

The campaign I wanted to create would now be based on an extended claim that "With the best in the World—McVitie's Bake a Better Biscuit." It would feature TV commercials shot all over the world. (Big ad agency creatives are always looking for the slightest opportunity to travel the globe shooting outrageously expensive TV commercials in glamorous locations at the client's expense. I went through several glorious years in which every TV script I wrote started with the line, "Camera opens up on palm tree fringed desert island in the South Pacific.") Each McVitie spot would demonstrate the exotic and nutritious ingredients going into every Ginger-Snap or Bourbon-Cream Delight little Johnny could munch on to calm his hunger pains while waiting for his gourmet dinner of baked beans on toast.

The various agency "suits" (creative-speak for account executives) scoffed at the idea that this kind of esoteric bullshit could possibly be of interest to Britain's "desperate housewives." (Sorry, I couldn't help that.) However, after much begging and pleading with the client that we should at least test the concept to see if it had any merit, it agreed. The campaign turned out to be a big winner, one of the very few times focus group research has paid off for me. It turned out that Britain's Mums did, in fact, care desperately what their kids ate. If they could feel a little less guilty about giving them the fat/sugar/grease/lard/MSG-infused "Better Baked Biscuits" to "shut-them-the-hell-up" between meals after being exposed to the claims of the "With the best in the World" campaign, they could enjoy a guilt-free five minutes with a fag (English for cigarette) and a can of beer before hubby came home and demanded his dad-sized gourmet baked beans on toast.

Anyway, the essential point of the story is that all of this information had been lying around under the noses of the McVitie Company and its ad agency for years. They just never sat down and thought through the implications of what they could do with it from an advertising point of view.

> Once you find your USP and you're convinced it is truly unique, then try to work it into all your communications, not just advertising. Don't let anyone, inside or outside your company, tell you it isn't relevant. If it's right, you'll know it's right.

The second and equally important point of the story is that all the other biscuit companies used exactly the same ingredients, but because they had never thought about it either, they allowed McVitie's to make this claim its USP and so consolidate its hold on the market. As Yogi Berra might say, "It's Gleam with miracle ingredient GL70, de ja vue all over again."

Because the campaign was based on an inherent and easily provable claim of ingredient quality and manufacturing expertise, both incidentally, features of great importance in the food industry, particularly with a product primarily aimed at children, it was very successful and ran for years. Plus, I got to go to exotic places all over the world for a few months at the client's expense. But you know what? At

FIGURE 2.2: *Xerox's Optical Character Recognition (OCR) software could have been explained in mind numbing pseudo-scientific language, or by simply using a strong visual metaphor.*

the end of the day, McVitie's sold a ton of biscuits and the increased sales proved it was well worth the money and effort.

The moral is that you should never let yourself assume that all of the nitty gritty stuff that goes into your product design, creation, manufacturing, distribution processes, and after-sales service is of no interest to your target audience. See Figure 2.2. There may be, as I've said earlier, some 24-carat nuggets of information in that whole mish-mash that could make the difference between survival and success. But because you're too

> The key to a great USP is it should be simple to explain and totally believable. There has to be that "Oh, I get it" element that's easily understood in the advertising.

close to it on a day-to-day basis, you will probably have to make yourself take a couple of steps back to appreciate what they may be.

YOUR TARGET AUDIENCE

Perhaps it can best be summarized in those words of Howard Gossage, "People don't read advertising; they read what they are interested in. And sometimes, it happens to be ads." Think about that for a moment. Then, put yourself in the position of your prospective target audience. Do you want to be bombarded with a repetitive, nonstop plethora of trite messages that do nothing more than promote the miraculous benefits of something you know is substandard crap, a me-too product, or the offering of a degenerate charlatan?

You and I both know your target audience is better than that. So, why not give it solid reasons to get involved with you, to want to know about your company, and to see how it can benefit it, rather than merely making it annoyed and determined to avoid you at all costs because your advertising is painfully intrusive, insulting to its intelligence, and just generally sucks.

Never forget advertising is now such an all-pervasive part of modern life that it's almost impossible to escape it. Even with the advances of TiVo and the many other electronic devices designed to allow you to tune out stuff you don't want to see or listen to, you would be forced to live on a desert island thousands of miles from anywhere to escape its all-encompassing and suffocating embrace. Even then, some 19-year-old wunderkind would come up with a way to bombard you with sky writing messages as you gaze upwards while lying on the coral pink sands sipping your chilled Pisco Sour Manisquqagui cocktail.

This makes brand building or even brand reinvention particularly difficult in these days of message overkill, overexposure, and overfatigue. There is only so much the human brain can take in. So, you'd better be damn sure you don't annoy the hell out of the people you want to make an impression on.

Think of yourself as that unspeakable clown who always calls in the middle of dinner to sell you some lifetime guaranteed house siding or cheap car insurance. You sure as hell don't want what he's selling, and even if you did, he doesn't have the brains to know that this is the world's worst time to call. (Even if he's calling from a subterranean office in Bangladesh, he should know what time it is in Boise.) The end result is you're so annoyed by the intrusive nature of the message and the sycophantic chat of the messenger that you'll be damn sure to make a point of buying it from someone else. That's why, in way too many respects, advertising has become its own worse enemy. In the next chapter, I'll deal with how you can hopefully avoid falling into any of the easy-to-identify traps far too many advertisers do.

NAILING YOUR USP

Whether you're a start-up or reinventing yourself, identifying the essential core elements that can help build your company's name and reputation will get you started on the road to fame, fortune, and fast cars.

As you develop a marketing strategy you can use as the foundation of your communications plan, some questions you should consider, and hopefully come up with solid answers to are:

- Are you unique?
- If so, in what way?
- Can you definitively prove it?
- If you're not unique, are you better at what you do than the competition? And if so, what exactly is it that makes you better?
- Can you demonstrate in easily understandable language (not bullshit) what it is that makes you better or different?
- Do you provide provable quality—either at a price or irrespective of price?
- Do you provide value? And that doesn't necessarily mean offering the cheapest prices or matching those of some fly-by-night outfit that could very well not be around tomorrow.
- If you believe you provide value, can you express it in 20 words or less, spelling out what is the unquestionable benefit you provide at a fair price to satisfied customers?
- Do you back up your quality products or services with rock-solid, no-questions-asked guarantees and unmatched customer relationships?
- Are you totally reliable? This goes beyond the above two points and is the reason why some companies have been in business for years, while seemingly

not being any different than other companies with similar products and services. Perhaps a better way of posing the question would be, Does your company have integrity?

- Do you give the impression that you've been around for a while and intend to be around for a good deal longer? That anyone dealing with you, (particularly in a B2B relationship), should be assured that you will unhesitatingly solve to their complete satisfaction any and all problems that might occur in your business relationship.
- Even though it may not necessarily be seen as an obvious bottom-line revenue generator, are you prepared to spend time helping solve customers' problems, irrespective of whether this is part of the service you normally provide?
- If you've been in business for a while, do you have solid and reference-proof case studies, particularly with locally recognizable satisfied customers, that you can talk about in your advertising? Can potential customers call your existing customers to verify their experiences with you?
- If you went out of business tomorrow, would anyone, apart from you, your mother, your dog, and your investors give a damn?

So, let's assume you can answer yes to at least one of the above items. (Perhaps, even more than one.) If so, congratulations, you have a USP. Put it down on paper. Avoid using business-speak. Do it in plain language. No charts, no graphs, no Power-Point slides. If you were unfortunate enough to graduate from business school or even worse, you've blown untold thousands of dollars acquiring an MBA, don't worry. You can overcome this handicap. All you have to do is start thinking like a normal human being, rather than the automations these establishments of the Devil are dedicated to replicating throughout the management hierarchies of America and, increasingly, the rest of the civilized world.

Just communicate your USP in simple, easy-to-understand, everyday language to your target audience so that it is both irrefutable and guaranteed to make a wonderful and hopefully lasting impression on them. (See Figure 2.3 for an example.) And because you'll be the first one out there claiming this impossible-to-ignore and unquestionable difference, your competition will be left in the position of

Change everything.

Finally, a network with the bandwidth that delivers the promise of the Internet.
It's called Qwest. And it can make all your expensive IT investments pay off. Because it's the network with
the bandwidth to maximize multimedia applications, put e-business into overdrive, and make your kids start
recognizing you again. Visit our Web site at **qwest.com** to find out about the bandwidth to change everything.

ride the light
Qwest.

FIGURE 2.3: *This is one ad of many my partner Joe Massaro and I did for Qwest Communications; it graphically sums up how you should position yourself and the approach you should take to your advertising, particularly if you want to kick the competition's butt.*

playing catch up. Or, to put it another way, "They'll be eating your dust!" Won't that be an enviable position to find yourself in?

The next chapter deals with how to use your marketing strategy as a foundation on which to build a communications plan that justifies the many reasons why potential customers cannot afford to ignore the benefits of doing business with your company. This is where it starts to get interesting.

CHAPTER THREE

The communications plan: how it can build your business, straighten out your mind, and drive your competition nuts

This chapter will show you how to create a communications plan that serves as a continuing guide for the preparation and implementation of all of the advertising and promotional activities necessary to help you build your business during its early stages of development. It will also serve as a benchmark against which you can measure the success of these activities.

But let's get one thing sorted out right now. This chapter will not be about how to write a ball-buster business plan. You should have created one of those before you embarked on this whole crazy venture. It will also not enable you to write a sales, marketing, distribution, enjoyable sex, lose-100-pounds-in-a-week diet, or any other kind of plan. I'm not qualified to write about those various mundane things. (Well, I could probably be persuaded to have a go at the enjoyable sex plan.) But anyway, if you're looking for the first three items on the list, Entrepreneur Press has many titles that cover them extremely well. For sex and dieting, you'll have to go elsewhere.

The essential thing to keep in mind as I go through the steps necessary to create your communications plan is that the primary focus should always be on the customer. Even though this may sound like a statement of the obvious, and in spite of the fact that anyone with an ounce of gumption would never forget this is the audience you must communicate with and sell to, most so called advertising experts who work in the Big Dumb Agencies (BDAs) of Madison Avenue either fail to recognize or choose to ignore that the vast majority of the audience they claim to address, does not, never has, and never will live in Manhattan. It certainly has never enjoyed the sybaritic pleasures of being chauffeured between a Soho loft and the high-rise mid-town offices ad people work in. It doesn't stop at the health club, spa, or acupuncturist on the way in to work. And, it doesn't stop for cocktails at the King Cole Bar, followed by dinner at Nobu before a chauffer-driven ride back to the Soho loft.

Many in the advertising profession insist on referring to what they do as branding, but that's not really what I should be talking about here. Even though the term *branding* can be, and very often is, used as a catchall for many of the ways agencies endeavor to liposuction money out of their clients, it's also an activity whose results are invariably difficult, and in many cases, impossible to measure.

> Even though many of the people who work on Madison Avenue came from average backgrounds, once they join the Adverati they immediately begin living a lifestyle that is diametrically opposed to that of the people their ads are aimed at.

In other words, branding is often used by advertising agencies as a reason to convince clients they should spend the majority of their budgets on campaigns that will enhance their brand images by creating consumer awareness and generating goodwill towards the brand. And because it's almost impossible to apply any kind of yardstick as to how effective this kind of advertising is, it reduces the risk to the agency of being held account-able for failure. That's why it's in the BDA's self interest to convince clients they should be "investing" their money in branding campaigns, rather than the ones that actually sell stuff.

Obviously, blowing your hard-earned cash on this kind of foolishness is not something you should consider doing at this stage of your company's growth, if ever. The communications plan you need to create must have a single purpose: to produce advertising that sells your company and its products. (See Figure 3.1.) Having said that, some would claim that selling your company is in itself a form of

FIGURE 3.1: *The headline from another Qwest ad illustrates exactly what your com-munications plan should do for you: Overcome any limitations and more than meet your expectations.*

branding. Yes, there is a certain element of truth in this, because everything you do that exposes you to potential and existing customers, including your advertising, will ultimately affect your reputation. And, your reputation is a very important part of your brand.

Simply be aware that what you need to achieve with your communications plan (and limited budget) is far removed from the multimillion dollar campaigns way too many companies get suckered into by their ad agencies, all in the name of branding. What you need to have your advertising do is have an immediate effect on sales.

GETTING STARTED

A communications plan should consist of four elements: What, Who, Why, and How.

> *What*: The current market situation as it relates to your business and an analysis of the competition you need to win market share from.
>
> *Who*: The target groups your communications should be aimed at and the objectives you must achieve against these groups.
>
> *Why*: The creation of incontrovertible reasons (the USP) why the target groups will be positively influenced by your communications.
>
> *How*: The development of a creative strategy that will achieve your objectives and the design of the creative elements that will implement it.

FINDING YOUR WHAT

I have to make the assumption that you started your business because you thought you had something to offer that would appeal to potential customers. Perhaps you were working for someone else and came to the conclusion you could do a far better job if you could run your own operation and didn't have to report to the intellectually-challenged person occupying the corner office. I doubt that you've just graduated from college with a nice new, very expensive degree tucked under your arm. Very few entrepreneurs start a business straight out of school: Michael Dell is a rare example. Bill Gates is even rarer, as he didn't bother to graduate. So after having spent way too much time in the trenches working for someone you wouldn't employ to wash your car, you up and decided to strike out on your own.

This means you must have had a pretty good understanding of the market you wanted to address, what the potential for a start-up was, and what you would have to do to optimize that potential. But having said that, it's worth taking a few minutes to evaluate the significant differences between doing something for an existing company, with the security of a guaranteed monthly paycheck, and doing it for yourself.

Are you sure the market you want to aim at is exactly the same as the one you've been addressing for all those years on behalf of your previous employer? Is this a market that's already oversaturated with companies offering comparable products and services?

Would you be better off targeting a niche segment of the market you think you know from top to bottom, or should you be considering a completely different one? Should you scale down your product offering by concentrating on fewer things but perhaps of better quality, or even design? Have you considered covering a different geographic area? Or better yet, should you go completely virtual as so many successful companies have, in which case geography is no longer a crucial factor in how you run your operation.

There are many decisions you will have to make before taking that giant leap into the unknown. And the only way you can make them intelligently is by doing your homework, which means research, and lots of it. That's the only way you can amass the data necessary to enable you to make the crucial decisions you need to make at this stage of building your business.

> Successful entrepreneurs never stop learning from the successes and failures of others. Then they take that knowledge and leverage it into marketing skills they can apply to their particular business.

But the great news is that today, unlike the situation facing entrepreneurs in the past, virtually all that information is out there, often in the public domain. It's easy to access, and the great majority of it is free. Because of the internet, information that previously you couldn't find or would have cost you an arm and a leg to buy if you could find it, is today out there for the taking. Someone once rightly said that if you can't find what you're looking for on the internet, it either doesn't exist, or it's classified.

As an example, let's assume your new business will have something to do with bicycles, whether it's manufacturing them, retailing and servicing them, publishing books or magazines about them, or even organizing cycling tours around the world. Thanks to today's search engine technology, you can kick off your research by going to any one of the dozens of search sites out there. Odds are you'll make your first visit to Google. Simply type in "The Bicycle Market," and you will get a listing of 5,460,000 potential hits relative to this subject. And by the time you're reading this book, it will probably be up to 6 million! OK, many of these hits might not be of much use to you in your research, but you will be pleasantly surprised at just how many will.

You'll find the web sites of manufacturer and retailer associations, all with tons of information on the current state of the market, as well as forecasts for the future. For example, the National Bicycle Dealers Association offers various studies and reports such as "The Cycling Consumer of the New Millennium" and "The Cost of Doing Business." At the time of writing, it was also offering a very comprehensive "Industry Overview for 2005." In addition, the web sites of hundreds of manufacturers, retailers, trade journals, and ancillary companies are also listed, so you can get a pretty good feel of what the competition is up to.

But don't limit yourself to any one of the expected search engines (besides Google there are Yahoo!, Ask Jeeves, and many others). In fact, you can save yourself time by using one of the search conglomerates such as Dogpile or WebFetch, which combine the results from many of the most popular search engines. You should also consider other web and internet tools that can deliver consumer survey information as well as domestic and international trade statistics. You can get tons of information from the U.S. government and major university web sites. There are more of these resources listed in, would you believe, the Resources section at the back of this book.

There are also a great many market research companies who make continuing studies on virtually any market niche you might possibly be interested in. Web sites such as www.researchandmarkets.com or www.packagedfacts.com are fairly representative of the better ones dealing with the U.S. domestic market. Should you be interested in conquering a particular market in the United Kingdom and Europe www.the-list.co.uk is a good place to start. Be very careful when buying research, make sure it's current, relevant to your market, and that you've already exhausted every avenue to make sure you can't get the same information for free. More of these companies are listed in the Resources section.

Another increasingly important source of information that can be incredibly helpful to you at this stage of your entrepreneurial career will be tapping

> **A** great resource for information on your market is your competition. Go to their web sites and sign up for all their newsletters, white papers, technical papers, industry surveys, and conference reports. Get on their e-mail lists.

into and sucking the life out of the many blogs out there. As you have no doubt heard, blogs are the fastest growing phenomena on the web and these personalized *web-diaries* are multiplying at the rate of thousands of new ones daily. OK, a lot are pretty pathetic offerings doing little more than recording the last time Boring Jim took Filthy Fido for a walk and how many times Filthy Fido cocked his leg up against a lamp post. None of this is stuff you are exactly tearing your hair out to know about at this particularly stage of your career.

An enormous number of blogs, however, are business based, and I can guarantee you, no matter what kind of empire you are intent on building, there are hundreds of bloggers out there doing something pretty similar to you. Most of them are more than happy to share their insights, screw ups, and all kinds of useful information with you. (Otherwise, why would they have a blog?) Even major companies such as Microsoft appreciate the value of blogs, not just as a promotional and PR exercise, but also as a tool that actually drives sales through the dissemination of useful information. John Scoble, a Microsoft employee, maintains a blog at http://scobleizer.wordpress.com that has not only generated an enormous amount of goodwill for Microsoft, but is also an extremely useful tool for people wishing to do business with the company.

Apart from my web site, www.parkerads.com, I also write two blogs. One is primarily my acerbic, somewhat vitriolic thoughts on the current state of advertising at www.adscam.typepad.com; a milder version is at www.adhurl.com. This deals with the ad biz in a rather more restrained fashion and is primarily for those of a more sensitive disposition. It's also because I get paid to write it for a very large online publishing company who would not relish the thought of defending the more outrageous points of view I am at liberty to expound in AdScam. Both blogs have generated a great deal of interest in this book as I have continually informed readers of my progress in the writing.

As I have chronicled my progress on the book, the feedback has been invaluable, not only in terms of determining what people starting and running small- to medium-businesses with limited budgets need in the way of advertising and promotion, but also in helping me stay current with the way small business principals are coping with today's rapidly changing economic landscape. That is precisely why blogs are becoming such an invaluable communications tool. Unlike virtually all other media, they are as current as the latest post, reader feedback, and comment, which may have been put online just a few seconds ago.

> There's a ton of really useful stuff out there in the Blogosphere, but don't be afraid of its sheer volume; use it to your advantage. Even if you have to take a class or a tutorial to better understand it, it will pay off handsomely.

To find blogs relevant to your business and market, you can use one of the many *blogrolls* such as Blogarama, Bloglines, and Blogwise. (There are dozens more out there, many of which you will find listed in the Resources section.) All of these act as search engines and aggregators for the millions of blogs seemingly growing at a much faster pace than the young Steve McQueen's nemesis in his never-to-be-forgotten movie debut, *The Blob*.

But, don't worry about being overwhelmed by the sheer volume of all the stuff out there in the Blogosphere, you can simply subscribe (more often than not for free) to one of the many feed sites out there, all of which, thanks to the wonders of RSS technology, will instantly advise you of new posts through e-mail alerts that then link you to all of the blogs you've designated as being of particular interest to you.

It's not brain surgery; it's common sense. Remember?

Finding Your Competition's What

Once you've started to get a handle on what the current size and condition of the market is for your business, you need to start thinking about what your competition is doing to reach this same market. Because whether you intend your business to be local, regional, or national in scope, it's absolutely essential that you identify and get inside the head of your competition. OK, I know this may sound somewhat obvious, but based on many, many brain-numbing years of experience, I can assure you I've come across an amazing number of clients who don't have the vaguest idea what their competition is up to. Even worse, they don't seem to see any reason why they should. Irrespective of whether it's an awareness of their competition's market share, product range, and differentiation, distribution, pricing, advertising, and promotional activities, or any of the many dozens of other essential facts that can help a company plan how best to steal the competition's customers away from them, most are blissfully ignorant. But then again, if you come to think about it, the surprising fact that so many businesses do indeed seem to operate in such an amazing condition of unawareness can only ultimately work to your advantage.

By talking to the competition's existing customers, you can find out what it is the competition did that attracted these people to do business with them in the first place. What are the things, big or small, they do that are key factors in maintaining their existing customers and generating repeat sales? Better yet, by talking to some of the customers your

> Before checking out and logging on for information on your competition's web sites, set up a series of anonymous e-mail accounts. No point in tipping your hand.

competitors have lost, you can find out what competitors did that drove these customers away. You also need to talk to your competition's suppliers and distributors. Find out what business practices they use, or perhaps fail to use effectively, that affect their relationship with essential parts of their supply chain.

Check out your competition's web sites. And don't just do it every now and again, do it daily. That way you can immediately see what promotional or seasonal offers they have, what kind of discounts they are offering, whether they give free shipping on orders over a certain size, or if they give free shipping irrespective of the order size? How about bundling deals, inventory clearances, and so on and so forth? No matter how insignificant or unimportant this information might seem to be at the time you access it, you never know; it could be potentially useful in the future.

Finding this information will require time and effort on your part. If you don't think you've got the time or don't want to expend the effort, you can always engage an independent research company to do it for you. (This also applies to the initial market research discussed earlier.) Whether you do it yourself or have someone do it for you, this market/customer/competitor research will, without question, prove to be invaluable when creating your communication plan.

> Depending on the size of market you're operating in, why not become the go-to person with the expertise for your business category? How do you think people like Martha Stewart and Click and Clack, The Car Talk Guys got started?

You should also find out if your competition attends trade shows. Do their principals and corporate management speak at conferences and seminars? Do they write for the local press or appear on local TV and radio shows? If they don't, then you should. If you can become recognized as the local expert on whatever it is your company does, you'll very soon become the person the media calls first for quotes and a point of view on the subject you know everything about. This is just one simple example of the many highly effective ways you can get your company name out in front of potential customers. I'll be dealing with more later, most of which enjoy such NewSpeak advertising descriptions as viral, guerrilla, and word-of-mouth marketing. The beauty of these tactics is that most people, including your competition, don't immediately recognize them as part of the expected way of doing things when it comes to mainstream advertising and promotion. Best of all, the great majority of these activities won't cost you a penny.

FINDING YOUR WHO

The first thing you must do when deciding on a target audience is to identify it. That may seem like another obvious statement of fact. Yet as I've mentioned earlier in reference to your competition, it's surprising how many clients I've dealt with over the years who have failed to follow through on the somewhat obvious procedure of searching out and cherry picking their potential customers. That raises an important question: Exactly how do you begin to find out whom you should address through your advertising? Even more importantly, when you've broadly identified them, how do you then go about discovering their many and different characteristics? These characteristics will allow you to pinpoint their socioeconomic habits so that you may then target your communications specifically at those who are not only interested in what you have to offer but also have the resources to purchase what you are offering at this time.

If you're starting a B2C company you might think you already have a fairly good idea of who your potential audience is. But if you really want to define and identify that audience, you'll very likely have more work to do. For example, as we discussed earlier, you may have created a business aimed at cyclists. But having broadly identified the category,

> One of the oldest rules in marketing is known as the 80/20 convention: 80 percent of goods in a given market niche are bought by 20 percent of consumers. If you can identify and target that 20 percent, you can take the lion's share of the market.

if you do not fine-tune exactly who your best prospects are, you could end up talking to a tremendous number of people. That's why you want to refine your potential audience a little more than just lumping together everyone who rides a bicycle.

There are people who cycle as a healthy and inexpensive way of getting to wherever they earn their daily crust. There are people who do it as a masochistic form of exercise. There are people who ride for sport, and there are even people who ride for a living (think Lance Armstrong). And within these broad categories, there are subcategories, people who ride different kinds of bikes, road, track, mountain, tandem, tricycles, and unicycles. There are even people who indulge in bicycle polo! Aiming their marketing efforts at these many different kinds of enthusiasts are companies that specialize in bikes, accessories, clothing, books, fitness programs, tours that recreate the agonies suffered by the pros as they cross the Alps in the Tour de France; you name it.

So, keep in mind that whether you intend to make your fortune selling bicycles or bologna, if you're talking to individuals (B2C), then you must identify them as precisely as you can by age, gender, occupation, other demographics, both social and economic, and any other interest they may have that allows you to develop communications that effectively address this precise market niche.

On the other hand, if your company is B2B, your priorities will be different. Here you must identify businesses or industries that would be specifically interested in the products or services you have to offer. In the past, this was primarily determined by geographical location, which is why the companies who made the widgets that went into the Fords, Chryslers, and Pontiacs of the '50s were usually located within a few miles of Detroit. Now, the vast majority of these companies

> If you concentrate on a niche market, rather than a mass market, you will benefit from being recognized as the resource customers must go to for products they cannot find elsewhere. They will also refer you to others as your reputation grows.

are several thousands of miles away in the Guangdong province of the Peoples Republic of China! Today, with the wonders of the internet and the many other forms of electronic communication, geography is no longer a dominant factor in reaching your customers. Now it's all about offering a superior product at a superior price that you can guarantee to deliver exactly when you promise, if not before.

If you are a B2B start-up, there's no question you wouldn't have gotten yourself into this situation if you hadn't had a list of prospective customers and perhaps promises of work from customer contacts you've made over the years while working for others. Even so, you must recognize it's absolutely essential that you don't take these promises for granted. If you're really going to make it, you'll have to get out there and prospect for new business. You'll have to invest in an ongoing advertising program that's based on a sound communications plan that delivers long-term returns. It all comes down to spelling out, as precisely as you can, exactly who you intend to sell your products or services to. Once you've done that, you can move on to the next part of the communications plan.

DEFINING YOUR WHY

The why is usually the hardest part of the exercise. Here you must discover, or if necessary create, the incontrovertible reasons why potential customers will want to do business with you. The good news is that it's your company, so if anyone in the world knows what makes it the best thing since sliced bread, it should be you. And because you are going to produce your own advertising, you can use your laser-like intelligence and God-given talents to produce the kind of kick-ass advertising companies rarely get when they rely on a Big Dumb Agency to do it for them.

Why are you constantly exposed to so much bad advertising? Well consider this, in your small business empire, unlike the leviathans that constitute corporate America, you don't have multiple levels of chicken-livered corporate marketing management scared witless to produce anything that might be perceived by senior management as possibly rocking the boat.

This state of affairs is usually compounded by the fact that these many layers of jello-spined, chicken-livered creatures are replicated at the Big Dumb Agency (BDA) by a bunch of account executives, otherwise known as *suits*, whose main function in life is to avoid doing anything that could possibly upset the client (and thus, endanger their own position). Consequently, the chances of the agency producing work that might be perceived as edgy by anyone who hasn't been dead for 50 years, is remote. That is why the vast majority of advertising produced by BDAs is weak, ineffectual, and very often a complete waste of money.

Anatomy of a Missing Why in an Ad Campaign

There are many reasons most Madison Avenue advertising doesn't have a Why. Here is an example of the steps that miss the Why.

1. *The client decides it needs an ad or a campaign.* It's nearly always the client who dictates when it needs something. Most agencies are totally reactive, usually lacking the nerve, or indeed the common sense, to think of acting otherwise. The agency suits fly in to corporate headquarters and get *briefed.* This usually entails taking the client's advertising director out for lunch or dinner, or both, writing down a few details about the new product, service, or whatever the client wants the ad/campaign to be about. Then the suits jump on a plane and fly back to the "real world" of Madison Avenue in time for predinner cocktails in Soho.

2. *The suit prepares a creative brief,* which supposedly contains the information necessary to get the caged animals down on the creative floor starting to think about producing the next award-winning campaign for the agency.

3. *The suit delivers the creative brief to the creatives.* This usually involves the suit reading the entire thing very slowly and very loudly to the art director and the copywriter team working on the account. Most suits are under the impression that all the creatives are Neanderthals incapable of understanding words containing more than two syllables, a perception usually reinforced, if not encouraged, by the way creatives talk, dress, and behave.

4. *The creative brief is rarely more than one page long* and usually consists of such earth shattering insights and objectives as "The client creates synergistic solutions to empower business leaders," "The client aspires to become the market leader," "The client is committed to customer satisfaction," and so on. These are often statements so banal and generic they could apply to virtually any company in the known universe. Rarely are there any insights, let alone any kind of meaningful information that the people tasked with actually producing the advertising can use to create anything remotely resembling a worthwhile campaign.

5. *As the brief usually requests initial ideas in a couple of weeks,* the creatives immediately repair to the nearest bar for 10 or 11 days to play shuffleboard, darts, drink, smoke, and generally do nothing that would involve thinking about the brief. With a few days left, they knuckle down and start looking through advertising award annuals, photo stock books, and the latest editions of hot magazines such as *Wallpaper* or *Black Book.* (I am sure by the time you read this there will be much hotter magazines.) In fact, they do anything else that might spark the beginnings of an idea they can use to create an *homage,* which is French for rip-off. (It sounds better in French.) Other sources of creative inspiration often include going to see all the new movies released that week, buying every art book costing more than $50 in Rizzoli's, and, when all else fails, returning to the bar and hoping something original pops into their respective heads after prodigious quantities of writer fuel have been imbibed.

6. *Without going into even more excruciating detail,* suffice it to say that some ad concepts are eventually produced and presented by the suit to the client. The client proceeds to demand numerous changes that will water down any originality in the concepts and guarantee they are like 99 percent of all the other ads out there. The "suit" praises the client for her insight and invaluable refinements to the concepts. He buys her lunch or dinner, then speeds back to the agency and briefs the creatives on the necessary changes. After the obligatory hissy fits and tantrums, a few days back in the bar bitching about the suit and the client, the creatives begrudgingly make the changes. The concepts are then tested.

7. *Testing usually implies doing a series of focus groups.* This involves getting together a group of housewives anxious to escape the tedium of suburbia by escaping to the mall and then being corralled into a windowless room with a large mirror on one wall, which is in reality, a one-way window, behind which sits the agency and client munching on M&M's as they listen to these ladies answer inane questions about prototype ads that are flashed in front of them by a failed psychology major. Focus groups serve two purposes: First, they allow agency and client middle management to cover their rear ends, because if the advertising fails to achieve any kind of success, which is usually the case, those responsible can claim "Well heck CJ, it tested like gangbusters in Dubuque." The second purpose of focus groups is to guarantee that any tiny remaining spark of originality will be beaten out before it sees the light of day. As someone once said, "Design by committee produces camels."

8. *This process is repeated* until either (1) the CEO of the client company is playing golf with his other CEO friends and one of them tells him he just saw his latest TV spot and thought it sucked, big time; (2) the marketing director of the client company leaves for a better job. The new Marketing Director instigates and goes through the motions of an agency review, which is basically an exercise in futility, because his intention all along is to steer the account to the agency that wined and dined him so well in his last job; or (3) the agency resigns the account because it is approached by another client operating in the same business category, but with a budget ten times bigger than the existing client.

That's why most Madison Avenue advertising doesn't have a why. But the great thing about your business situation is that you don't have to go through this kind of stupidity, not only because you can't afford to, but also because you're too smart to fall for the sheer craziness of it all. Big companies are content to create me-too advertising that rarely presents a USP to their intended customers because these companies can rely on the overwhelming volume of advertising they put out there to make an impression. If you are new in a particular market, it isn't enough to be seen as just showing up. You have to communicate you are the best vendor in that market by offering not just a similar product or comparable service to everyone else, but one that's perceived as unique and exactly what the customer needs and wants right now.

If you are lucky, or perhaps a genius, you may have invented something that is unique. The first company to invent a cure for cancer or, even less dramatically, a cure for the common cold will truly have the world beating a path to its door. But rest assured, in today's overcrowded marketplace, it'll still have to get the word out there. It will, however, be a lot easier to do this in its case than if it had merely come up with another nasal congestion spray or headache pill.

The odds are you haven't come up with something destined to get you a Nobel Prize. But hopefully, what you have come up with is something marginally better than most of the other stuff out there. So, in order to create your USP, you have to carefully analyze how you can present that discernable difference in such a way as to make your potential audience consider it something it cannot live without. As I've said before, there will always be something intrinsically different about your product, or how you make it, or even how you distribute it; you simply have to dig and dig until you figure it out.

Some years ago, I was tasked with doing an ad campaign for a very large U.S. telecommunication modem manufacturer. As usual, the creative brief was exactly like the ones I've described above—useless! So, being an awkward bugger, I insisted on visiting the factory where the modems were made. I was told in no uncertain manner by both the client and the BDA I was freelancing for that a visit would be pointless as it made its modems in exactly the same way everyone else made modems. I insisted until I got them to agree on my making the trip.

After spending a great many boring and pointless hours looking at boiler-plate PowerPoint presentations by armies of management, marketing, and R&D people, I was eventually allowed down on the production line where the stuff was actually made. Among many stupid and seemingly pointless questions that I directed at the chief engineer, my final one was why the modems went through the line, were taken off at the end, carted up to the beginning of the line, and put through again. He replied that they did that so they could double solder all the connections to guarantee no loss of connectivity, irrespective of operating conditions. I asked him if the competition did that. He shrugged his shoulders, looked at me as if I had just asked him if the moon was made of green cheese, and said, "To be honest, I don't know. Why, is it important?"

That was the Eureka moment, because, as it turned out, no one else knew either. And more importantly, no other manufacturer knew or talked about it in any part of their marketing communications. For all I knew the competition may in fact have triple or quadruple soldered everything that went down the production lines, but no one talked about this part of the manufacturing process. So, the client's "unique" double soldering manufacturing technique became the USP upon which all the ads I did were based. It served to emphasize the absolute reliability of the client's products.

This is the kind of USP that works best, because it relies on one, easily understood, differentiating fact. You've heard of the elevator speech, right? The one that goes as follows. You get in an elevator on the 25th floor of a building. In the elevator is one other person. It might be the world's most beautiful man/woman whom you would love to spend the night with. It might be the guy who wants to foreclose on your house because you haven't made any mortgage payments in six months. Or it might be the customer you want to convince to buy your incredible new Gizmo. In the time it takes to get to the ground floor, you have 15 seconds to convince that man/woman/loan shark/customer to sleep with/forgive/buy from you, otherwise you will be frustrated/homeless/out of business.

If you look at most companies' so-called USPs, which, in essence, are their elevator speeches, they usually go something like this:

Acme Global Infrastructures create the world's most innovative, interoperable, and scaleable business solutions based on leading edge research and development programs. Our passion is to bring these solutions to business enterprises, irrespective of size and geography, and to do it with a guaranteed superior ROI. All Acme Global Infrastructure solutions are backed up by our unmatched teams of after-sales and service specialists, each and every one dedicated to the delivery of ultimate customer satisfaction.

By the time you've managed to get someone to listen to, let alone understand, all that gobbledygook, the elevator would have crashed through the 12th subbasement.

Your USP should go something like this: (You choose the applicable words.)

Acme Inc., designs/manufactures/delivers the best value product/service/ selection of widgets backed up by an absolute satisfaction/money back/no questions asked guarantee.

Better yet, if you can say something like this: (You fill in the xxxx's.)

Acme Inc., makers of the worlds only atomic powered xxxx widgets, guaranteed to outlast and outperform ordinary widgets by 10,000 percent at half the price of other widgets.

You'll have their attention before you hit the mezzanine, guaranteed.

It also means you have nailed exactly what it is that makes you different from everyone else (see Figure 3.2 for a classic example) and why a prospective customer has to consider you when it is in the market for what you are selling. Even better,

FIGURE 3.2: *Simple, straightforward, and believable!*

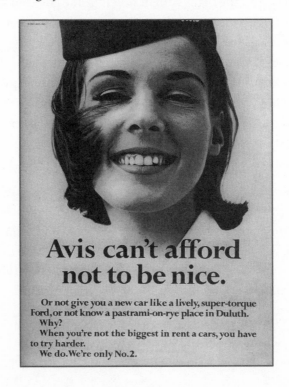

what if you can come up with the ultimate solid gold, diamond encrusted USP that is so remarkable it will attract customers for your product or service even when they are not in the market for it? Now, even though that might be pretty hard to pull off, it's not impossible.

The biggest pitfall, the one you need to avoid at all costs, is trying to be all things to all people. The big companies can afford to take this lazy route. They can end up with the kind of me-too communications that only partially succeed because of the weight of their advertising expenditures. Your USP must help you carve out a specific market niche, one that gives potential customers a reason to prefer you over and above the rest of the competition. One that leaves them with the perception that you provide a unique product or service delivered at a price point that is seen as delivering value. Show them you may not be the cheapest, but there's no question, you are the best (see Figure 3.3).

The least desirable scenario is one that reduces you to competing strictly on price because you have not made the effort or taken the time to succeed in differentiating yourself sufficiently from your competition. If you fall into this nasty trap, it will never fail to end up as a zero sum game. There will *always* be someone who can beat you on price. Much better to compete on value.

So, why not define your USP by

- being the first on the market with a new product.
- making or selling better stuff.
- offering a wider range of inexpensive things.
- offering a smaller range of super high-quality things.
- making it really easy to buy stuff.
- making it pleasant and fun to buy stuff.
- being the best at what you do.
- being more effective at what you do.
- being more flexible in how you manufacture
- being more flexible in how you stock.
- being more flexible in how you sell.
- being more flexible in how you do everything.
- Men hate to shop. Make it less of a pain.
- Women love to shop. Make it more than love. Make it ecstasy.

FIGURE 3.3: *Even though IBM's O/S2 operating system was superior to Microsoft Windows, it was being killed in the market place until O&M repositioned it as a server operating system. The ad campaign showed customers worldwide enthusiastically endorsing the product.*

And so on and so on.

Your USP is there. Either it is in actuality staring you in the face, or intrinsically, it is waiting to be dug up out of the everyday processes you have come to rely on and take for granted as the normal way of doing business. Just be careful that you haven't allowed yourself to accept these processes and see them as the things that make your business like everyone else's, rather than identifying those significant enough to make yours different. Time to get digging.

Finding Out How

Assuming you've come up with a rock-solid, atomic-blast-proof USP, the next thing you need to do is decide exactly how you're going to communicate it to the masses out there desperate to buy your stuff. Don't worry, I'll deal with how you go about creating gangbuster ads and exactly where you should run them in later chapters. Right now, what we need to concentrate on is making absolutely sure your USP becomes an integral part of all your communications. That means it should have an influence on everything from business cards and stationery, to catalogs and literature, even to how you and your employees answer the phone and greet customers.

You must never lose an opportunity to communicate what it is that makes your company different. If you are sublimely lucky enough to be the only manufacturer of atomic-powered widgets in the universe, then by golly, you are unique and you'd be incredibly stupid not to make sure you make that fact known to every potential customer out there. If on the other hand, you haven't come up with something capable of recreating Chernobyl, then as I have repeated ad nauseum, you must take something you have and communicate it in such a way that causes the merely ordinary to become extraordinary.

> The key to a successful advertising program is building a relationship between you and your customers by continually treating them with respect and giving them the information that will compel them to want to do business with you.

HOW SMART COMPANIES MAKE THEIR USP UNIQUE IN EVERY RESPECT

Here are four examples of truly great USPs and how the companies who created them relentlessly applied them throughout all their communications to radically change the market's perception of who and what they were. Be sure to notice that none of these USPs are based on anything that is intrinsically different from what their competitors already had. What they did that separated them from everyone else was to find a way of presenting the ordinary in an extraordinary way.

Smirnoff Vodka
"It leaves you breathless"

In the 1960s, America's perception of vodka was as a cheap, fiery Russian peasant drink made from potatoes. (In fact, contrary to the commonly held belief, very few vodkas are actually made from potatoes; like whiskey and gin, they are mostly made from wheat or rye grain.) Smirnoff's success was to take the implied strength of vodka, talk about filtering it through "mountains" of charcoal (a process virtually all alcoholic spirit makers use) and so imply that you could drink it without it leaving an alcohol after taste on your breath. This way, by drinking Smirnoff Vodka you could enjoy the best of both worlds. You could get hammered without making it obvious.

And long before today's avalanche of buzz—viral—guerrilla—word-of-mouth advertising (WOMA) and other nontraditional media activities, Smirnoff was hosting parties, tastings, running cross promotions with other drink and food companies, competitions, and sponsorships, and other activities that virtually created the U.S. market for vodka by making it a respectable and desirable drink. It owned the lion's share of the market for years until the advent of designer imported vodkas in the '90s.

Harvey's Bristol Cream Sherry
"Never serve the coffee without the cream"

Sherry had traditionally been seen as a rather genteel aperitif favored by little old ladies who might perhaps have the odd thimbleful along with their afternoon crumpets and Dundee cake. Heublein, the American importer (who was also the manufacturer of Smirnoff), wanted to expand the market by repositioning it as a more "robust" drink suitable for both sexes and all kinds of occasions. Hence, the juxtaposition of a cream sherry with after-dinner drinking, something normally reserved for cognac or port.

All the advertising majored on Harvey's implied USP—that it was perfectly acceptable, even desirable, to drink Harvey's along with your coffee after dinner. As with Smirnoff, this USP originated in the 1960s and was heavily merchandized through all aspects of the bar and restaurant trade, along with major consumer promotions and events. Ever since then, Harvey's has maintained and built upon its position as the largest selling brand of sherry in the United States.

Sun Microsystems
"The network is the computer!"

Until the mid-1980s, Sun Microsystems was recognized as one of the major designers and manufacturers of work stations, an advanced type of desktop computer designed to handle sophisticated computational tasks such as mathematical and graphics intensive applications. However, Sun determined that if it were to grow and be perceived as more than a niche market player, it needed to expand into other hardware and software product lines. It was one of the first companies to realize the future of computing would be in seamlessly connected, transparent environments.

By offering servers, operating systems, and multiplatform development languages, it was able to position itself as a total networking solutions company. Hence the brilliance of its USP—"The network is the computer!" While others sold stand-alone box solutions, Sun was able to position itself as the company with the single-source answer to enterprise-wide computing. Sun stayed with the theme for many years, using it in all forms of corporate communications and marketing materials. In fact, at the time of this writing, there are rumors that they may be bringing the line back.

IBM
"Solutions for a small planet!"

For many years IBM had been viewed as a monolithic giant, only interested in dealing with major companies on a global basis. Even though in the early 1980s, it had made the personal computer an acceptable purchase within the rarefied atmosphere of corporate America, it was still regarded as remote, stuffy, and only interested in customers who were prepared to spend significant amounts of money. When Lou Gerstner took over as CEO in the 1990s, IBM was losing business to the smaller but rapidly growing, more agile, and reactive companies that were starting to make significant inroads into areas of business IBM had traditionally maintained a stranglehold on.

Gerstner consolidated all IBM's advertising at Ogilvy & Mather, with a total combined budget of nearly $1 billion. (It had previously been using more than 80 different agencies world wide.) The reinvention of IBM in the minds of the consumer began with the long-running and very successful TV campaign featuring IBM customers who were not the traditional "CEO as God" types seated behind three-inch thick mahogany boardroom tables. Instead, these were people who had small vineyards in Italy, a furniture company in England, a boutique in New York, even an "organ grinder" in Hungary. All spoke in their native language with subtitles at the bottom of the screen. Everyone's business was helped in some direct fashion by an IBM product or service. The tag line for all the spots (repeated in all other forms of communication) was "Solutions for a small planet!" It completely repositioned IBM from being this big, impersonal organization to one that was happy to deal with business owners, irrespective of size or location. The campaign ran for several years, and I believe would still be as effective if it were running today.

Each of these themes was not only used extensively throughout each company's advertising and marketing programs, they were also used for very long periods of time. One of the major problems I've had with some clients in the past is that they are under the impression that the public is as aware of their advertising as they are. Believe me, that is far from the truth. If you are creating your own advertising, which is more than likely if you are a small- to medium-sized business owner, then you are going to see it every day. But your potential customers will not, unless you are prepared to stand outside wherever they live night and day wearing a sandwich board plastered with your message.

> The audience of one is much more attainable on the internet. Amazon has the most sophisticated interpretation of this with its highly personalized customer web pages and sophisticated, targeted e-mail programs.

Instead, you have to develop a creative strategy that will allow you to get your message through the clutter of advertising out there and do it in the most efficient and cost-effective way. In later chapters, I will discuss media and other communications options that allow you to do this. For now, let's consider what your strategy should be to communicate to your target audience the benefits of doing business with you. How can you make your USP particular to that *audience of one*— your customer.

Firstly, you have to let them know you *exist*. That means getting their *attention*. For years, far too many advertisers have done this simply by being loud and obnoxious. The problem with this approach is that there are already too many advertisers out there doing just that; think of your local car dealerships. They almost all subjugate potential customers to the same old boiler-plate advertising approaches car dealers have used for years. Every inch of the space they buy in local newspapers is crammed with cars, trucks, SUVs, starbursts, banners, money off, low financing, no payments for 100 years. Then, they offer free hot dogs and soda, worth at least a couple of dollars, if you "come on down" and test drive a $60,000 Hummer. As for the TV spots they subject the viewing public to, they should be ashamed of themselves. So, if you are a car dealer, it's time you changed your ways. If you consider that most people are bombarded by hundreds of advertising messages every day—90 percent of which are simply tuned out—there's a good chance that 90 percent of the money being spent on any kind of advertising is wasted. Do you want it to be yours?

Remember the words of my two favorite dead ad men, David Ogilvy's "The consumer isn't stupid, she's your wife" and Howard Gossage's "People don't read advertising; they read what they're interested in"? Both seem pretty obvious and quite logical statements to me, yet for years the vast majority of people who spend money on advertising have chosen to ignore these irrefutable truths. So, why not make a promise to yourself that whatever you have to say in your advertising will be interesting, relevant, and best of all, meaningful to that *audience of one*?

That means you should not try to be all things to all people by aiming at the lowest common denominator. How much better to grab a smaller but more profitable part of a big market than going for the buckshot effect and getting none? Position yourself (and your USP) as answering a need this *audience of one* is anxious to throw money at. Get its attention by being *specific*; spell out what there is about you (and your USP) that is the significant difference. Don't be afraid to do it in detail, and depending on the choice of media, at length. One of the biggest *canards* advertising experts use is that people do not read long advertising copy. This may very well be true when it's done in such a way that the reader sees no reason to pay any attention to it. But, as Howard Gossage said, "People read what they are interested in." Make your advertising so interesting they can't ignore it.

Then, when you've got your audience's attention and interest and hopefully convinced it that it must do business with you, give it an extra reason to do so. Maybe a sale, special offer, free shipping, two for the price of one, it doesn't have to be extravagant, just something to give it that extra nudge. Then make it easy for it to take that final step, in person, on the telephone, through the web, via e-mail, or by smoke signals, if necessary.

Take a leaf out of the direct marketer's book. The offer doesn't have to be as cheesy as those TV spots pushing NoFatso pills that make you lose 500 pounds in 5 days, or the Aberzizer for a six-pack belly in 10 days if you use it for 10 minutes

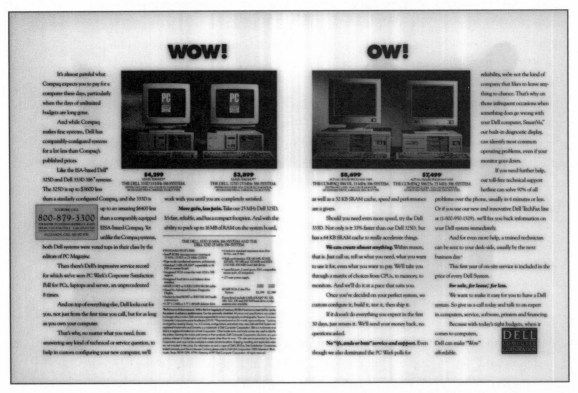

FIGURE 3.4: *Just one of the hundreds of ads I did for Dell that helped build it into the world's largest manufacturer and seller of computers, creating a multimillion dollar company.*

a day. Instead, look at the ace direct-marketer of all time, Dell Inc. It doesn't matter if it's via TV, newspapers, magazines, inserts, or direct mail. Dell's advertising always gives you tons of information, backed up some special offer that drives you to respond for more information and special pricing or bundling deals. It doesn't treat customers like idiots. Instead, it respects their intelligence, which is why Dell is now a multibillion dollar company. (See Figure 3.4.)

Finally, when you've got that *audience of one* interested and anxious to do business with you, close the sale. Depending on what kind of business you run, that means getting it into your store or factory, talking it into committing to a purchase over the phone, or designing your web site in such a way that purchasing decisions for customers are intuitive, easy, and hassle free.

In later chapters, I'll get into the actual mechanics of how you can cost effectively and intelligently create the advertising elements necessary to get your customers interested and enthusiastic about buying from you. For now, concentrate on getting the What, Who, Why, How sorted out. They will be the foundation upon which everything else you do will be built.

CHAPTER FOUR

Do I really have to spend an arm and a leg on advertising? Or can I do it on the cheap?

I won't pretend to be an expert on budgets, whether they are for what you should spend on advertising or how you should manage your personal finances so you're guaranteed an early retirement at the ripe old age of 30. Goodness knows, there are enough books around dealing with the latter subject to fill a landfill somewhere in the southern hemisphere.

But when it comes to spending/investing/blowing obscene amounts of money on advertising, I've spent too many years in the ad biz watching vast sums of cash being wasted on ineffectual and outrageously expensive campaigns and schemes that even the most creatively challenged ten-year-old would immediately recognize as a criminal waste of time and money. Much of it I've witnessed in the thickly carpeted halls of Madison Avenue, where, because of the intrinsic ad agency business model, it's an inescapable fact that the more money the client spends, the more money the agency makes.

It's no surprise that when, 20 years ago, the Ted Bates agency was sold to Saatchi & Saatchi for $507 million and the agency chairman walked away with $112.5 million, clients began waking up to the fact that most of this money was coming from what they had been paying their agency in fees and commissions over many years. Today, the few remaining independent agencies of any size are being acquired, not for millions, but for billions (including long suffering and many times courted Ted Bates, which has been sold yet again). It just proves there's still quite a bit of money to burn on Madison Avenue, even with the great majority of agencies garnering their ill-gotten gains through fees rather than on rebated media commissions. Yet for some archaic reason, the industry still calculates its agency league tables based on the sum total of each agency's media billings, rather than its income.

But having noted and commented on these less than desirable qualities of the agencies of Madison Avenue, I'll be the first to admit there have also been many occasions when I've worked directly with clients as a consultant or freelancer where I've witnessed much the same profligate waste, bad planning, and ineffectual execution of advertising programs that can be only be described as being on a par with some of Madison Avenue's worst excesses. Perhaps this is simply further proof that advertising is one of the most inexact and least accountable ways companies can spend large amounts of money it has taken them a great deal of effort to acquire in the first place.

> In a recent study, as a percentage of revenues, small companies (assets of less than $250K) spent an average of 1.6 percent on advertising. Medium companies (assets of $500K to $1 million) spent 1.7 percent. Large companies (assets of more than $1 million) spent 5.8 percent. Yet, advertising agencies spent an average of 1.2 percent.

YOU WORKED HARD FOR IT, SPEND IT WISELY

So, rather than fall into either of those highly undesirable situations, how can you best execute your communication plan without it costing you the equivalent of the GNP of a small African country? Surely, there must be ways to spend money wisely when you do your own advertising. And there are.

As I keep unapologetically stressing, it's all about applying logic with a generous heaping of common sense. You know the market you're in, you know what your competition is up to, and you can easily find out what they're spending on their advertising and where they're spending it. Do the math; it's not brain surgery. Then comes the hard part. Once you've found out what everyone else is shelling out for their advertising, you have to decide whether you should match them or go for the brass ring and spend more. Or, better yet, is there a third way, one where it's possible to spend less, but spend smarter? Obviously, the third way is the most preferable.

How do you spend your limited ad budget smarter? You do it by (1) recognizing the essential components that you need to create as the core of your ad program; (2) costing out what it will take to produce them; and (3) then establishing what you can afford to spend running them in the media best suited to have an effect on the target groups you need to make an impression on. As to what those media choices should be, I'll deal with which ones and how you should go about sorting those that will be right for you in Chapter 5.

You must zero in on what you can best achieve with the minimum number of advertising exposures, both in terms of the ads themselves and where you choose to run them. You cannot allow yourself to be persuaded by others that you need to change what you instinctively, and perhaps through experience, know is the right approach for your business and your market.

A Sorry Story

Let me illustrate. Many years ago I was consulting for a small ad agency that handled the account of what was then America's largest manufacturer of telephone head sets, those that people in call centers wear so they can work hands-free to input data on their computers. The company had an 85 percent market share of the installed base, and as this was before the outsourcing explosion moved many call centers overseas, it meant that the company controlled virtually all of a substantial American market. Most of the client's budget, which was about $1 million, was spent in a limited number of trade press publications, marketing directly to companies with large sales and service organizations. The media advertising was backed up by well designed and written product literature, sales promotion, and support materials.

After several years of doing an excellent job for the client, the agency was fired by the client's brand new marketing director, who moved the account to the BDA (Big Dumb Agency) on Madison Avenue that he had worked with at his previous job. Over lunch at the Palm and after the third bottle of wine, the agency suit persuaded the client's marketing guy that what his company needed was a big-push to expand its brand franchise. This is Madison Avenue speak for "Why-Not-Blow-It-All-In-A-Giant-One-Shot-Campaign?" By wrapping this scam up in macho, General Patton/Vince Lombardi-style language, the agency impressed on the client that this would create an "event" out of the advertising, thereby making his budget stretch even further and work harder.

If you'd been around BDAs as much as I have, you know an event is simply a less outrageous way of saying, "We really don't have a clue about your business, your market, or who the hell you should be talking to. But, speaking as the ad experts of Madison Avenue, how about this for a barn-burner of an idea. Let's take the entire ad budget and not dribble it away over a 12-month period with the odd media insertion here and there, followed up by the occasional promotion or special offer. We'll go ape and blow it all in one big media extravaganza—like buying lots of network TV and a pile of double page spreads in *People* magazine, and we'll do it all over a four-week period." So, after a couple of cognacs, the client goes for it, spends several million dollars over the four week media blast, at the end of which his market share is still 85 percent and there's no money left for the next 11 months. And because the client didn't have any money left to spend for the rest of the year, the agency then resigned the account.

The agency's rationale for the big-push was that by going on network TV and running ads in *People* magazine they were reaching and influencing the end-users of the client's product, i.e., the ladies (in those days it was mostly ladies working in call centers, airline/hotel/travel reservation centers, and other companies with large telephone sales and service operations) who wore the head sets. Of course, what you or I could have told the agency, and the client who should have known better, is that it might very well be the call center ladies who wear the product, but they weren't the ones buying them. That was the responsibility of the management people within the companies operating the call centers who purchase office equipment and communications products. All of whom had been reached very effectively by the previous program of trade advertising and direct mail, and incidentally, they'd been reached for a fraction of the money the new agency had blown on its massive TV and the consumer press campaign.

> The cost of producing the "Headset" TV spot (not the cost of running it) was the profit the client needed to make selling a million headsets.

The moral of the story, apart from avoiding alcoholic lunches at the Palm with BDAs, is to stick with what you know, particularly when it comes to your budget and what kind of return you expect to get from it. In the case of this particular client, someone should have been asking the question, "If I already have an 85 percent market share, why would I want to spend millions to try and nudge it up a couple more points? It only means my cost per new customer acquisition will be through the roof."

ADVERTISING FOR START-UPS

If you are a start-up, deciding on exactly how much of your seed capital you need to spend on your advertising program can be a problem. If you worked in a similar kind of company before striking out on your own, you may have a fair idea of what your previous company spent on advertising. And while this is a good starting point, you have to bear in mind your previous employer ran a company that was already established and had a large existing customer base.

You, a future captain of industry, are starting from scratch and so will have to spend substantially more to establish yourself in the marketplace and attract customers, even if you manage to skim a few from your previous employer. And let's be honest about it, you've probably already had a few tête-à-têtes with many of those customers before you decided to strike off on your own. But even if you had a few promises of future business, and who hasn't, to make a go of it and get your

> "Most major advertising budgets are based on the premise that it takes a billion dollar hammer to pound a ten cent thumb tack!"
>
> —Howard Gossage

TransGlobalWidget Company off the ground and started on the way to an IPO worthy of the front page of the *Wall Street Journal*, you're going to have to cast your net a little wider. That means knuckling down and deciding just how big a budget will be necessary in order for you to be up and running with the gangbuster advertising program that will be capable of doing the job for you.

Before I get into the nasty details of dollars and cents, remember this: A well-thought-out and properly planned advertising budget must be one capable of funding a program that achieves two objectives:

1. Winning customers
2. Retaining customers

Even though the first one sounds as if it's purely acquisition focused and is therefore strictly about sending out targeted messages in an effort to encourage new customers to try out what you have to offer, it should also be about building a distinctive character and unique tone of voice which will separate you from the competition. In other words, it's about beginning to build a brand.

The second objective is about safeguarding your brand. OK, you may consider at this stage in the development of your company that it's perhaps a little premature to be talking about safeguarding a brand that hardly exists. Nevertheless, it's something you should be aware of. Who knows, a couple of years down the road, or maybe even sooner once you start to become successful, some newcomer may attempt to do to you exactly what you are currently trying to do to your competition. A small amount of money included in your current budget allocated to that purpose now might save you a great deal of money and aggravation in the future. Evaluating your customer retention rate also gives you a good indication of whether or not your advertising is doing more than merely attracting sufficient numbers of new customers to replace those who have moved on.

One of the critically important things to consider at this stage of your development is that the money you put into your advertising program should be seen as a business investment rather than as a business expense. If you don't do this, you'll only spend whatever is left over from the day-to-day costs and expenses of running the company. Your advertising will end up being ineffective, and you'll wonder why.

Don't limit your company's growth by putting your advertising budget into the same cost column as general office expenditures. Doing this will only leave you in the unenviable position of putting the worth of your advertising investments on a par with how many nickels and dimes you saved this week by buying bargain-priced boxes of garbage disposal

> "I avoid clients for whom advertising is only a marginal factor in their marketing mix. They have an awkward tendency to raid their advertising appropriations whenever they need cash for other purposes."
>
> —David Ogilvy

bags or that load of Korean coffee filters you got a special deal on. Meantime, you'll be left scratching your head and wondering why the advertising program you depend on to help grow your business is producing such poor results.

HOW MUCH SHOULD YOU SPEND?

Classic marketing theory, that is, what most MBA courses are based on, would have you believe there are two broad models or methods to be used in determining from a quantitative point of view, how much you should spend on your advertising. These are cleverly named the "let's look backwards approach" and the "let's look forward approach." No wonder these guys make the big bucks!

Let's Look Backward Approach

The let's look backwards approach, otherwise known as percentage-of-sales-or-revenue approach, is a very conservative and static strategy. It's OK if you're selling products or services that have no discernable difference over your competition. All that's required is for you to take last year's sales figures and forecast what you want this year's to be. Then, you incrementally increase last year's advertising budget by the same percentage you want this year's increase in sales to be. You can even use a formula based on how much other companies in a similar line of business spend on their advertising. (See the Resources section at the end of the book.)

Many low-tech B2B companies, like those involved in less exciting industries such as guano removal and recycling or nuclear waste disposal and Geiger-counter repair will spend less than 2 percent of their revenues on advertising. The more visible and glamorous high-tech, financial, and consulting B2B companies can spend up to 10 or 12 percent of their ill-gotten gains on high-profile TV advertising campaigns, flooding the cable TV financial channels day traders love to watch on one of their half-dozen computer screens while eating Twinkies and drinking Jolt Cola. On the other hand, many B2C manufacturers of mass market items in the highly competitive grocery, toiletries, and pharmaceutical products business have been known to spend upwards of 20 percent of their revenues on ongoing, and in many cases, highly intrusive and irritating advertising campaigns.

All you have to do is find the industry average for your line of business, forecast how much you want to achieve in sales, and then work out what you have to spend to achieve this. Sounds like a no-brainer, right? The problem is, it's almost certain you'll be operating in a different environment from most of those who make up the industry averages, which are compiled from statistics at least 12 months old. The market, the economy, your competition, your sales, cost of goods and raw materials, shipping, labor, and on and on—all will have changed in the last year, and I guarantee they'll all have changed for the worse. So this static approach should only be used as a very general rule of thumb because if you rely on average forecasts, you're bound to end up with average results, maybe even worse. And why would you want to settle for that?

Let's Look Forward Approach

This is much more objective and requires a seat-of-the-pants attitude on your part. But you're an entrepreneur, remember? So forget last year's sales and forecasts. With this dynamic approach, it's all based on what you want to achieve this year and how much you're prepared to invest to reach those goals, always remembering it's your money you're throwing around.

Depending on the nature of your business, the cost of making the sale can vary. In B2C and most retail situations, it can be a large percentage of the buying-in cost of the merchandise. For luxury goods, such as that Cartier Santos watch you've been lusting after for years, it can be most of the profit. For B2B goods and services, the marketing and advertising costs can be substantially lower, but will ultimately depend on the size of the order. After all, if you're hoping to sell a nuclear-powered battle cruiser to the East Mashenova Peoples Republic, you're definitely not running prime time TV campaigns to help make the sale. Instead, you're more than likely making a healthy donation to one of the President's sons to help him set up that tennis academy for disadvantaged teenaged girls. In the final analysis, it all comes down to the immortal words of Inspector Callahan when he asked, "Just how lucky do you feel today, punk?"

Being aggressive and lucky is merely the reverse side of the coin from mediocrity. If you can answer in the affirmative to the question, "Are you prepared to invest sufficient money in an advertising program that will help you annihilate your competition?" Then, you're beginning to grasp what it takes to use advertising as one of the most powerful and effective ways to build your business. This doesn't necessarily simply mean throwing lots of money into your advertising budget. It could also require you to look at target audiences and market segments you wouldn't initially consider as prime prospects for what you are selling, or maybe being open-minded enough to consider taking chances on unexpected media choices and promotional opportunities.

LEVERAGE YOUR AD BUDGET FOR GREATER EFFECT

If you are a start-up, small- or medium-business, which is probably why you're reading this book, then your ad budget will be small. So, you need to leverage it to the point where it will be more effective than your competition's. Think of it like this: a truly effective ad budget is designed to deliver maximum results for reasonable resources. What constitutes an effective ad budget? It's one that's based on the three things you must to be crystal clear about when preparing it.

1. The priorities
2. The risks
3. The opportunities

All three are equally important and must be considered if you want powerful, cost-effective advertising.

The Priorities

What do you want to achieve with the money you are allocating for your ad program? If a start-up, your main objective will be recognition, letting the world know you exist, what you have to offer, and why it makes sense for prospective customers to give you a try.

If you are already in business, then your number-one priority will be achieving greater market share in comparison to your competition. A secondary priority may be customer retention if and when you're being threatened by new competition in your geographical area or particular business category. Other priorities might include new product or service launches, branch openings, mergers, etc.

As a start-up, for at least the first year you will have to spend at a high rate to establish yourself. This must be acknowledged in your business plan as an essential cost of beginning to do business. If you are already in business, but branching out into new markets or developing new product offerings, the same criteria apply. You will have to spend at a higher rate than what might be considered a normal maintenance ad budget.

The Risks

In a nutshell, the risks are you may spend too much or you may spend too little. Most people err on the side of spending too little. But don't get me wrong here; I am not advocating you should spend more than you can afford on your advertising. As you will read later in the book, I often recommend that when it comes to ad production, that is, what you spend to produce ads as distinct from what you spend to run them, you expend the least amount of money possible to get the job done. This encourages you to be more creative in what you say and how you say it.

There's a tendency, particularly among many advertisers, both large and small, to treat the ad budget as a kind of slush fund that can be drawn on in times of financial stress. On many occasions when I've been consulting for a BDA working on a large multinational account, I've been informed that the client's ad budget has just been slashed by $20 million or so because the client needs to tap into it to "meet this quarter's numbers." Small clients simply stop spending until they have recovered from whatever financial crisis they find themselves in. Interestingly, very often when this happens the competition continues to spend on advertising at its usual ferocious rate. The client then finds it necessary to spend at double its normal rate through the next quarter to make up for the market share its lost in the quarter it cut back. As I said, if you choose to regard advertising as an expense rather than an investment, you will often be tempted to look at the advertising budget as an immediate remedy for a sickly bottom line. Unfortunately, it's a remedy which only works temporarily while often causing long-term damage to the company.

Another risk many companies fall into when determining their ad budget is the belief that advertising will do more than can reasonably be expected of it.

Remember my story in Chapter 1 about the company with the terrible after-sales service record? No amount of money spent on advertising could fix that problem. It was an internal company dilemma that was entirely the responsibility of management to put right. The same is true of allocating significant sums of money for advertising to support a new product launch. I have been involved in more of these than I've had hot dinners (old English saying I picked up from my mother). The vast majority has been a complete waste of money and effort. It's

Big companies dislike risk. Entrepreneurs accept it as a cost of doing business. That's why a great deal of big company advertising is safe and mostly ineffective. Exceptional big companies such as Apple still act entrepreneurial, and this is reflected in their products and how they advertise them.

a sad, but true fact that four-fifths of new products fail within six months, although nearly all have gone through extensive product testing, focus groups, and myriad other forms of qualitative research.

Years ago I worked on a product for Hunts Foods called "Crazy Peaches." Aimed at kids, these were canned peaches that actually tasted like oranges, pineapple, cinnamon, and so on. Tested like gangbusters in focus groups with kids and mothers, the product failed miserably in the marketplace because in real life, not the artificial atmosphere of the testing situation, kids wanted peaches that tasted like peaches. So, if you've come up with the latest atomic-powered rotary widget, great. Just don't blow your entire ad budget on it; keep a little back to support the good old steam-powered model that pays the bills.

The Opportunities

When you determine what your ad budget should be, try to keep some in reserve. Anywhere from 10 to 20 percent will do nicely for the odd great deal that comes along. You need to be ready when a particular opportunity with a media vehicle you know through experience delivers good results gets a late cancellation from another advertiser and offers space to you at a significant discount.

There may be situations in which you are offered the opportunity to go in on a cooperative venture with one of your suppliers or customers. Depending on the nature of your business, this can also apply to the sponsorship of an event or occasion that has a particular relevance or a useful association to your business. Who knows, once in a blue moon sponsoring the local WhakoBungeeJumpolla event might make sense. Not very often, I'll admit, but if it came along and was a golden opportunity because you are the western hemisphere's largest manufacturer of elastic bungee cords, you'd be kicking yourself later if you had to pass on it because you hadn't had the foresight to keep a few measly dollars in reserve in your ad budget.

WHERE SHOULD YOU SPEND IT?

What you should be concerned about now when drawing up your ad budget is how to break down what you will spend and how you will spend it. (Various media options are discussed in Chapter 5.) In a start-up mode this is tough, because you have no prior experience to draw on. However, if you came from a similar kind of business, you will know where your previous company advertised and have a fair idea of how frequently. Depending on your responsibilities with that company, you may also have some idea of how effective its advertising was.

If you've developed a solid communications plan as discussed in Chapter 3, you will have a good sense of who your potential customers are and what you need to say to convince them that you're someone they should consider doing business with. If your company is a B2B one, you should be familiar with all the trade magazines that reach your prospective audience. If B2C, you should also have an idea of the kinds of periodicals and broadcast channels your target groups are reading, listening to, and viewing.

> You get more bang for your bucks when you concentrate your bucks. Don't try to run ads everywhere. Avoid being suckered in by media reps who bombard you with great deals. They're rarely that great.

What Kind of Business Are You In?

If you have a B2B company and are not an IBM or General Electric, the odds are you can rule out TV and multipage print insertions in *The Wall Street Journal*. Until a few years ago, most B2B budgets had been spent on trade journals and direct mail programs. Now, creating an ad budget based on these kinds of media is becoming increasingly difficult because of the growing influence and effectiveness of online advertising. This new advertising venue has led to a remarkably swift decline in the number of hard-copy trade journal titles out there, particularly those dealing with technology, telecommunications, and dotcom industries. Several survive on the internet as web sites and newsletters, but even these are a poor reflection of the couple of hundred page issues many of them flaunted in the high flying days of the '90s.

Big B2B companies still spend the lion's share of their ad budgets—usually as much as 75 percent—in mainstream print and broadcast media, particularly TV. (There would be precious few golf tournaments on television if B2B companies pulled the plug on their sponsorships and advertising support for the seemingly thousands of these events that go on year round.) Smaller companies are realizing they can get more for their money and reach a much more targeted audience by investing a substantial proportion of their ad budgets in online media.

Depending on the nature of your business, I would recommend standing the traditional division of your budget on its head and opt for putting most of your money into online media. Exactly what choices these offer will be spelled out in Chapter 9. In the case of B2C companies, unless you are in the business of selling direct to your customers, you will still primarily rely on traditional media vehicles. This means local newspapers, weeklies, TV, and radio. But having said that, depending on the nature of your business, where you are situated geographically, and how narrowly defined a market you're addressing, I would encourage the adventurous to look at the possible advantages of putting a significant proportion of your ad budget in online media, particularly if your competition is outspending you in the more expected media vehicles.

What Can You Realistically Expect Your Money to Get You?

I'm assuming that you've got all your ducks in a row as I discussed in Chapter 1, and that after some consideration you're convinced that it makes good business sense for you to invest in an ongoing advertising program. You have to be realistic in the way you look at what the possible return on investment (ROI) will be for that investment. But please, be aware that the key words I insist on stressing are, yet again, *investment* and *realistic*.

I appreciate that you might be getting a little tired of my going on and on about your looking at an advertising budget as an investment. But to really beat this thing over the head with a big gnarly stick, I will reiterate just one more time that it's nothing more than the application of common sense and logic. Think of it as if you were investing in the stock market. What if every time the stocks you hold drop a couple of points, you sell and buy something else? Unless you are some kind of financial genius, most experts agree that this strategy will ultimately be a recipe for disaster. On the other hand, if you have the patience and fortitude to listen to the Warren Buffets of this world, you will unfailingly look at all your stock market investments as being made for the long haul. Ultimately, they will result in all those snotty-nosed great grandchildren you never had the time of day for to reap the rewards of your earlier prudence. So, why not try to think of it in these terms when it comes to considering how much you should invest in your advertising program. What you need to say to potential customers, and how best to say it, are the subjects of other chapters. This one is strictly about how much you need to spend to capture their attention.

> Don't waste your money advertising where you don't exist. An amazing number of people actually spend their hard-earned money on media that doesn't effectively target their audience or run where their products are available.

How Can You Evaluate the ROI I Might Expect Over an Extended Period?

You can only evaluate ROI over an extended period based on what you have spent in the past and what you anticipate spending in the future. If you can identify the sales you made as a result of last year's advertising budget, then you would hope that increasing your budget by 10 percent in the coming year will increase sales by 10 percent. Unfortunately, there are factors other than advertising that can affect your sales: increased competition, loss of distribution, problems in manufacturing, the general economy, and many more. You can use your advertising to counter some of these, but that will usually require increased spending. The return you'll get by doing this will be impossible to determine in advance and so will come down to your making a judgment call as to whether you believe the increased spending will generate increased sales.

There will also be occasions when you need to look for an immediate response and financial payback from your advertising, particularly if you are in the retail business or promoting a special event or offer. New product launches, the announcement of new services, and extra distribution areas are all events that will need to be supported by increased advertising and should be included in the planning for the forthcoming year.

It goes without saying that if you are in direct sales, your advertising has to work on a 24/7, pick-up-the-phone or visit-the-web-site basis. You should pay very careful attention to what the major direct sales companies are doing and how they continually fine tune and modify their efforts. For these guys, advertising is the life blood of the company. If the ads don't continually drive massive amounts of customer traffic to them through the web site and 800-telephone numbers so prominently featured, they're going to be out of business. Notice also that most of their advertising has a very recognizable character and tone of voice that has been carefully built up over a great many years of consistent advertising, not to mention the investment of many millions of advertising dollars.

Where Does the Realistic Part of the Formula Come In?

It's simply realistic that you should never expect your ad budget to work miracles. If you are a one in a million entrepreneur fortunate enough to have a miracle product, the job your advertising needs to do will be that much easier and the world might very well beat a path to your door.

But what if you have a me-too product or are offering a service not markedly different from many others? (Hopefully, this will be corrected after you've worked hard on developing your USP and translated it into the core component of your magic formula, the communications plan outlined in Chapter 3.)

> Eighty percent of new package goods products fail within six months of launch, yet virtually every one tested in research as a guaranteed winner.

Then, you'll be forced to realize that unless you have unlimited amounts of money to spend on your advertising, you'll have to set yourself some attainable goals. You can set attainable goals by creating an initial budget based on the following information:

1. Industry average spent as a percentage of sales/revenues.
2. Your last year's sales.
3. This year's forecast sales.
4. Total overall number of customers last year.
5. Number of new customers gained last year.
6. Total number of customers forecast this year.
7. Deciding whether to spend above or below the industry average.
8. Going with the entrepreneurial gut that got you where you are today.

The first seven are all fairly obvious items to consider, but the eighth is probably the most important. If you feel the money you intend to spend on a well-thought-out and well-constructed advertising program is going to help you grow your business, then it's imperative that you fund it properly, continue to work on improving it, and give it sufficient time to do the job. That requires more than numbers. That requires conviction, not to mention nerve.

TIMING . . . OH, YES . . . TIMING

A final thought on when you should do what you intend to do with your advertising budget. Most ad budgets are based primarily on media expenditures. These are invariably based on buying flights of ads. Buying flights is the hoary old chestnut beloved by the BDAs of Madison Avenue and is based on the premise that you should take your yearly budget and break it down by quarter. Then, over the period of any proposed campaign, you come in with heavy exposure for a few weeks, drop out for a month or so, and then come back with another flight of ads for a few weeks.

The agency bombards the client with Gross Rating Points (GRP) for TV campaigns, a long since broken formula that supposedly indicates how many people will watch your commercial over a certain period of time. This measurement of effectiveness is

> If you are in a seasonable business, there are times when you must advertise. This is also when your competition is advertising. Try not to say the same things as they do, and don't say it in the same places.

about as useless as the Nielson ratings, which supposedly tell advertisers how many people have watched the latest abysmal reality show or *SmackDown—WrestleMania*. For print media, agencies will do the same with circulation and readership studies purporting to show that the audience of expatriate East European violin players you consider to be the prime target for your catgut resin is actually 90 percent of the paid circulation of the *New Jersey Home Decorators Gazette.*

All media statistics are based on studies that usually bear no relationship to the way people actually read newspapers or magazines, listen to the radio, or watch TV. And now with the advent of the internet, TiVo, DVDs, iPods, and the numerous other ways electronics have changed the way people get their news and entertainment, traditional media studies are often barely worth the paper they are printed on. Never forget the words of Lloyd George, "There are lies, damn lies, and statistics." He may have said that after lunch at the Palm with a media rep.

Depending on your business, you know when the busy times are, when you need to presell merchandise or services prior to a heavy period of demand, or when you need to get rid of excess or dated inventory. So you should be planning your media buys and expenditures well ahead of these events. Do not wait until they are almost upon you. Delay will not only cost you more in terms of booking the media late and paying rush fees for the production of your ads, but also the ads themselves will not be as effective as they could be because you didn't take the time to think them through. As in all things, think and plan ahead. Your budget will be all the better for it.

IF ALL ELSE FAILS, GET SOMEONE ELSE TO DO IT

In Chapter 10, I will be talking about how you might work with freelancers and consultants for the creation of your advertising. This might also make sense when it comes to managing your advertising budget. Even though you will probably have your own controller or financial manager, she may not be well versed in the arts of media and production buying. Bringing in a specialist for a few hours a week could save you far more than her cost. You will also get better results for your money.

You should be able to find these people through local trade organizations and groups. In the Resources section at the back of the book, I list some of the services that handle local and regional experts who are available on a freelance basis. Just be sure that if you do decide to use an outside budget consultant make sure he is conversant in the advertising and media disciplines. And remember, in the final analysis you're the one who has to make the call on where and how you want to spend your money.

CHAPTER FIVE

Where should you spend your advertising budget? So many bad choices, so few places to hide!

At the time of writing, there are many forms of advertising communication: old media, new media, electronic media, viral/buzz/guerilla/gangsta/ youth/you-name-it/media. All are recognized and consistently hyped as advertising in one form or another. But whatever version or flavor you end up using, be aware it will undoubtedly cost you money, lots of money, 'cuz there's no such a thing as a free lunch on Madison Avenue. You should also realize that many of the activities considered as *free*, such as PR, attending trade shows, getting involved in local charities and good causes, providing tee shirts to the neighborhood bowling league, even giving a luncheon speech at the local Rotary club, invariably involve time and expense in preparation and execution. So they are not, by any stretch of the imagination, free.

Before considering what you should expect from a well-structured and well thought out ad program, look at some of the many and varied components and choices available to you when thinking how best to get your message out to your potential audience. In later chapters I will deal with the actual nuts and bolts, mechanics, and expenses you will face when creating the ads to run in these different media.

MEDIA ADVERTISING

This is what most people starting and building a business think of when considering advertising in its broader aspects. It's no surprise that advertising is seen as the world's second oldest profession when you consider that such examples of media advertising as billboards have been around since the Greek and Roman republics, as have signs outside tradesman's shops and taverns. (Interestingly, the Romans were also responsible for the world's most obscene graffiti, some of which still exists at Pompeii.) Then, with the invention of paper, handbills appeared, to be quickly followed by advertising in news broadsheets, then newspapers, magazines, etc. Today the destruction of the Amazon rain forest continues to provide the raw materials necessary to stuff your mail box to bursting with fliers from your local hardware store, preapproved credit card applications for your dog, Victoria's Secret catalogs, and all the other wonderful things guaranteed to give your mail carrier a hernia. But enough of the history lesson. It's time to consider the various primary media advertising vehicles currently available to us.

DAILY NEWSPAPERS

In most entrepreneurial business situations, newspaper advertising will mean the use of local newspapers. (Unlike the rest of the world, there are few national newspapers in the United States and those there are tend to be prohibitively expensive and thus well outside the scope of a small- or medium-sized company's ad budget.) How you use local newspapers will depend on where you and your target audiences are situated and the consequent demographics and circulation of the relevant papers.

Ad rates in the dailies can vary from a few dollars to multiples of thousands. All periodicals will gladly send you a *rate card*, which gives you an indication of the cost of running an ad in their newspapers or magazines. Obviously, the cost is determined by the size of the ad, whether or not it uses color, and the number of times you run it. (Multiple insertions obviously generate a bigger discount.) But be warned, once you contact them for information, the publication's salespeople will make your telephone glow. At this stage of your media research, tell them you'll call back when you've evaluated all your options.

You need to explore all your media possibilities before drawing up a plan. Depending on your business category and location, you may have almost no choice but to throw yourself on the tender mercy of the local *Walla Walla Bugle*, particularly if you are in the business of selling secondhand cars or escort services. But as I'm pretty sure owners of neither of these kinds of businesses will have purchased this book, I'll let you in on a secret. There are a large number of new and surprisingly inexpensive advertising media vehicles increasingly opening up to advertisers. This is beginning to

> Local daily newspapers are becoming less attractive as advertising vehicles with the growth of both the internet and free local weeklies. Combined with their declining circulations, the ROI they deliver continues to shrink.

decimate the ad revenue, (particularly that from the classified sections), of many daily newspapers, which in turn is allowing advertisers to exercise considerable leverage on the publication's ad sales reps. Although this is unfortunate for ad reps, it's good news for you. These are a few factors you should consider before deciding if dailies might indeed be a logical part of your ad program.

- Even though most dailies have been in existence for a long time and profess to enjoy both local integrity and community awareness, most of them belong to a limited number of national media conglomerates that are driven by bottom-line considerations rather than some altruistic spirit of local pride. Much of the editorial content relies on wire services and retreads of news stories from the nationals. This is particularly true of the international and national news, living, and business sections. Depending on the nature of your business and who you need to talk to, if you want to use the local daily newspaper, your best bet for reaching customers within your target markets will usually be through the entertainment, local news, and sports sections.

The head offices of the organizations owning these dailies very often drive advertising policies and guidelines to the point where local ad reps are expected to generate specific levels of income and meet preset targets. This is particularly true when quarterly and end-of-year revenue numbers assume Draconian importance to the number crunchers back at the head office. This situation can work both for and against advertisers when negotiating rates and frequencies.

> Local newspapers are heavily retail in advertising appeal, with maximum advertising content leading up to seasonal holidays and other events.

If the paper is booking more advertising than it can find space for, it can afford to be tough when negotiating your contract. But believe me, the odds on this actually happening are virtually zero because all papers are perpetually, ravenously hungry for ad income. When the reps are facing their inevitable shortfall in advertising revenues, you can demand lower rates for single insertions or even a number of bonus free insertions for your ads if you are prepared to commit to an extended schedule.

- Dailies enjoy a very short shelf life; they are quickly read and then discarded. Weeklies and monthlies, on the other hand, tend to sit around and be referred to over a longer period of time. Indeed, some copies of the *National Geographic*, particularly in dental offices, have been known to enjoy a lifespan of years, eventually ending up in a next-millennium garage sale. You should remember the short life of a daily paper if the nature of your ad program depends on promoting extended periods of specials or sales. No one is going to refer to last week's paper to see what is on sale today.

- Most of the ads in local papers tend to look *local*. Unlike ads from big national advertisers that use high-quality photography and artwork as well as well-written copy, way too many local ads look amateurish. In reality, there is no excuse for this because there are ways of producing high-quality, impactful advertising without it costing an arm and a leg. Indeed, I shall be covering exactly how you can do this in Chapter 6.

- Copy dates, that is, how far ahead of the ad's appearance date you need to get your materials to the publication, for dailies can be as short as a few hours. This allows you to make last-minute changes or updates to the artwork. But do this only if absolutely necessary. Burning the midnight oil and having second thoughts about whether to do the headline in day-glo orange invariably screws up the original concept and integrity of the ad and in the cold reality of dawn usually looks far less brilliant than it did through last night's alcoholic haze.

WEEKLY NEWSPAPERS

Virtually all cities and many towns now boast at least one example of what used to be called the *alternative press*. Many of these papers started off as shoestring operations cobbled together by some guys who had a great time getting drunk while putting together a college newspaper and so decided to break into the wonderful, wacky, world of journalism for real with their very own title. A surprising number of them have done rather well. A few garner circulations rivaling some of the city dailies, for example, the *Village Voice* in New York. However, there are certain things you need to consider about local weeklies before opting for them as part of an ad program.

- Because these papers are free, circulation figures don't mean much. However, they usually boast a very loyal readership.
- Most of that readership is young and their primary interests are the local film/music/club/dating/drinking scene. Consequently, you'll notice a great many of the advertisers cater to this audience. You'll see few ads for police equipment stores or church bake sales.

It's easier to do trades and barter deals with weeklies than dailies. This way you can make your ad dollars go further. Of course, it depends on what kind of business you are in and what you have to trade.

- The paper sits around for a full week and is referred to on a frequent basis for local entertainment/eating/drinking/etc. news and venues.
- While space costs are relatively inexpensive, the target audience you need to address may be a very small part of the paper's overall readership, unless you happen to be in the hemp clothing and bong business.
- The presentation and content of a lot of the ads in the weeklies can be off the wall. Your professional looking ad will tend to stand out more. But, this could be a double edged sword, depending on what kind of product or service you are promoting.
- Copy dates are usually three to four days ahead of publication date, less if you can wangle an extension. But doing this is not recommended on a regular basis. It can get you identified as "that awkward sod who does everything at the last minute," which makes it increasingly difficult, if not impossible, to ask for genuine favors when you need them.
- Because they are relatively inexpensive, you can use the weekly paper as a test bed for ads you may consider running later in the more expensive daily paper. You can fine tune or modify the ads until they are generating the response you are looking for, then splash out on the more expensive daily.

INSERTS

These are really a subset of the above two categories. Usually, inserts are preprinted pieces that are "tipped-in" to that day's or week's edition, turning the paper, particularly on Sunday, into an arm-breaking workout session. First off, although they are usually a cheaper buy than actually having an ad in the periodical, unless you pay the periodical to design and print the insert, you have to take care of all that hassle yourself. Unless you are in the retail grocery trade and need to run a special on all those 50-pound blocks of Crisco you have to shift before they turn into a rancid Mount St. Helens, I'd forget about inserts.

MAGAZINES

These can be weeklies or monthlies covering all aspects of news, sports, general interest, financial, and every category of human activity you can think of. There are literally hundreds of magazines out there catering to almost any person residing on the face of the planet. For the purposes of this discussion, I will ignore the well known heavys such as *Time* and *Newsweek*, primarily because of their cost. Many of these national magazines do, however, produce more affordable regional and city editions. If you produce, distribute, or sell a niche-specific series of products such as a dog grooming equipment and accessories, then there are at least a dozen magazines aimed at dog owners and probably a half a dozen others talking to the kennel and professional grooming trade.

What are the facts you need to consider before putting money into a magazine ad campaign?

- The majority of the magazines you probably want to advertise in will be monthlies. This means you must be prepared to commit to an ongoing, year-long program, preferably front-loaded with an ad every month for at least the first two or three months, followed by every other month or even on a quarterly basis. You will always get a much more favorable rate from the publication if you sign on for multiple insertions. Also, merely running the odd ad now and then will usually be ineffective and therefore a waste of money.

- Magazine ad space is usually more expensive than local dailies and weeklies. However, because these publications are aimed at specific interest groups, your ads will be much more targeted and should therefore deliver a higher quality of response.

- The advertising you run in magazines should be specifically written to appeal to a well-defined audience and designed to make full use of the higher production values found in most magazines, such as the quality of its stock, that is, the paper it's printed on, and the superior reproduction of your artwork that will hopefully make a more impactful impression on the reader.

- The larger the space your ad occupies, the more impact it makes. The optimum space is a spread (side-by-side pages), but obviously, these will be expensive, depending on the

> Some magazines will offer to prepare your artwork for you. That is tempting because of the cost savings you can make. Still, it's much better do your own. That way you can maintain better quality control.

magazine's ad rates. Most small advertisers settle for a page, or even what's called fractional space, a half or quarter page, single or half columns. But don't be afraid of initially using *small-space* advertising if your budget is limited. Some of the best, most interesting, and effective ads are the fractional pages that run at the back of magazines. The *New Yorker* magazine is a prime example. Several very successful companies got their starts by running quarter-column ads at the back of that rather prestigious magazine. Remember the J. Peterman story earlier in the book?

• Look for niche-within-a-niche magazines to stretch your ad dollars to the maximum. I recently did a campaign for a client who was importing very small digital video recorders. We positioned them against the Extreme sports market, with an emphasis on skate boarders who could wear them on their helmets when doing insane stunts. We found out that the mainstream skateboarder mags are surprisingly expensive. (There's an amazing number of skateboarders out there.)

So, I discovered a small-circulation fringe mag called *Concussion*. It caters to those boarders who are considered "beyond insane," the ones who do really freaky stuff, hence the title of the magazine. But these are exactly the guys who want to capture on video their very last moments before flying headfirst down the stairwell of the Empire State Building or base jumping off El Cap strapped to a skateboard. Anyway, for a lot less money than buying space in the mainstream books, and also avoiding being surrounded by hundreds of ads selling nonskateboarding stuff, the client sold a ton of recorders and even had a great word-of-mouth campaign going as "the video gear hard men favor."

The moral of the story is that no matter what kind of business you're in, there are plenty of niche magazines out there that can reach substantial portions of your target market for less money than you might think. But, you'll have to do some digging around to find them. Spend some time doing a Google search; you'll be amazed how many periodicals, web sites, and blogs out there that cater to your market.

• Let's assume you commit to a long-term ad program in a magazine or series of magazines. Unless you have a constantly changing inventory of products or services needing to be featured and updated on a regular basis, you shouldn't have to create more than the two or three ads necessary to carry you through a 12-month campaign. It's always worth investing money in creating a few good ads, rather than lots of bad ones. (More on ad content and production in Chapters 6 and 7.) Don't fall into the trap of thinking you have to constantly change your ads. Just because you see them all the time doesn't mean the public does.

OUTDOOR

Unless you enjoy a specific geographical location that allows you to plaster your name all over Times Square or you need to direct traffic from the interstate to your brand-new SuperSuddsy car wash, I wouldn't recommend the use of outdoor advertising at this stage of your business venture. In spite of what the billboard companies will tell you, there are far more cost-effective ways to spend your ad dollars. Plus, there's way too much crappy advertising disfiguring the highways of America already.

RADIO

Now here's one media option in which, no matter where you're doing business, you'll find yourself overwhelmed by the number of choices available to you. This has good and bad aspects. In any large urban market, there will be dozens of AM and FM stations offering everything from 24-hour news and talk, to top 20, to classical, to heavy metal, and so on and so on. Every radio sales rep will try to convince you his station demographics fit exactly with your target groups. Obviously, this is nonsense. If you live in the market, you will probably be familiar with the content and have a feel for the popularity of particular stations. If you don't, it gets a lot harder.

Consider some of the things to bear in mind before deciding if radio is right for you.

- Radio can be a very *immediate* medium lending itself to *instant* sales promotions, like Krazy Karl promising to set fire to everything

> Radio advertising is immediate, personal, and cheap, which is why there's so much of it about and why it gets so cluttered. Do not let your spots add to the clutter.

on his used car lot if you don't get your butt down there and buy something—right now! That's why retailers love it so much. With radio, they can control and manage their inventories at very short notice through the use of sales, specials, discounts, and promotions.

- Local business can use radio very effectively to move people to the next point of contact along the sales chain, that is, using radio spots that feature 800 numbers and Web addresses to encourage instant purchases while building a powerful sales tool through the compilation of a database of existing and future customers.

- A great deal of the program content of radio is extremely cluttered, particularly on many of the AM stations that often seem to carry more advertising messages than entertainment segments. That's why care should be taken in the selection of the stations to carry your ads. Evaluate not just their cost effectiveness but also the rub-off effect that can come from having your name associated with schlocky, overly commercial stations.

- The geographic coverage claimed by different stations can be as important as their audience share and demographics. AM stations usually have far greater reach (although this also depends on the strength of their signals) than FM ones. But in turn, the AM dial tends to be much more cluttered, with stations drifting in and out of reception. Remember, radio is very much a drive-time experience, and if you are trying to reach people who commute in from the suburbs, you will need to use stations that give overlapping coverage of various driving corridors.

Stan Freeberg once described radio as "theater of the mind," meaning you can use it to create pictures and images in people's heads. (Remember Orson Welles's famous Mercury Radio of the Air production of *War of the Worlds,* which created so much panic in 1938? I'm not suggesting that you actually listened to the original broadcast, but I think you get my drift.) Unfortunately, when you listen to so many radio spots today, the only image you want to conjure up is a picture of the announcer wearing a gag. I shall be talking more about how to produce the kind of radio ads your audience might actually enjoy in Chapter 8.

- Radio is one of the few media choices that lends itself extremely well to the use of humor. Having said that, it depends very much on the kind of message you are trying to get across to the audience. The use of humor to promote the benefits of a funeral services company would have to be discouraged. But irrespective of what you are considering using humor for, always remember that its use should invariably be judicious, rather than profligate. A single banana skin can create more guffaws than a whole truckload.

- Radio production, that is, the cost of creating the spots themselves rather than the cost of the air time to run them, is usually very inexpensive compared to production costs for most other media. In many cases, the station you choose to run your advertising on will offer to produce the commercials for free as part of the overall package. However tempting this offer may appear be, proceed with caution. The end result, even though it will be professionally done, will often be homogenous in nature, with a tendency to blend into the overall program content, particularly if your ad is read by the same announcer who's hosting the show. Unless the station can persuade Walter Cronkite to come out of retirement, it's far better to expend the extra dollars it will take to have some independently created and produced spots make your campaign stand out from everyone else's. I'll talk more about radio production in Chapter 8.

- Never forget that the Public Broadcasting Service offers a rather sly form of advertising on all its radio and TV stations. These used to be in the form of "This news broadcast is brought to you by the Joe Blogs Foundation for greater understanding between cats and dogs," or something like that. But now, with the tightening of government funding, many local PBS stations are offering to run what are almost regular commercials promoting not only the community spirit and generosity of the sponsor but also a generous dollop of selling.

> Sponsoring program content through the local affiliate of National Public Radio is an incredibly inexpensive way to get your name out in front of the public, while making you seem to be a responsible member of the community.

Another benefit is that these spots are cheap to make and run, and best of all, you come off looking like a philanthropist.

TELEVISION

Ah yes, television, the Holy Grail of the advertising profession. The media that for many, many years was the big agencies' license to print money. Until recently, it was considered by many to be the most effective vehicle for the creation of brands and the launching of new products. Now with the advent of cable, satellite, videotape, DVDs, TiVo, and the many other electronic ways to avoid commercials, circumstances have changed dramatically, not that you would think so when you look at the price of a 30-second spot on the Super Bowl.

With all the caveats, TV can still be a very important and effective part of any advertising campaign. But as a small budget advertisiser, you just have to be very careful how you approach it. Consider:

- To do it well, television advertising requires the expenditure of substantially more money than all other forms of advertising. It also requires a bigger input of time and effort from the advertiser to do it right. If you are not working through an ad agency, you'll have to be prepared to get involved in everything from campaign planning, to media negotiating and buying, to concept creation and copywriting, to supervising the actual production of the commercials. It's a lot of work, and if not done properly, it can leave the end product looking amateurish and the sales results rather pathetic.

- Depending on your budget—because ultimately everything depends on your budget—and the nature of your business, you can look at TV advertising either as a brand-building exercise or as a sales tool. But be well advised, unless you have a huge amount of money, it's hard to achieve both of these objectives with the same campaign. They require completely different approaches. So let's assume at this stage of building your business, you're more interested in seeing a definite return on your advertising expenditures. This means generating sales. High-faluting brand imagery can come later. I hasten to add that you should never fail to be conscious of the fact that everything you do at every stage of your business cycle will continually define your brand and make a lasting impression on customers, suppliers, and staff.

- Using TV to build sales by increasing customer traffic to your store or driving them to a web site or 800 number is a tactic used with great success by retailers and direct marketers. Look at the difference between the corporate TV spots for Ford Motors vs. the ones for the local Ford distributor. The brand spots are primarily about image, styling, power, features, and talk about the integrity of the brand. The dealer spots are all about getting you down to the dealership where they can concentrate on the immediate hot buttons that will drive you to say, "I have to have it now." Dealers repeatedly use the same old triggers, such as end-of-year sales, financing, trade-in values, and even such seemingly mundane things as free Coke and hot dogs along with balloons for the kids. (Do you think that any of these things actually work, or are people to assume that car dealers are so unimaginative they've been unable to come up with an original advertising idea in years? Actually, when you consider the average car dealer's TV spot, I've just answered my own question.)

- So brand stuff is long term, whereas most selling stuff is immediate, allowing advertisers to feature specific products at specific price points as well as to promote seasonal sales and limited time offers. And because it lends itself to accurate measurement through the monitoring of sales after the ads have run, its effectiveness can be quickly determined. Through the constant testing, refinement, and measurement of their TV advertising, such well-known direct marketers as Dell and Sharper Image have built multibillion dollar businesses while national, regional, and local retailers are consistent users of TV in conjunction with continuing local press campaigns to help build store traffic and sales, all the while being unremitting in nonstop measurement and evaluation of their advertising programs.

- Leaving aside the actual content of your TV spots (I'll get to that in Creating TV Ads in Chapter 7), there are basically two factors to

> Nothing looks worse than a "cheap" TV spot. Notice, I didn't say *inexpensive*. Think of the enormously successful *South Park* series. It consists of nothing more than the torn paper characters you made as a kid.

consider when putting together a television campaign: where to run it and when to run it.

If your business is in a single location, or even if you have several branches but they are all within a tightly defined geographic area, then where you should run your TV campaign is obvious. All you have to decide is whether you should run on the local affiliates of the major TV networks or on cable TV by buying these channels on a regional basis. Of course, if you're loaded, which I doubt or you wouldn't be reading this book, you can do both. Buying the network affiliates allows you to run your spots during the most popular shows that usually get the largest audiences. So if, for instance, you need to reach a certain segment of the population that is likely not to be gainfully employed right now and whose major worry in life is fixing the leak in the trailer roof, daytime network TV is the way to go.

The problem is that like everything else in life, you have to pay for what you get, so the network programs that have the biggest audience are also the most expensive. On the other hand, if you really want to target people who live in trailer homes or drive RVs, there's more than likely a cable channel carrying programming specifically aimed at them. (In the interests of avoiding possible law suits, I shall decline to name it right now, but if you really need to know which cable channel has the most appeal to trailer park residents, drop me an e-mail.)

In a nutshell, the major difference between network TV and cable TV is the size of the audience and the reach. With network TV, you can get to a bigger audience, whereas with cable you can impact a more targeted audience. So if you can really define your audience, there's a good chance cable will have a channel offering programming specifically aimed at it. That revolutionary nutmeg grater you intend to make millions from is a natural for the Food Channel, or those fake chinchilla-lined driving bootees you're about to start importing from China will be perfect for the Speed Channel.

> Local TV can be as cheap as radio, but only if you buy those strange time slots when most people are in bed. But depending on the nature of your business, insomniacs might just be in your target group.

You should also recognize that your audience, with the exception of the guy with the leaky trailer roof, is not usually watching television 24/7, whether it be network or cable. That's why timing can be just as important as demographics. Buying network TV, even on a local basis, during prime time, such as the morning shows and early evening news programs is expensive, but, of course, it guarantees that you will reach a larger audience. On the other hand, spending the same amount of money

> You can, of course, buy local spots and have them run in national network programs. They will only get shown in the geographic areas you pay for, but you can run them in the most popular shows.

on a cable TV campaign that reaches more of the people unquestionably within your target audience will more than likely be a better investment. Working out the various planning and buying permutations that will allow you to estimate the proper return on your TV campaign investment is covered in Chapter 12.

SUMMARY

So, how should you pick the media that will do the best job for you? As I said in the introduction, none of this is some kind of mythical magic formula known only to the Madison Avenue Adverati. Like most things in life, it's merely the application of common sense. If you've gone through the steps discussed in Chapter 3 regarding the preparation of your communications plan, you will be well on the road to knowing what media is going to do the best job for you. By working through the plan, you've already defined who you need to reach, decided what you want them to know about you, and developed a strategy on how best to convince them of these inalienable facts.

All that remains is to determine how much you need to spend to achieve your objectives because that will determine what kind of media you can afford and where you should spend the money. The problem is that this is the classic chicken-and-egg situation. Most advertising budgets are decided on the basis of a predetermined percentage of sales being devoted to the program, which means if sales go down, so does the ad budget, even though common sense would dictate that this is precisely the time you need to spend more. In reality, spending more rarely happens because most businesses see advertising as an expense rather than an investment and cutting the ad budget, although temporarily, makes an immediate and seemingly, beneficial impact on the bottom line.

Worse still, many companies see advertising as a damn nuisance, something to be barely tolerated because of the principals' deep-seated perception that it rarely delivers value. (Remember the complaints of John, Henry, Genghis, and Adolph earlier?) Based on previous experience, there is a certain amount of justification for this point of view. However, the flip side of the coin is companies such as Apple, Nike, Dell, and others who have built huge brands based on their belief in brilliantly executed advertising and a commitment to run it over long periods of time.

It's also worth remembering that all these companies started out in garages, the trunks of cars, or athletic locker rooms. They also started out with minute advertising budgets. But what they had, they used creatively. And dare I say, fearlessly, as any entrepreneur worth his or her salt would!

CHAPTER SIX

Creating print ads the old fashioned, excruciatingly painful, yet strangely rewarding way

Today, irrespective of the ever-expanding wonders of digital technology and the online communications age, the vast majority of advertising still sees the light of day through traditional media vehicles: newspapers, magazines, billboards, radio, TV, and direct mail. In this chapter, I deal with how you can best create and execute advertising for the print media. In subsequent chapters, I deal with how you can then progress to the production of communications for the other media. But, first things first.

All advertising, irrespective of where and how it appears, can only be successful if it has an impact on the audience it is addressing. And the only way you can be sure of achieving this is if the content of your communication is so compelling that it creates a desire within those reading, watching, or listening to it to want to know more. There are certain proven triggers you can use to flag down the reader who would rather be reading the comics or sports section of their local newspaper, but once having done that, please don't insult their intelligence by boring their pants off or talking to them as if they were idiots. Nothing is guaranteed to turn readers or viewers off more. Even worse, you may even drive your audience to convince their friends and neighbors that you're someone no one in their right mind should think of doing business with.

So before I get into the specifics of creating advertising for particular media, I'll talk about creating great advertising in general. It doesn't matter if you are in a B2C or a B2B business, never fail to recognize that your advertising will always be a reflection of your company's character. As I've said, the worst example of how this works is with local auto dealership advertising. With few exceptions, it is unbelievably schlocky.

Check out the ad in Figure 6.1 as a prime example of how not to design an ad. Even worse are the ones that feature the owner of the dealership, often a loud, obnoxious, badly dressed character who any sane person would normally cross the street to avoid. When featured in TV and radio commercials, these people seem to be under the impression that their potential customers are deaf, so they need to be screamed at. Even in print advertising, the equivalent of this ranting is translated into day-glow colors, giant star-bursts, snipes, and other intrusive graphic devices usually characteristic of the desperate and stylistically illiterate, all plastered over thousands of hard-to-read, postage-sized images of similar looking trucks, SUVs, and sedans. I don't know whether this is because of laziness, ignorance, or an endemic insistence on spending the least amount of money possible on something so essential to the success of their business. It makes you wonder why they bother to advertise at all.

FIGURE 6.1: *Not pretty. Even if you're a car dealer.*

To a lesser degree, a similar communications paranoia seems to filter down to local retailers of furniture, home appliances, carpeting, and hot tubs. Compounding the felony, all these people seem to think that by offering huge "24-hour only" discounts because it's President's/Mother's/Valentine's/Ground Hog/Whatever Day, people will beat down the doors of their establishments to sign up for "No-Interest, No Payment" financing until the next millennium. Did it ever occur to them that when *everyone* in their business category is doing exactly the same kind of advertising and everyone is offering *exactly* the same promotions and deals, perhaps they should try doing something different?

In other words, why not zig when everyone else is zagging? This means taking the time and effort to create advertising that is an indication of what is unique about you and your company and what you have to offer—that certain something which separates you out from the crowd. It's called your USP, remember?

As for all the free balloons, hot dogs, sodas, T-shirts, and pony rides for the kids that your competition will undoubtedly rely on, do you honestly believe any of these run-of-the-mill incentives has ever convinced someone to sign up for a $75,000 Hummer? If you do, you might be well advised to close this book now and start selling cars. You and I know better. So, you should begin by treating potential customers with a little respect, giving them the credit of having a great deal of common sense, even a modicum of intelligence. That means if you're going to capture their attention, simply make a statement acknowledging this fact. Plain English, with a twist, will do it.

GET THE WORDS RIGHT

Some headlines couldn't be ignored because they struck a chord:

- *At 60 miles an hour the loudest noise in a Rolls Royce comes from the electric clock!*
- *When you're number 2, you try harder.*
- *Think small.*
- *Do blondes have more fun?*
- *I can't believe I ate the whole thing!*
- *It takes a tough man to make a tender chicken.*

With the exception of the first one, the product name is not included in the headline, yet I'm sure you can name the majority of the companies they represent. Incidentally, something else worth considering is the fact that all of these headlines are more than 30 years old!

Each of them, at the time they were written, went contrary to all the accepted rules of advertising—proof of the old adage "Rules are meant to be broken." And, even though today, they would all be described as having "attitude." They also grow out of a discernable product attribute. The Avis "When you're number 2, you try harder" is a perfect case in point. Created by Doyle, Dane, Bernbach in the mid-'60s, it flew in the face of all conventional wisdom. At a time when everyone was trying to claim they were number one in whatever they did, why would anyone in their right mind admit, let alone boast, to being number two? Because this admission of not being the market leader is backed up by the crucially important second part of the line, "You try harder!" The implication being you will get better service and value by dealing with someone who is currently number two but is busting its chops to become number one. This fairly obvious interpretation only serves to emphasize what I cannot stress enough, that most good advertising is simply a process of logical thinking.

Even the Clairol line "Do blondes have more fun?" relied on the commonly held perception, reinforced by the popular press as well as the movie and TV industry at the time, that blondes such as Marilyn Monroe, Anita Ekberg, and others seemed to be the ones leading the most glamorous life style. It also had subliminal sexual connotations that were surprisingly risqué for the period.

So, assuming you've got a killer USP, how do you translate this into advertising that will grab attention and drive customers to action? Let's imagine that you're lucky enough to manufacture one of the finest automobiles on the face of the planet, the Rolls Royce. Your USP would probably go something like this:

No other car is designed and built to such uncompromising standards using the highest quality materials and components.

Most of the Adverati of today's Madison Avenue would then proceed to show a pristine Rolls traveling along that portion of Route 101 that crosses the bridge perched atop Big Sur in California, the same location used for the vast majority of U.S. car commercials since our grandparents graduated from the horse and buggy. (Further proof that BDAs rarely come up with anything original, in spite of their exorbitant fees.) One or two agencies might progress beyond the facile and predictable by creating advertising that talks about the weeks of craftsmanship and skilled labor it takes to complete a single Rolls Royce, or the hundreds of hand-tanned leather hides discarded before the right half dozen are selected as worthy enough to create the glove-like interior, or the fact that the average life span of a Rolls Royce is beyond 37 years, or even that this is the automobile that has been the preferred mode of transport for kings, presidents, emperors, and dictators since the beginning of the 20th century.

All this interesting stuff is fine and should unquestionably be part of the overall messaging within the ad copy to serve as reinforcing arguments for the USP. But how to encapsulate this in an attention-grabbing headline? One that is immediately understandable, while driving home the impression that when you buy a Rolls Royce you are not merely buying a means of transport capable of getting you from point A to point B, you are also buying what is considered to be the finest car in the world.

At 60 miles an hour the loudest noise in a Rolls Royce comes from the electric clock!

Yes, I think that does it nicely.

Getting the words right is the key to all successful communications, It doesn't matter if you disseminate them via newspapers, magazines, radio, billboards, or even skywriting. In all these cases the medium is not the message. The message is the message. Another famous, long dead ad man (I promise to try and find some worthwhile quotes from a couple of living ad people soon), Leo Burnett once said, "The greatest thing to be achieved in ad copy is to be believed, and nothing is more believable than the product itself." This is precisely what the Rolls Royce headline does.

As I said at the beginning of the chapter, the most important element of any advertising communication is content: *What you say.* The second most important factor is style: *How you say it.* Content will be determined by what it is you create as a logical extension of your USP, whereas the style in which you say it will be a reflection of what kind of company you are. Even if what you say is that you have the greatest products in the world, that you offer them at the very best prices, and you back everything up with unmatched service, should you communicate these facts in the used car dealership

> Your product doesn't necessarily have to be a thing. It can be a service, your location, even the way your company looks. Just make sure it's part of your USP.

style we talked about earlier, you will be perceived as loud, pushy, and unpleasant to deal with. Most importantly, you'll come across as being exactly like every other car dealership out there. Why on earth would you want to give customers that impression?

So, when it comes to creating your advertising, irrespective of where it will run and what kind of media it will run in, you should turn to a very important stage of the communications plan that occurs between the USP and producing the actual ad. Sometimes described as the Big Idea, it's much better described as the *concept*.

THE CONCEPT

This is the platform on which you build all your *current* advertising. I use the word *current* because as you grow, when your market alters, or things beyond your control change, such as the economy, the environment, loss of hair, your advertising might need to take a new approach. This will require you to develop new concepts. But having said that, you must stick to this *unbreakable* rule: The concept should always grow out of the specifics of your USP, while maintaining a broad enough appeal and flexibility that it will work in any kind of media.

Unfortunately, most of the big Madison Avenue agencies seem to be capable of only coming up with concepts that work primarily in one media (more often than not TV) and are rarely capable of working in others. Many will probably disagree with me, but I insist on saying definitively that if it doesn't work across the board in *all media*, it's not a viable concept. See Figure 6.2 for the print execution of an idea that worked equally well on TV. BDAs focus on one medium all the time, particularly those hooked on using celebrities in their advertising. This is because they invariably think about a TV campaign first, then attempt to shoehorn every other media execution into a gerrymandered version of the original TV concept whether it runs as print, online, or direct marketing. This blinkered approach is rarely effective and more often than not the unfortunate client is left paying through the nose for a lot of stuff that doesn't work.

And who, you may ask, is to blame for this sorry state of affairs? Well, it's no one in particular. It's a combination of the agency creatives wanting to shoot hugely expensive TV commercials with Cindy Crawford, Paris Hilton, Tiger Woods, BoBo the Chimp, or whoever the current celebrity or jock du jour is.

FIGURE 6.2: *A print ad I did that worked equally well on TV. Compaq was being hammered by Dell (I'd earlier done most of the Dell ads). The idea was to position Compaq as the original, while Dell was merely a copy.*

Adding insult to injury is the agency account management team for not suggesting other avenues of communication worthy of exploration, or even if they do, not having the balls to fight for their beliefs. Compounding the felony are the marketing people on the client side who would sell their souls for the chance to play a round of golf with Tiger Woods, or Cindy Crawford, or even BoBo the Chimp. And the final icing on the cake is provided by the BDAs' management, who still see mainstream TV buys as a wonderful license to print money. And when you consider that most of the major ad agencies in the world are now part of three or four huge conglomerates, all of which are publicly traded companies, this means making the numbers every quarter becomes far more important than producing the best work for their clients.

> Even though you may not be big enough to afford Tiger right now, don't get suckered into using the school football coach in your ads. Support the team instead.

So, how do you develop great advertising concepts, ones that will differentiate you from the competition and give customers solid reasons why they should patronize you? Go back to Rolls Royce, and use that as an example. And before you say "What the heck has Rolls Royce got to do with the kind of business I'm running?" let me assure you that it has a great deal to do with how you should think about and create the advertising concepts that will drive your advertising.

Remember, the USP?

No other car is designed and built to such uncompromising standards using the highest quality materials and components.

Remember the headline?

At 60 miles an hour the loudest noise in a Rolls Royce comes from the electric clock!

Can you imagine what the concept was that grew out of the USP, that then became the platform on which the headline was based? (This was only the first of many headlines of many ads that ran for years in the Rolls Royce campaign.)

Here, you will have to trust me, because even though I had the pleasure of meeting David Ogilvy a few times, first as a student from England straight off the Queen Mary (the original one now a convention center in Long Beach, California), then later when I did a great deal of freelance work for O&M throughout the '90s. But, I never had the opportunity to question him on his methodology in developing this famous campaign.

How the Rolls Royce Concept Came About

So, even though I am making this up, I'll wager, I'm not too far from the truth of how it all came about. Unlike today, as described in Chapter 3, the AD/copywriter team goes off to the pub and throws progressively dumber ideas about while getting inebriated at the agency/client expense (it's usually referred to as a *working lunch*, which often seamlessly rolls over into a *working dinner*). David probably strolled down to his local Rolls Royce distributor in Greenwich, Connecticut, where he lived (no big surprise there) and conned them into loaning him a Silver Cloud for a few weeks so he could check it out on drives between his home, the yacht club, the golf course, and the polo club.

Never make claims about your products that are not based on fact. If you say in your advertising that Acme Widgets have 20 times more XXX power than everyone else's widgets, someone will check it out, and woe betide you if it isn't true.

Now I am sure that as David drove his Roller around in regal splendor, stinking up the interior with his pipe. (He invariably smoked a large curly briar stuffed to the brim with evil smelling dark shag.) He was perhaps thinking of producing advertising with up-market associations using crenellated castles, thatched roof cottages, gnarly yokels enjoying a pint at the local, all taking place against panoramic views of the rolling English countryside and accompanied by the Royal Philharmonic playing Elgar's "Enigma Variations." He was also for many years responsible for the splendid British Tourist Board's advertising in the United States, a daunting mélange of regal palaces, Anne Hathaway's Cottage, and Westminster Abbey, topped with a frosting of the Beatles, Carnaby Street, and subtle hints of the vicarious thrills available to dollar-wielding tourists in swinging London.

Then, in the middle of one of his jaunts at the wheel of his test-drive Roller, David's epiphany happened. It suddenly dawned on him how extraordinarily quiet the interior of the car was. That got him to thinking about how this fact could be used to reinforce the product's USP.

So, instead of coming up with one of the much-expected, soporific concepts about how a Rolls is so smooth it makes you feel like you're flying at 35,000 feet on diaphanous clouds, how its Super-Hydro-Squishy-Torquomada drive train gives you the impression you're riding in a goose-down filled bed, or any of the numerous appalling clichés car makers inflicted on the unsuspecting public via their advertising in those days, David very cleverly turned everything on its head and created a completely different concept. It featured a relatively insignificant component, but used it as a riveting demonstration of how Rolls Royce's time-honored tradition of broken fingernail craftsmanship, the accumulation of the sweat of centuries, the commitment to use only the highest quality components, etc., etc., would result in the epitome of the automobile builders art.

So, the concept became,

Use unexpected features to dramatically demonstrate our painstaking attention to the details other car makers don't even think about.

This somewhat revolutionary idea (for its time) was then utilized throughout the campaign. In other ads, the perception that a Rolls Royce cost a great deal of money—and it certainly did—was turned on its head with the argument that it actually worked out as a very prudent investment when you consider its lifespan compared to other luxury cars.

Other ads in the series made a big plus out of the fact that because the styling rarely changed, it wasn't necessary to keep up with the Jones's by trading in for a new model with bigger tail fins every couple of years. (Curiously, a similar argument was used later by Volkswagen, but was applied much further down the socioeconomic scale.) All these sound, rational arguments promoted the car as a prudent investment. Other ads in the ongoing series talked about the car's inherent safety, stressing that the longer than normal guarantees for parts such as the engine, clutch, and drive train gave the purchaser greater peace of mind.

> As I've said repeatedly, don't rely on BS to sell your company. There are solid, worthwhile reasons customers should deal with you. Take the time to find out what they are; then, spell them out in your advertising in a straightforward fashion.

A somewhat dubious claim was even made that the cars had lower overall maintenance costs because everything lasted longer and actually saved you money. Best of all, there was even an ad recommending you should buy the company president a Rolls because it would not only make him less stressed and guarantee him (sorry, in those days, it was invariably a him) a longer life, it would also be a reflection of the company's inherent good taste, conservatism, and high regard for quality. On a personal note, it's worth remembering all these arguments, because when you've really made it big, you might be able to use them to convince your board of directors to buy you your very own Rolls Royce, particularly if it wants to reduce your stress levels, keep you at the helm of your wonderful company, and put you in a frame of mind that guarantees continuing to pay exorbitant directors' fees and expenses for the next few years.

The important thing to understand here is that it doesn't matter if you're selling one of the world's most expensive and prestigious automobiles or merely a bunch of ten-cent widgets, truly effective advertising that is not a chore to read will always come out of the product. And it won't hurt if you can create that advertising with style and wit.

I am particularly struck by the fact that in spite of the impressive volume of advertising David Ogilvy was responsible for over a great many years, he was always particularly fond of the work he did for Rolls Royce because, as he put it so well, it was advertising that relied on facts, not hype. That's something to be considered when developing your own advertising. Eventually, hot air and BS always lose out to solid information.

GETTING STARTED

It all starts with words, no matter whether you are creating an ad for print media, TV, radio, or even a billboard. It doesn't matter if you are working on a computer, with a pencil and paper, or using a sharp twig to scratch on clay tablets. Start at the beginning. Put something down, anything. Just get it down. If all else fails, start off with a line that reads something in the vein of, "My product will change your life forever . . . because . . . ." Then start filling in the blanks.

Think about the benefits your product or service will bring to the customer. This doesn't mean putting together a list of product *features*; it's about the *benefits* these features might bring to the user. Retailers such as Home Depot don't sell tens of thousands of hardware products; they sell the things people need to improve their homes. They sell all kinds of mundane stuff like plumbing fixtures and spackling compound that will eventually improve their customers' quality of life. Hardly anyone goes into Home Depot on the hunt for sheets of plywood; they're looking to convert their basement from an

> Words are wonderful. Throughout history, every important document in the world, from the *Iliad* and the *Odyssey*, to the Bible, to the works of Shakespeare, to the Declaration of Independence, has relied on words to achieve its impact.

unfinished hell hole into a family playroom. People want the things they think will help them look or feel better, give them a better standard of living, feel financially secure, enjoy a better sex life, lose ten pounds, grow three inches taller, get out of debt, maybe even make their pets love them for more than just for their next meal.

So, don't just let your concept lie there, give it a twist. This means going beyond the expected and normal way to express what it represents. Throw caution out the window, just as Ogilvy did for the Rolls Royce ads. No one in their right mind would think you could sell one of the world's most expensive cars by talking about a feature that is possibly one of the least costly things in it. But in reality, he wasn't selling the clock; he was selling the perception that if it was the only thing you could hear when you were driving at 60 miles an hour, then you could be damn sure everything else in the car was designed and constructed to the same excruciating standards. If you're selling ten-cent widgets, sell them as if they're $100 widgets, and give me the reasons why I would be better off spending a $100 for your widget, rather than ten cents for someone else's.

Are your widgets better designed, are they better made, do they use better raw materials, are they safer, are they more hygienic, do they protect the environment? If you can say yes to any of these propositions, then tell me so, but do it in an easy to understand, thoroughly interesting fashion. Show me why I shouldn't have the slightest problem coughing up a $100 for one. In other words, what are the benefits I will enjoy? Will I get my work done quicker, will they make me live longer, will they make me feel like a teenager while I live longer, will my children's grandchildren and future generations reap the rewards because I haven't polluted the atmosphere? Do not bore me rigid with features; everyone else does that all the time. Simply tell me about the benefits, benefits, benefits. See Figure 6.3 for some print ads that do this.

Force yourself to think outside of your own and your company's world. And whatever you do, get one thing straight. Your customers don't care about you. They care about themselves. They want to know what's in it for them. So, start thinking like them. For some reason, this is the single most difficult thing companies and many of the people who run them seem able to do. Why is it after years of hearing advice such as "the customer is always right" or "the customer is king," we are still subjected to far too many ads, brochures, web sites, and other forms of company

FIGURE 6.3: *Three ads out of a campaign of more than 20 that I did for Hasselblad cameras many, many years ago. Each ad was stuffed with information about one of the world's most expensive cameras. At the end of every ad (each more than 2,000 words) was an offer for a free brochure. Hasselblad had to reprint the brochure seven times.*

communication we throw away in disgust because all they do is toot their own horns? For some reason or other, this seems to be particularly true of banks, brokerage houses, insurance companies, and other financial institutions I've had the misfortune to work with over the years. Perhaps having all that readily available cash flying around affects their perspective on the rest of the world. Certainly, the outrageous amounts of money the principals of most of these institutions take home at the end of the day seems to indicate that, as F. Scott Fitzgerald once so insightfully put it, "The rich are different from you and me."

THE HEADLINE

The headline along with what is known as *the visual,* the photograph or illustration that usually takes up a significant proportion of most ads, is what captures the initial attention of a prospective customer. The two should work hand-in-hand to telegraph the core message of the ad. The body copy and any supplementary visuals are usually used as support arguments to the central premise of the ad. See Figure 6.4 for a great example.

Because most small- to medium-businesses operate in a confined geographical area, they often start with an ad or a limited campaign in their local newspaper. Unfortunately, most of these are often badly concepted, written, and visualized. This is because they are tactical, rather than strategic. Local newspapers are full of cheaply produced ads screaming about "Closing Down Sales," "Last year's inventory must be cleared to make way for this year's inventory," "Special shipment of Black Forest cuckoo clocks," "No payments 'til 2020," "Employee discounts to every customer." And so on and so on. Every one of these clichés has been used a million times, yet retailers continue to beat prospective customers over the head with

FIGURE 6.4: *One of many ads produced for* The Economist *by my friend Hubert Graf that rely simply on a short, witty, and sophisticated headline.*

them. Is it because they actually work? Well, even if they ever did, which I sincerely doubt, they have by now become so hackneyed that there is no way they can possibly have the desired effect on an intelligent reader.

Remember what I said at the very beginning of this chapter, "All advertising, irrespective of where and how it appears, can only be successful if it has an impact on the audience it is addressing." I then went on to point out that, "The only way you can be sure of this is if the content of your communication creates a desire within those reading, or listening to it, to want to know more." If it's that simple, why do so many advertisers fail to do it? It's because they continually fail to put themselves in the customer's shoes. I don't care if you have too many cars on the lot, I don't care if you have a surplus of merchandise, and I certainly don't care if you're going out of business, particularly if you've been running ads saying that for the last three years.

I want you to give me a few concrete reasons why I should do business with you. No, check that, just give me *one* concrete reason why I should do business with you. How about you selling me one of those last year's model cars you've got cluttering up your lot for 10 percent less than the price any other dealer within a 100-mile radius is willing to offer me. And don't give me any of that baloney about matching other dealer's prices. Matching prices with every other dealer in town doesn't get me up off my backside and give me a reason to run over to your place! On the other hand, if you had the gumption to run an ad that said:

Brand new Stinker XL's for 10 percent less than any other dealer's price—Guaranteed!

If I'm in the market for a Stinker XL, I'm going to come and see you first. That's what tactical advertising is all about: solving an immediate problem, like having too much inventory. If on the other hand, you've got the insight to realize that running tactical advertising will only get you off the hook right now, and it's not in your interest to be coming up with one promotional gimmick after another, month in and month out, when you should be concentrating on developing and running a business, then you need to be looking at advertising from a strategic point of view. That's the kind of advertising that will build your business long term.

Let's assume you're the owner of a gift shop, maybe even the one with a closet full of Black Forest cuckoo clocks. So, what do you advertise, the clocks or the store? Or, should you try and do both? The answer is yes, do both. By all means advertise the clocks, after all you need to empty that closet but at the same time use them as a vehicle to promote the store. Never fall into the trap of just promoting merchandise. Doing that leaves you open to giving potential customers the impression you merely sell one-offs bought from wholesalers who act as middlemen pushing whatever was in the latest container load from Bangladesh. Far better to first establish the perception in the mind of your potential customers that when it comes to buying gifts, they'd be crazy not to come see you first, because:

- You have better quality stuff.
- You have unusual stuff.
- You travel the world looking for stuff.
- You have more choice of stuff.
- Your stuff is priced reasonably.

There are lots more reasons you could come up with that might form the basis of an interesting and informative ad campaign. Just because you're a gift shop doesn't mean you should only feature the expected gift-like objects. Once you've seen one cuckoo clock, you've seen 'em all. Become The Gift Expert, The Gift Guru, The Gift Big Kahoona. Go beyond simply flogging individual items to people who need to purchase a gift once in a blue moon for some particular occasion; have your advertising become a font of information and entertainment by talking about the tradition of gift giving and the history behind the various gift-giving seasons. Offer lists of suitable items within given price ranges. Create lists geared toward different age groups, lists suitable for members of the family, lists for all those occasions when you are forced to buy gifts for people you hardly know and certainly don't care about.

Occasionally feature items that are really unexpected: shrunken heads from the upper Orinoco, voodoo dolls complete with color-coded pins for inducing headaches, stomach aches, whatever. You don't have to stock a ton of this stuff, just enough to use in the advertising and have yourself talked about. Get a reputation for being different and certainly worth checking out because you always have just the right thing, even if it's something completely off the wall. If you create your ads in the same vein, you'll get yourself a reputation as the place to go. So, instead of a headline that says,

Acme has the finest selection of gifts in town.

Wake up the neighborhood with something like this:

Shrunken Heads to Crunchy Frogs. Acme Gifts has it all.
No one will ever forget you (or possibly forgive you) for your gift!

On the other hand, if this approach is a tad on the strong side for you, you can always go the route that promises discerning customers the expectation that unlike other gift shops, you don't stock the usual mass-produced, shoddy line of goods made by people in Guangdong province earning two cents an hour. (Figure 6.5 shows how to go with the unexpected.) Something like this might do the trick:

FIGURE 6.5: *There are enough DVDs and videos out here to sink a ship. So how to make the BBCs stand out from the crowd? Present the titles in a tongue-in-cheek combination of the titles that takes advantage of a rather British and somewhat sardonic sense of humor.*

*The only thing you'll find made in China at Acme Gifts
is the mat you wipe your feet on as you enter!*

As you would expect, a suitable visual would be the actual doormat sitting outside the store's front door. It will, of course have a large "Welcome" written on it. Maybe in Cantonese. Naaahh, a little too obtuse for our purposes.

The point I'm trying to make here, yet again, is that whatever business you're in, widgets or shrunken heads, never fall into the trap that over 95 percent of all advertisers (that is most of your competitors). Namely, running advertising exactly like the advertising everyone else runs. Where's the sense in that?

BODY COPY

There are two schools of thought when it comes to advertising body copy. The first school would have you believe no one reads body copy. If you follow this line of reasoning, all ads would have a headline spelling out what is being sold, accompanied by a picture of it. In this case, David's famous Rolls Royce ad would consist of a visual of the car and a headline saying:

The new Rolls Royce, yours for $26,000, complete with electric clock!

I doubt that would have had the same impact as the ad he produced.

The second school of thought insists on cramming every single iota of information about a product or service into every single ad, whether it's relevant to the purpose of the ad or not. Demonstrated by a phrase I've since picked up, one which is particularly apt at describing how a great many clients view their advertising, it goes like this:

S**t expands to fill a vacuum!

I leave you to fill in the blanks.

Because you buy a page in a magazine or newspaper doesn't mean you have to fill every square inch of that space. Sometimes you can be more effective by saying very little in a large space. You just be sure that what you do say will capture the reader's attention and then prompt a reaction. (See Figure 6.6.)

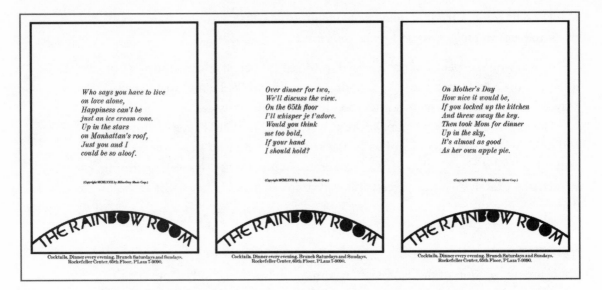

FIGURE 6.6: *Three from a series of ads I did for a famous New York restaurant which not only reflected the art deco atmosphere of the place but also used the ad's white space to enhance the sophisticated feel of the copy which was written in the style of 1930s song lyrics.*

As I keep repeating, advertising is a form of communication. So for goodness sake, use it to communicate. But do it in such a way that it invites prospective customers to make the next step, whether it be visiting a web site, sending an e-mail, calling an 800 number, stopping by your store or factory, or even when hiring a third party to do a job such as remodeling a kitchen or installing new carpets telling whoever is doing the work that they must use your cabinets or carpeting as part of the job specification. All of this will be dependant upon your advertising having motivated them to make that step.

I guarantee you, this technique will invariably require you to give readers of your advertising more information, rather than less. Well-written body copy should present information in a dramatic, interesting, and easily digestible fashion. A better writer than I will ever be once put it rather well in his rules for writing a speech:

- Begin strongly.
- Have one theme.
- Use simple language.
- Leave a picture in the reader's mind.
- End dramatically.

He also, upon being appointed First Lord of the Admiralty in 1939, was reputed to have sent a memo to every admiral of the British Fleet—and in those days, the British fleet groaned under the weight of several hundred admirals—requesting an immediate update on the current state of the British navy. Appended to the memo was a handwritten footnote requiring them to, "Pray do this on one side of one sheet of paper." If you haven't guessed, the writer in question was Winston Churchill.

Yet paradoxically, in many other ways Churchill was not necessarily the soul of brevity. He was a prolific writer who over a period of 60 years wrote dozens of books, including his five-volume *History of the English Speaking Peoples*, and a five-volume history, *The Second World War*, in addition to churning out thousands of news reports, articles, and commentaries for numerous magazines and newspapers.

> When you consider that language is based on combining 26 letters in certain ways to express love, sorrow, joy, and every other human emotion, why on earth would you want to use it to insult the intelligence of anyone reading your advertising?

What Churchill did grasp was the need for brevity in communications when it is necessary to impart information quickly and create an immediate response, particularly from an audience with little initial enthusiasm for what you have to say. If on the other hand, you're addressing readers you've identified as having a definite interest in what you're selling, then you can afford to take a more detailed, long-copy approach, which will allow you to expand on all the reasons why people should buy your product.

Another trap it's easy to fall into when writing ad copy is to start talking to your audience as if they were indeed an audience and are all seated in the back row of a theater, while you are the great actor performing on stage. So you shout, you declaim, you act out a part, you might even toot your own horn. Without realizing it, you do everything you wouldn't dream of doing if you were having a normal conversation with a friend. It's a well-known fact of life that people dislike loud-mouth churls even more than they do bores. So, why attempt to be either?

The best-written ad copy is done in such a way that it could very easily be a relaxed chat between two people—not loud or strident but with easy-to-understand statements, phrases, and words delivered in a calm manner. Some of the worst offenders for badly written ads are those from B2B advertisers. Chock full of business-speak gobbledygook, this copy insists on destroying the English language with such gems as "Bleeding edge technology," "Multiple synergistic opportunities," "Empowering entrepreneurship," and far too many other meaningless phrases. I recently did some work for an agency handling the account of a large business consulting company. After getting the usual bare-bones briefing from the agency, I started doing my own research, which included visiting the client's web site to get a feel, not just for what it is and what it does, but to appreciate the manner and kind of language it employs to describe itself to its audience.

This is what it said about itself on its "About Us" page:

> We provide strategic consulting, application services, technology solutions and managed services to Global 2000 companies and government organizations. We help customers achieve results by identifying mission critical issues and implementing innovative and customized solutions designed to generate revenue, reduce costs and access the right information at the right time. As business systems integrators, we align our clients' business processes and information systems to enable them to access the right information at the right time, empowering them to achieve their desired business results and create enterprise value.

To me, this is almost unintelligible. I really have no idea what it is the company could do for me. I certainly get the impression it is self centered, pompous, and not shy about blowing its own trumpet. But, in terms of how I might benefit from a possible business relationship with it, I haven't a clue. I do, however, get the feeling that unless I am a huge multinational company prepared to spend dumpster loads of money, I shouldn't waste my dime giving it a call.

I also know that this eye-glazing example of corporate-speak was crafted by a team of at least 20 people around a giant conference room table on the 65th floor of Global Headquarters. As the lowest level flunky scribbles away at a giant white-board, people are shouting: "We're in most of the *Fortune* 2000." "We have to talk about business processes. That's hot right now!" "For crying out loud, don't leave out mission critical." "Hey, they should know we create enterprise value." Anyone who's ever sat in one of these nightmare meetings will know exactly what I am talking about. They will also know that after the 100-word masterpiece is finally bludgeoned into an unreadable piece of mush everyone is happy with, it goes to the CEO who, depending on what he just read in the *Harvard Business Review* or what fellow CEO and drinking buddy James Doe said to him at golf last Sunday, will fine tune it to the point of it being completely meaningless drivel.

Compounding the felony of all this meaningless rubbish are the corporate lawyers (which at this stage of your development, hopefully you are not yet cursed with) who will always insist on the use of politically correct, purposely bland language, and inoffensive visual representations of the company, its employees, and possible customers. Although the reasoning for this insistence on putting all forms of communication into a legalistic straightjacket is supposedly to protect the company from possible legal action, in reality, it is little more than an excuse by those who do this . . . to do it . . . because they can. (See Figure 6.7.)

> Whether it be known as corporate-speak, geek-speak, gangsta-speak, or any other kind of speak, it's jargon or in the vernacular, bullshit. Using these words or phrases doesn't make you familiar with the reader, it confuses them.

It all comes back to what I said earlier about not looking at your company from your own point of view but from your customers'. Never stop asking yourself what you can do for them. No one, with the exception of you and your family, cares what you can do for yourself. Tell prospective customers what's in it for them if they do business with you, but don't think for a minute you can bore them into buying what you're selling. Get them interested in what you have to offer, then convince them why they should buy it. Write brief, snappy sentences with short paragraphs while avoiding using obtuse words, such as obtuse. Unless you are in the unique position of having a business that sells sophisticated products to a sophisticated audience, realize that the great majority of Americans buy and refer to far fewer newspapers and magazines than they have ever done, read less than one book

FIGURE 6.7: *The original headline for this IBM speech recognition software ad was: "For years mad scientists have talked to their computers. Now you can too!" The IBM lawyers killed it; as it was offensive to mad scientists. Great art direction by my partner Joe Massaro.*

a year, get most of their entertainment from TV/DVDs and games, and are increasingly accessing their information from the internet.

They live in a world in which they are exposed to thousands of messages a day, and a great many of them are ads, which is why ad agencies are engaged in a never-ending quest to find new ways to capture consumer awareness. Unfortunately for their clients, most of these new approaches don't work. Fortunately for the ad agencies, they provide new revenue streams for them as traditional media vehicles continue to shrink.

The day is rapidly approaching when even the largest clients will realize that the traditional agency/client relationship is broken beyond repair. Fortunately, as a small- to medium-business entrepreneur, you don't have to suffer through that learning curve. You can start with a clean sheet. Even if you worked with ad agencies in your previous business life, take the knowledge you gained from that experience and use it to your benefit. Even if eventually you grow to a size where you may use an agency (more on that in Chapter 11), doing it yourself at this stage will be invaluable to you later.

> The American Association of Advertising Agencies continues to hold numerous conferences in Fiji, Cannes, and other glamorous venues where agency principals make speeches about changing their ways to not rely on the 30-second TV spot for all their clients needs. Then they go home and produce more 30-second TV spots.

NOTHING BUT THE FACTS, MA'AM

As Joe Friday used to put it so well on *Dragnet* (the original TV series, not the movie remake with Dan Aykroyd and Tom Hanks), there is something intrinsically honest and appealing about simply laying out the facts of what you have to offer and letting the customer decide whether or not they want to buy. Having said that, you'll get a much better response if you can make the facts more interesting, appealing, and of some value to the reader. There was a great Apple Computer ad from the early 1980s with a headline that said, "Will someone please tell me exactly what a personal computer can do?" (See Figure 6.8.) This was before the IBM PC and the Apple Mac, and well before IBM's PC had started to make serious inroads into the business computing environment. The ad showed what you could do with the Apple II (as I said, this was pre-Mac days), including everything from keeping your business accounts to filing your favorite recipes. It was an eye opener for people who hadn't yet considered how a computer could change the way they did business and organize their lives.

You can use the same approach without necessarily buying the large space required to list dozens of reasons. I've done it with ads that say "55 Incredible things you can do with the Acme Widget." But, you only need to list the first half dozen or so, then at the end of the ad, you tell the reader that "For the other 49 wonderful ways

FIGURE 6.8: *This is an eight-page ad written by Steve Hayden that actually spelled out 100 different things you could do with the Apple II. At that time, in 1983, it was an eye opener.*

to benefit from the Acme Widget, go to www.acmewidget.com." Then, if you've made the copy sufficiently provocative and enticing, they'll go to your web site, which will be costing you peanuts compared to what you've paid for the ad space. Once they get there, you can bombard them as much information as you need to complete the sales pitch. Just be sure that you also make that interesting and easy to access as well; don't make it an online data sheet or one of those plumbers catalogs I talked about at the very beginning of the book. More on web sites in Chapter 9.

TELL ME A STORY

Storytelling is an essential part of human culture. From childhood, people have listened to stories. The reason the Dickens, Brontes, Grishoms, Clancys, and Cartlands of this world have sold millions of books is because they weave tales that initially capture the reader's interest, then hold it through the twists and turns of the plot until arriving at a satisfying resolution at the end. Advertising copy can be written in exactly the same way, simply by talking to potential customers as if you were telling them a story.

The story can be a true one based on how the product or service you are selling solved a problem, answered a need, or resolved a situation. If you can do this by using an existing customer who will endorse you and your product, it is known as case-study advertising. Research has shown that, particularly for B2B companies, case studies are extremely powerful because they provide reassurance to potential customers that others have had a positive experience with you. You can also create stories about hypothetical situations in which your product or service could provide the perfect solution to a problem. Obviously, this is not as strong as an actual case study in which you can name and get the endorsement of a real customer. But if the copy is written in a sympathetic manner demonstrating than you understand the problems and needs of the customer and what you are selling could very well solve those problems or satisfy their needs, then you are on your way to a sale.

Lots of B2B ads are what I call "bastard child" case studies. These are the ones that talk about a "major hospital," "nationally recognized manufacturer," or a *Fortune* 500 Company" being users of the advertiser's products. This is usually because the customer doesn't want to be featured in someone else's advertising or perhaps because their experiences were not sufficiently rewarding for them to want to endorse the advertiser. Either way, this is not a route I would recommend.

SHOW ME

Another very powerful form of advertising is known in the ad biz as *product demos*. The worst example of these are the infomercials late-night TV viewers are subjected to as Billy Loudmouth shouts at the top of his voice about the incredible stain removing properties of OxyBaloney, or the long-lasting NeverDull kitchen knife collection. The reason these monstrosities have been around since the invention of television is that, unfortunately, they actually work. My problem with them is they all seem to use the same awful script: "If you call 'right now' we'll double your order, and if you're one of the first ten to call, we'll throw in the bagel slicer for free."

Why not be different? Remember what I said about trying to avoid doing the same formulaic stuff everyone else does? Be different, develop a personality, give yourself some character, have some fun, and above all, avoid being schlocky!

For my sins, when I first came to America in the 1960s I worked on the Timex Watch account. Remember John Cameron Swasey with his immortal "It takes a lickin' but keeps on tickin" campaign all those years ago. Maybe not, unless like me you're a semi-geriatric. But the pay-off line will live in perpetuity. It was based on a long-running TV and print campaign, known by those of us who worked on it as "The Timex Torture Test." The watch was always placed in situations where it would undergo a great deal of stress, "taking a lickin,'" yet survive and "keep on tickin.'" And the watch did indeed survive, not necessarily on the first take; sometimes we would go through dozens of watches before one would live through the ordeal of being attached to the propeller of an outboard motor or survive repeated cliff dives at Acapulco. But we never swapped watches in the middle of each torture test. The same watch had to perform throughout the take, even if we destroyed hundreds of watches to get the final result.

The campaign created a brand that stood for inexpensive, but extremely reliable watches you could count on. Occasionally, the ads featured real stories, such as one we did about the farmer who lost his Timex, only to find it after it had "passed through" one of his cows that had eaten it days earlier. But the vast majority of them were dreamed up by people at the agency desperately looking for the next interesting and dramatic situation we could use to prove the inherent value of the product. And even though it was obvious to the people watching the ads that these were all staged demonstrations, no attempt was made to do them as anything else, so over time they acquired their own validity. Plus, the fact that we used an extremely well-recognized ex-network newscaster as the spokesman for the brand helped give it a certain gravitas.

Even though most of these demos were told in a very dramatic fashion through the medium of television, they also translated very well into a long-running newspaper and magazine campaign. Print advertising can be extremely effective using the show-me approach. With all that space, you can afford the luxury of going into far more detail than when limited by 30 seconds of TV time. Just make sure the detail you go into is interesting and relevant to your selling message. Use the visuals to reinforce the arguments you make as to why the product does what you claim it does.

TESTIMONIALS, CELEBRITIES, ENDORSEMENTS AND OTHER DUMB IDEAS

You all know what a testimonial is, right? Sometimes they can work very well for you, but only if they are seen by the reader as genuine. The merest hint that a glowing recommendation is a paid-for endorsement immediately devalues the message. After all, as everyone knows, given enough money you can get anyone to say anything. If you have a customer who really has a great story to tell about how your product *honestly* worked wonders on their baldness, made them rich, improved their sex life, or any other benefit they've enjoyed as a result of using what you're selling, testimonials can work.

The worst kind of advertising endorsements are those using over-the-hill actors, sports personalities, and retired political hacks who start off by saying, "Hi, I'm Joe Schmoe for the First Bank of Palookaville." Simply remember the first rule of using celebrities in an ad, if they have to tell the audience who they are, they're no longer a celebrity. The second rule is that if by chance someone does recognize them, their reaction might very well be, "Oh my God, I thought he was dead. Would ya look at him? He is dead."

At this stage of your business development, you can't afford to start throwing money around on the likes of Tiger Woods or Michael Jordon as spokespeople or endorsers for your company. And even though it might be tempting to use the local celebrity you met on the golf course last weekend, be very careful before you commit to a program using such a person. Just how dangerous this can be was recently demonstrated to me by several local advertisers in

> If you ever consider using a celebrity spokesperson, ask yourself this, "Am I doing this because I have absolutely nothing of any worth to say about my company, so I will have to rely on borrowed interest?" If the answer is yes, close the company.

the city I now live in after escaping from New York. (Sounds like the title of a bad movie.)

The much glorified football coach of the city's biggest university was being used by several local businesses to shill for roofing, lawn care, car dealerships, and various other products that, in spite of painfully delivered exhortations to "Get with the program," "Show some team spirit," or "Go the extra yard," had absolutely no connection with the game of football. Compounding the idiocy of it all, after repeatedly professing his undying loyalty to the school and its team, halfway through his five-year contract Coach XXX skipped town to go to another university for more money. This turn of events not only made the local crazed football fans even crazier, it meant the companies that had invested substantial amounts of money to feature him in their advertising had to scramble to change everything while somehow putting on a brave face and desperately distancing themselves from this ill-thought-out association.

Never forget, celebrities big and small, are only endorsing your stuff for the money you pay them to do it. Next week someone may offer them more.

Small scale sponsorship is OK for businesses that do it for local teams and charity events. (See Figure 6.9.) The thing is to be smart about how you do it. Just because every other business in town sponsors or supports the local football/baseball/basketball team doesn't necessarily mean you should. Why not go out of your way to find a sport or activity that is less mainstream and put some money into that? The ROI will be significantly better, because even though there may be fewer participants and fans, they will be more hardcore and appreciative of your support. You will become indelibly associated with whatever team or event you sponsor, particularly if you use advertising to make a logical connection between it and yourself.

Be careful, however, to realize these associations work best and pay off over the long run. Pulling out of a sponsorship can have very negative effects and leave the fans with a sense of betrayal. A perfect example of this was Hewlett-Packard's sponsorship of the Woman's Challenge, one of the premier women's multistage cycle races in the world. Supporting this event cost HP less than $200,000 per year and generated a tremendous amount of goodwill for the company, particularly in Idaho where the race was held, because Boise is home to one of HP's largest and

BULLDOGBANKERS

We're proud of the Bulldogs. And their long championship tradition. We wish them continuing success.

We'd like to think we have a few things in common. We're both local. Successful. And have been around for some time.

Our decisions are made on the spot. Not by management, hundreds of miles away.

We both have a number of plays. They have quarterback sneaks, flare-outs, double reverses and red-dogs. We have checking and saving options, IRAs and lines of credit.

Now it's true Westside players are a bit older. And pass deposits and loans better than footballs.

But, you'll still see us out practicing every business day to be the best team around. Like the Bulldogs.

Visit our Tracy office and receive a financial game plan for your upcoming championship seasons. And don't forget to pick up a Bulldog game schedule.

WESTSIDE
THE RESPONSEBANK

60 West 10th Street • Tracy • California • 95376 • (209) 836-5500
120 E. Center Street • Manteca • California • 95336 • (209) 239-4434
13 Plaza • Patterson • California • 95363 • (209) 892-3540

Member FDIC

FIGURE 6.9: *An ad I did many years ago with my partner Robert Hendricks for a small California bank. The Bulldogs were the local high school football team. For peanuts, the bank became their biggest booster and the town hero.*

most profitable divisions. Yet, one of the first things new CEO Carly Fiorina did when she was appointed to head HP was cancel the sponsorship of the cycle race and instead invest many millions of dollars in a Formula One motor racing team. Not only was the ROI on this new multimillion dollar venture minuscule, pulling out (at very short notice) of the Women's Challenge race caused its permanent cancellation and led to the alienation of many thousands of people who had favorably associated HP with the sponsorship of this unique event.

After wasting many millions of dollars on the International Grand Prix motor racing circuit, HP's team no longer exists, and Ms. Fiorina is no longer CEO of HP. She did, however, get to go to the Monte Carlo Grand Prix several times and drink vintage champagne while watching the race from the balcony of her suite at the Grande Hotel, Monaco.

DUMB THINGS YOU SHOULD AVOID

Even though this chapter is primarily about print advertising, there are several recommendations I make here that apply equally to all forms of advertising. And even though our focus is advertising for small- to medium-companies, most of these no-no's apply to all businesses, irrespective of size.

- *Borrowed interest.* Avoid trying to associate yourself with things that have no relevance to what you do. If you're in the roofing business, talk about roofing, show roofing, and explain how you're the world's unmatched authority on roofing. Don't show pictures of animals and babies. I don't care what you've read in other books, animals and babies might get people's attention, but unless they're in the market for one, these cute and cuddly objects won't help you make a sale. Don't talk about your ancestors, where you grew up, or where you went to school—unless you graduated Phi Beta Kappa from the National Roofing Academy. Stick to what you're best at—roofing.

- *Event sales.* Refrain from jumping on this bandwagon. Even if it is the 1,200th anniversary of the signing of the Treaty of Blognovia, this event has no relevance to the fact that for the next week you are having a four-for-two sale on hubcaps. Far better to simply spell out the great savings customers can get while making their '65 Valiant look like it just came out of the showroom. Far too much local retail advertising, including that from our favorite villains, the car dealerships, falls into this trap. If you're going to have a sale, have a sale. What's the point of having a Presidents' Day Sale when every other retailer is having a Presidents' Day Sale on exactly the same Presidents' Day?

  And even when it's not used as an excuse for a sale, try to avoid falling into the trap of running the same advertising and promotional themes everyone else is running because they woke up one morning and found they were seven days away from St. Valentine's Day. The worst example of this is when the Olympics roll around every four years and everyone starts running ads with inane headlines such as "Blogs Electric is going for the gold" or "At VideoRama we're raising the bar to new heights." Remember, it's all about standing out, not blending in.

- *Ego trips.* Don't put yourself in the advertising. You think you're great. Your family thinks you're great. Even you're employees think you're great. (Would they tell you otherwise, even if they thought you were an imbecile?) But guess what? Your prospective customers don't know you from a hole in the wall, and your smiling face isn't going to convince them you have the best stuff within a 100 miles. Any time I see a CEO or company president in an ad, I can smell the desperation oozing out of the page. Either the person pictured in the ad is suffering from a bad case of egomania or the ad agency has reached the stage were the client has turned down the last dozen campaigns and out of desperation they come up with the what-the-heck-do-we-do-now chestnut, "Hey CJ, why don't we feature you in the ad? Kinda serious, but approachable, on the factory floor, or walking on a beach looking out to sea, the visionary thing, maybe in a black turtle neck, very Steve Job'ish. Waddya think CJ?" Don't ever go there. It never works. Smart CEO's save themselves for PR. Look at The Donald of Trump and Branson of Virgin; they're everywhere, except in their own ads.

- *Different media, different ads.* Don't run ads that bear no relationship to each other in different kinds of media. As I've said earlier, if a concept is good because it's based on an original idea, it should work in all kinds of media. Your core advertising message need only change if your business changes. Yes, you can certainly fine tune your advertising and messaging, but only to improve it. Don't change for the sake of change. No one sees your advertising as much as you do. Give your prospective customers the chance to see and be affected by it.

- *Advertise everywhere.* Make your ad budget work harder for you by specifically creating ads that work in a limited selection of media. (I've dealt with media options in the previous chapter.) Find out which of the various media options have the most readership with your target groups, then put all your money in those. If you have a limited budget (who doesn't?), you can't afford to waste your money in generalist publications. Find the ones that appeal to the specific niche who will be the prime market for what you have to offer. Then create your ad content to suit.

- *Overdoing the ads.* Do not create too many ads. Use your money to create a few really good ads. Invest in superior art work. Take the time to write (or have written for you) intelligent, pithy copy that people will take pleasure in reading. Make it interesting and informative. Write it so the reader will want to know more and will make the effort to do so by going to your web site, returning a prepaid reply card, calling a phone number, or even coming round to your place of business.

Only create ads you're proud of. Don't be satisfied to say to yourself, "Yeah, they may look like crap, but they sell a ton of stuff." Life's too short not to be proud of what you do. Create ads that look great—and sell a ton of stuff.

CHAPTER SEVEN

Creating TV ads: welcome to the wonderful world of showbiz, excitement, glamour, and acid reflux

Everyone has grown up with TV. But back in those dim, dark, prehistoric days, choices were somewhat limited, just three networks. And if you lived in a major metropolitan area, you might get a couple of really crappy local stations putting out a diet of sitcom reruns, traffic reports from Chopper Six, (actually a guy in the studio playing a recording of a helicopter from the sound track of *Apocalypse Now*), and every five minutes Chief Meteorologist Skip Mahoney would

The average cost of producing a network-ready 30-second TV spot is about $400,000. The cost of running it networkwide can run into the millions.

stand on the roof of a car park trying to make you believe he really was a meteorologist, even though the week before he'd been the sports editor.

The commercials in the early days were as primitive as most of the programming. There were lots of rings around the collar, white knights chasing out stains, earring-wearing bald men with muscles making sure your kitchen floor was squeaky clean, anvils pounding in your head, raging fires in your belly. All of it was brutal stuff, and all of it talking to the viewing audience as if it were a bunch of morons. But today we've moved on, thanks to the wonders of computer graphics and multimillion dollar production budgets.

TV ADVERTISING TODAY

Now, most of the TV commercials we have to sit through as we nosh on our microwaved mac and cheese look like 30-second versions of *Star Wars*, *The Matrix*, or *Lord of the Rings*. Unfortunately, most of them still treat the audience like cretins; they just happen to be spending a heck of a lot more money to do it.

Remember what I said at the very beginning of this book? Most good advertising is based on logic. So, why is it the one thing the great majority of advertisers never seem able to acknowledge about advertising on TV is that it is the one media choice that is totally intrusive? When you pay good money to run a TV commercial as part of your killer advertising program, never forget you are going to be interrupting the viewing pleasure of the audience you're attempting to sell to, and you're probably doing it at exactly the point when something exciting or dramatic is about to happen in the program they're watching. So, they really aren't in the mood to hear about your new miracle cure for hemorrhoids. And they certainly don't want to see your message if it's boring, trivial, or heaven forbid, offensive.

One of the major reasons why TV advertising in general in the United States has always been much more "in your face" than in Europe, particularly the United Kingdom, is that commercials have long supported the radio and TV business. But in Europe all the broadcast media were run by the state and didn't have to rely on advertising to fund the programming. It was only when commercial broadcasting was introduced in the late 1950s and early 1960s that TV and radio advertising became possible. But because the audiences had become accustomed to watching commercial-free television, they were not inclined to be very receptive if innumerable advertising breaks interrupted what they were watching. Consequently, when the ads came on, most viewers decided it was either time to put the kettle on for a nice cup of tea or to go to the "loo" to relieve the pressure built up from drinking too much tea.

Consequently, advertisers and ad agencies were obliged to create commercials people might actually want to watch, ones that entertained and informed, often using humor, telling stories, and casting real actors playing real roles. It was not unusual for such thespian luminaries as Sir Lawrence Olivier, Sir John Guilgud, and Sir Richard Attenborough to appear in TV commercials for banks, credit cards, and even gas companies long before American actors decided it was not beneath their dignity to appear in such commercial ventures.

Many of the spots were miniature vignettes representing believable, true-to-life situations and stories that managed to make selling points without hitting you over the head with them. The American versions of these real life situations, known in the ad biz as *slice-of-life* commercials, are as remote from true life as the twisted minds of Madison Avenue can make them. They usually involve a couple of women seated at a kitchen table having a cup of coffee. The conversation moves on from such weighty topics as the current state of global warming to an erudite review of the family wash. One tells the other how she's having problems with her whites. Her friend, who's just popped in on the way home from teaching advanced neurosurgery at the local university, then produces a five-gallon container of Miracle Whito, which she obviously carries around with her at all times in case she is faced with one of these "washing emergencies."

> Many American actors who still refuse to do television commercials in the United States are more than happy to do them for enormous sums of money in countries such as Japan. Sylvester Stallone is paid millions to appear as the spokesman for Ito Ham.

This shining example of feminine pulchritude then proceeds to give her pal a detailed lecture on the cleaning properties of Miracle Whito, accompanied by a

The ultimate TV commercial character would have to be Mr. Whipple, played by the same actor, Dick Wilson, for over 34 years. To my embarrassment, I admit having written a few in my first job in the United States as a writer at Benton & Bowles, New York.

series of animated slides showing the deep-down scrubbing action of Miracle Whito's patented dirt-blasters. The spot ends with the newly enlightened woman profusely thanking her pal as if she's just come up with the cure for cancer.

Now you know I haven't made any of this up, because you've seen this two-women-sat-at-the-kitchen-table spot or something very much like it hundreds of times over the years, for everything from detergents, to deodorants, to dog food. And rest assured, you will see it many more times, because some of the biggest advertising spenders in the world, including Proctor & Gamble, General Foods, and others continue to rely slavishly on this format. Why do they do it? I honestly think, because they don't know any better. It's like having a terrible addiction they can't break, only their habit doesn't have anything to do with nicotine, caffeine, or smack. It's those dreaded slice-of-life TV spots. But don't worry, you'll never fall into this trap, because you're going to create TV spots that will be creative, entertaining, and original.

ACHIEVING THE UNEXPECTED

Exactly how will you create great ads? Well, as I said at the beginning of this chapter, you must accept that you are intruding on someone's viewing, so you have to make it worth their while to stick around and listen to what you have to say. Don't give them a reason to channel surf, pop some corn, or go to the bathroom. You must also never forget that if you do manage to get their attention, you will only have it for 30 seconds. That is a very, very short amount of time. Under no circumstances must you fall into the trap so many advertisers do of trying to fill every one of those seconds with stuff you consider as vital to the sale. Because believe me, it won't be. Those few, precious 30 seconds will allow you to say just one thing. Not two and certainly not six. Just one.

Let me give you an example. In my opinion, one of the best TV commercials ever made was—no, not the Apple Macintosh, 1984 Super Bowl commercial. It was indeed a great spot, and is probably the most famous television commercial ever made in terms of the publicity it continues to receive to this day, twenty two years after it first ran. (See Figure 7.1.) And although it was at that time the most expensive commercial ever made, it only ran once. Providing one more example of the marketing genius of Steve Jobs and how he has made Apple into one of the great global brand names. But, for me, a truly great TV spot is one that puts over the products USP in a memorable fashion and leaves you wanting to know more. Which is why in my opinion, the best commercial ever made ran back in the 1960s and was a black-and-white spot for Volkswagen. Here's a brief description as it's almost impossible to get any frame clips from the spot. It opens as a car is climbing a steep hill in the middle of a snow storm. Most of the action is shot through the windshield of the car as the wipers try to keep the glass clear of the accumulating snow. The car reaches the summit and pulls in behind a very large barn. The front door of the barn opens, and we hear the roar of a large and powerful engine. Headlights beam out through the door, and then we see an enormous snowplow pull out and proceed to go off down the hill. The sound of the engine recedes and a VW logo pops up against the dark of the open door. Then an announcer voice over says,

Did you ever wonder how the guy who drives the snowplow, gets to the snowplow?

FIGURE 7.1: *More than any other TV commercial, the Apple 1984 spot that launched the Mac, turned the Super Bowl into an advertising extravaganza where viewers tune in for the ads as much as for the football, and companies spend tens of millions to buy air time.*

Think about it. Why would you want to say anything more? You have captured the viewer's attention with the drama of the opening. What is going on? There is a hint of implied danger and mystery. Where is this car going in this kind of weather? The pause between the car arriving and the reveal of the snowplow serves to heighten the tension and sense of drama. The announcer's resolution of the mystery is perfect. It doesn't embellish the situation. There is no need, as most other car commercials would, to go on about the turbo traction nonslip transmission that makes driving in snow storms easy. To wax eloquent about the car's all-weather heating and ventilation system that provides blissful comfort in all conditions. Or, the luxurious interior that takes the stress and tedium out of lengthy journeys. Apart from the fact that the VW of the 1960s didn't have any of these wonderful things, they would actually have gotten in the way of the message and diluted its impact. But trying to convince most car manufacturers of this, both then and now, would have been impossible.

One other thing worth noting, the spot was actually a 60-second one, so for the first 30 seconds, all you saw was the view through the windshield of the snowy road. This only served to increase the tension and reinforce the resolution provided by the announcer's tag line at the end. You could make that spot today, even as a 30-second one, and it would still be far more powerful and effective than many of those you've seen for four-wheel drive vehicles sloshing through mud, ice, snow, rivers, etc. as they end up on top of Mount Whitney or an ice floe in the middle of the Arctic Ocean or various other places you wouldn't dream of taking a car. This is why so many car commercials are totally unbelievable and often ineffective. I don't want to climb the Himalayas in my car; I want to get to Aunt Maud's for Thanksgiving dinner when it's snowing.

Great TV is simple TV. The simpler the concept and execution the easier the message will be understood. It will also be less expensive to produce.

For some reason when people create and produce TV commercials, they seem to acquire the delusion that they are now in show business, forgetting the primary function of the spot is to sell something—not boringly, or tediously, or repetitiously but hopefully, with humor, intelligence, and style. But unquestionably, it should sell.

TEN NONBREAKABLE RULES OF CREATING GREAT TV ADS

If you don't like the idea of rules, consider these as guidelines. Either way, they are things I've learned and relied on over the years to help me make better TV commercials.

1. Always remember the viewer has a remote, TiVo, VCR and/or DVD recorder, and many better things to do than watch your commercial.

2. The second rule is KISS (Keep It Simple Stupid). Say one thing, preferably the incredible benefit the viewer can look forward to if he uses your product. But just one. If it cures wooden legs, don't say it's also good for headaches. A cure for wooden legs is impressive enough.

3. Although this may sound a little strange, spend the least amount of money as possible when producing the spot. This clarifies the mind by not allowing you to compensate for a lousy idea by throwing money at it through computer graphics, fancy sets, or exotic locations. If it's a great idea, you can shoot it with a home video camera in a broom closet.

4. TV is a visual medium, so think visually. Do not have presenters (particularly yourself) standing there as if they've been stuffed and mounted while delivering a speech from cue cards. Do not show factories, store fronts, show rooms, and used car lots. They all look the same—boring. If viewers turned the sound off, would they have the slightest idea what this wonderful thing is that you're trying to persuade them to buy? Avoid the use of what are known in the trade as "Snipes, star bursts, scrolling text, and day-glo banners," and all the other graphic gimmicks beloved of our old friends the used car dealers. They are cheap and nasty devices. They make you look cheap and nasty.

5. Again, because television is a visual medium, do not use the dialogue or announcer voice-over to repeat in words what is happening visually on the screen. Use the words either to reinforce (not repeat) the action or to act as a counterpoint to it in a way that enhances the drama.

6. If you can do a product demo, do it. But, do it only if it's a great one and will elicit a gee-whiz response from the viewer. And by a product demo, I mean something that fizzes, or sparkles, or makes beautiful noises. It

Be aware that it is illegal to fake product demonstrations that have been rigged to make the product look better than it really is. If it doesn't work on camera, then it won't work when the consumer buys it.

should also be believable. I know when I see commercials for miracle cleaners, polishers, stain removers, or whatever that the surfaces, rugs, or floors they are demonstrated on don't look anything like the awful ones I have in my home. So I am immediately suspicious that they've been specially prepared to work in the demo. Don't do a product demo that you think looks great because it's your product and you've sweated bullets to create and bring it to market. Don't think *me*. Always think *them*. What's the unquestionable benefit to the viewer? The viewer doesn't give a damn about you or your company.

7. Try to avoid producing one-offs. Make sure the idea for your TV spot has *legs*: meaning can it be the beginning of a campaign? Can you produce future executions based on the same concept, ones that will stay fresh and continue to capture the interest and attention of the viewer?

8. Your TV should tie-in with the rest of your advertising. This doesn't necessarily mean it must be a video version of what you're doing in print. It should make use of the inherent visual functionality of the medium, particularly through the use of drama, music, mobility, the acting ability of any talent used, and the visual possibilities of good camera work. Unlike print advertising, TV is not limited to a two-dimensional visual presentation. Television is a medium that overcomes the limitations of the flat art you are forced to use in print advertising.

9. Try to capture the viewer's attention early. This doesn't mean you have to do a Crazy Al by threatening to take a sledgehammer to a used Chevy if someone doesn't get down to your car lot "right now" with $500 in cash to take it off your hands in the next 15 minutes. You can be provocative (without being stupid), entertaining, interesting, even mysterious (think of the VW snowplow spot). But above all be original and give your audience credit for brains. Nothing is worse than me-too advertising, yet we are exposed to it all the time. It will cost you no more to create and produce a great TV ad than it will to produce a terrible one. In the words of Apple Computer, "Think Different!"

10. Make sure you see what your competitors are doing for their TV advertising. Also, whenever you see what you consider to be a really good TV spot—for any product or service at all—write down what appealed to you or made you think it was particularly good. And do not fall into the trap so many do of remembering what they consider to be a great TV commercial, but having no idea what it was advertising.

When you see stuff you like, don't be afraid to "borrow" from it. This doesn't mean you should rip off an exact copy of someone else's ad. But, think through what it was that you liked and thought was effective about it, and then apply those principles or that approach to your ad. There's nothing to feel guilty about doing this. Believe me, it happens all the time on Madison Avenue, and these guys are making millions doing it. Consider that there are very few original ideas out there; most of them are variations on the same themes: sex, adventure, aspiration, envy, babies, animals, and so on. Anyway, on Madison Avenue they don't consider plagiarism to be a sin; instead they call it doing an "homage." It sounds so much better in French.

11. I know I said TEN rules, but this is an extra one. If not quite 11, consider it as really 10A. The 10A rule is always feel free to break the first 10.

If you've definitely come to the conclusion that television is one of the ways you want to use to promote your company, then the rules listed above should be considered when you sit down to concept and write a TV campaign. There are, however, a number of other things you should think about before you commit the money necessary to produce it. We'll discuss those next.

NINE BEST WAYS TO PRODUCE YOUR TV COMMERCIAL

1. *Start with an idea.* Remember your USP? That should be the basis of all your messaging. Just because TV is one of the most powerful and pervasive kinds of media around, it doesn't mean you have to treat it differently from all the other elements of your communications program. Don't attempt to overthink problems, and don't get lulled into believing that because TV is different, whatever you run on it should be different from everything else.

2. *Integrate your message.* The ROI on your ad budget is magnified many times over when each element in the program synergistically amplifies its effectiveness. There should always be a connect, a family resemblance, a something that allows the viewer to remember a print ad, radio commercial, or a direct mail piece that reinforces the overall message, even when it's delivered in a more dramatic fashion via the TV screen. The ability to make every element of your ad program work together seamlessly is the key to successful, cost-effective advertising. Many companies, irrespective of size, forget this and wonder why they aren't getting better results from their advertising.

3. *Forget about storyboards.* When faced with the task of coming up with a TV campaign, most agencies create storyboards as the working blueprint for their TV ideas. These consist of a series of hand-illustrated frames showing the key visuals that will occur during the course of the commercial. Under each frame is the copy. This is usually the dialogue spoken by the actors or the presenter. It will also include directions for sound effects, music, camera movements, and any titles that may pop on the screen at particular times throughout the spot. The storyboard is usually used as the key selling tool by agencies when they present ideas to their clients. It is also used by agencies when they research ideas through the much-abused use of focus groups, a subject I'll be discussing in a later chapter.

But, as far as you're concerned, there's no reason to do a storyboard. You are the client. Write a script instead. It's always seemed an anomaly to me that novels, stage play and movie scripts, even those for television plays, soaps, and sitcoms are created in the form of the written word. So, why is it that agencies feel the need to have their television commercials painstakingly worked out, frame by frame, like miniature comic strips? Perhaps, to paraphrase David Ogilvy, someone should tell them, "The person you're presenting to isn't stupid, she's your client."

The vast majority of TV commercials are initially concepted as scripts. Storyboards only get made after the script is written and are primarily used by the agency as a crutch to help them sell the idea to the client. In most of the presentations I have made to clients, I've always simply acted out a script. The beauty of this is that if you have the confidence to do it well, you then allow the audience to conjure up the visuals they themselves want to see as you take them through the spot.

It's what Orson Wells described as "theatre of the mind." His famous Mercury Theatre radio production of H.G. Wells' *War of the Worlds* in 1938, the one that created panic along the East Coast as listeners visualized what they were hearing on the radio, would never have been as powerful if the audience had been looking at a bunch of badly drawn two-inch-square TV screens on a storyboard. It worked like gangbusters because the audience imagined and created the pictures of alien creatures invading the world in their own minds. Best of all, in the case of your TV campaign, whether you create it yourself or with the help of others, until it gets on air, the only audience you have to sell it to is yourself.

4. *Production costs.* If your brilliant idea requires you to use a location, use one that enhances the idea rather than one that overpowers or detracts from the message. Find one where you can shoot for little or no cost. Just be sure you get the owners' permission to use it; otherwise, you could end up with legal problems when they recognize it the first time you air the commercial. If you are shooting in a studio, get as close in on the action as you can using, if possible, what are known as a *table-top* shots. All these are production details that should ideally be handled by the production company or TV station producing your spot. However, it is worth bearing some of these things in mind when writing the spot.

5. *KISS is the answer.* To achieve great TV writing, do not over embellish your idea. Continually ask yourself what is the leanest, meanest, most direct way you can visually and with the use of as few words as possible put over this great idea in that incredibly short (30 seconds) span of time. Plus, the nicest bonus from this way of working is it often ends up being the least expensive way of doing it.

6. *Getting the spot produced.* You have the choice of producing your spot either through an independent production company or the inhouse facilities of the station you intend to air the commercial on. The latter has

financial advantages. The station will often throw in the cost of producing the spot if you've committed to buying a reasonable amount of air time. Weighing against this advantage will be the reality that it will obviously not be prepared to shoot a complex, expensive commercial, and it will only be "free" if you run it on this station. Using an independent production company frees you from these constraints—but will cost you money, if not necessarily as much as you think. The key on costs is to keep the spot simple and not to go overboard with special effects, multicamera shots, nonstock music, too many graphics, and expensive acting talent. Either way, you only have to present the station or the production company with the idea you want to get over in a very simple script form. They will produce a more finished version for your approval. If they don't, ask for one.

7. You could take the easy way out and have the production company or TV station come up with the original idea for the commercial and then write it for you. This is not recommended, because most stations use the kind of on-staff creative talent that normally gets paid a pittance for grinding out all those memorable "Closing Down Sale—Must Clear Last Year's Inventory—St. Patrick's Day Everything Green Must Go Sales." That's not the kind of thing you want to have associated with your business. On the other hand, if you choose to go with the production company, they will almost certainly use better quality talent to write your spot, but it will nearly always be local freelancers who you could very well hire directly yourself. (There will be much more on how to work effectively with consultants and freelancers in Chapter 10.)

8. *Be decisive.* When you've come up with something you like, do it. Don't ask anyone else's opinion of your idea. If you ask someone who works for you, he'll tell you he thinks it's the best thing since sliced bread. That's assuming he wants to keep his job. Don't ask your family; they'll think you should be spending your money on something more worthwhile, such as a new extension on the house or a family vacation in Hawaii. And definitely, don't ask your golfing or drinking buddies, 'cuz even though

everyone in the world is an advertising expert, most people wouldn't know a good TV commercial if it hit them on the head from 30,000 feet.

9. *Remember*, it's your company, it's your idea, and it's your money.

HOW TO WRITE A TV SCRIPT

I'm not going to give you a set of rules for writing a TV script, just three examples. They can be found on my web site at www.parkerads.com along with many other examples of how to think through, produce, and execute effective advertising. All three scripts are for very different kinds of commercials with very different objectives, yet all are for the same client. The first one cost a couple of hundred thousand dollars to produce and the second cost $2.5 million. OK, before you start screaming that these costs are way out of the ballpark in relation to what you expect to spend for your TV campaign, know that the third commercial only cost a few hundred dollars and was as effective in meeting its objectives as the other two. The purpose of showing such a diverse spread of concepts and costs is to give you an idea of what you can hope to achieve and how much you may have to spend to achieve it.

Before going through the scripts, you should be aware that there is a certain protocol to writing a TV script. You don't have to hold rigidly to this format, but it will help when you get to the production stage of your spot. Also, if you include your video and audio instructions on the script, it will do away with the need for a storyboard.

To help you prepare your script, or understand one written by someone else, here are some of the most commonly accepted terms used in preparing a TV script:

Video: *The visual taking place on the screen.*

VO: *The announcer's voice over the action.*

SFX: *Sound effects.*

Title: *Any text or graphic superimposed on the video.*

Super: *Text, usually at the bottom of the screen.*

Commercial 1: Qwest 30 TV Light Bulb

Video: *Open on black screen. In the center is a suspended, illuminated light bulb.*

SFX: *A faint, high pitched whistling effect starts.*

Video: *Camera starts slow pull in to the bulb.*

SFX: *Whistle continues and gets louder.*

Video: *In the top right hand corner of the screen we see the head of a hammer.*

SFX: *Whistle continues and gets louder.*

Video: *The hammer continues towards the light bulb.*

SFX: *Whistle continues and gets louder.*

FIGURE 7.2: *This was the first commercial I did for Qwest with my art director partner Joe Massaro. The campaign was written up in everything from* The Economist *to* The Wall Street Journal, *and was described by Bob Metcalf, the inventor of Ethernet networking, as the single best explanation of the benefits of broadband he had ever seen.*

Video: *The hammer hits the light bulb, but instead of the bulb breaking, the hammer head shatters into many fragments which fly off in all directions.*

SFX: *There is a breaking sound as the hammer shatters. The whistle stops.*

VO: *"The promise of the internet is not in the future . . . It's now."*

Title: *Qwest logo pops on followed by . . .*

VO: *"Ride the light . . . Qwest."*

This commercial was produced in the fall 1998, during the heyday of the dot-com and telecommunications boom. Its primary purpose was to position Qwest in the minds of the financial and investment communities as a leader in these new broadband technologies. At the time, all these financial experts were dedicated to creating a feeding frenzy among the ubergamblers of Wall Street in their never-ending search for "the next big thing." It didn't matter if you were selling broadband networks or sockpuppets; it was all about the *virtual future.* A future where you didn't actually have to make anything; you just had to be involved in the highly rewarding process of moving digits around. All of these companies were at that time being touted as the next GEs, Intels, and Boeings, companies representing a technology cornucopia from which untold treasures would spill, and anyone smart enough to invest in them would be guaranteed untold riches.

By associating itself with this tsunami of technological optimism, Qwest acquired a legitimacy that soon made it a darling of the investment community. The "Hammer" commercial was the first in a campaign that ran primarily on the news and financial cable channels. It was also used as the introduction for a major analyst's conference in New York City attended by representatives of the international investment community. The purpose of this spot was to leapfrog Qwest into the big leagues in this booming market, changing the way it had been perceived, as a small regional Bell operating company.

Commercial 2: Qwest 90 TV Christmas

Video: *Open on a barren desert setting. There is a rather strange looking house in the distance. It shimmers in the heat haze.*

SFX: *We hear the drone of flies.*

Video: *Cut to front of house as the screen door crashes open and a young boy runs out allowing the door to swing back with a clatter.*

He looks around, squinting his eyes against the oppressive heat. He scuffs the ground with his boot. It is dry and arid. He looks very disappointed.

He closes his eyes and clenches his fists. We see that he is muttering something to himself as he concentrates intently.

SFX: *We hear the clank of metal.*

Video: *The sky starts to darken as storm clouds race across the screen. A metal windmill starts to rotate rapidly as the wind builds.*

Cut to a mule in a corral as it brays in fright as the wind becomes even stronger.

FIGURE 7.3: *A wonderful spot for the holiday season conceived by writer Travis Ashby and art director Chris Parker (yes, my son!) I was lucky enough to be the creative director and driving force that got it approved and shot, for $2.5 million.*

The camera rapidly follows a cable from the windmill to a generator and then to the house.

Video: *Cut to close up of old gramophone in the house as the power comes on and it starts to play.*

SFX: *Old recording of "Jingle Bells."*

Video: *Cut to exterior, we see a Christmas tree light up in the front window of the house.*

SFX: *The recording, the wind, the mule, everything stops.*

Video: *The wind stops, the windmill grinds to a halt. There is absolute silence.*

Cut to close up of the boy's face shot from above. As we watch, a single snow flake enters frame and lands on the boy's cheek.

SFX: *Music enters.*

Video: *Cut to door of house as the boy's grandfather comes rushing out.*

Cut to long shot to reveal that the desert is now full of snow. The boy, his grandfather, and the boy's dog play in the snow.

VO: *The future belongs to those who believe in the quality of their dreams...*

Title: *Qwest logo . . . "Ride the light . . . Qwest"*

SFX: *Music sting as logo runs.*

VO: *Ride the light . . . Qwest.*

OK, so that spot (Figure 7.3) cost $2.5 million to shoot, primarily because we had to do it in a hurry, when the client decided that it wanted a Christmas holiday commercial at the last minute with just a few weeks in the year left. Then we had to cast the commercial, set up all the preproduction details, find the location, build a house from scratch in the middle of the California desert, then make it snow while it was 90 degrees in the middle of the day. On top of all that, the client wanted both a movie (90 seconds) and a TV (60 seconds) version. You can see the end result of all this money and effort on my web site at www.parkerads.com

along with the "Hammer" spot and some other commercials in the long-running Qwest campaign.

Commercial 3: Qwest 30 TV Voice-Messaging

Hopefully, when you've built your business into the next GE, Intel, or Boeing, you'll be able to start throwing your money around on expensive stuff like "Hammer." In the meantime, here's what you can do for very little money (Figure 7.4). Interestingly enough, it was also done for Qwest. And it was done very quickly for a few

FIGURE 7.4: *The only visual in the entire 30 seconds. Proving you don't have to do* War and Peace.

thousand dollars. It's the kind of spot you can do very easily with a local production company, or even a local TV station. All it takes is a solid idea.

Video: *Open on close-up shot of a wall-mounted telephone. Under the phone is an old tape recorder answering machine.*

SFX: *Phone ringing.*

Video: *Phone continues to ring for 10 seconds, then the answering machine clicks on.*

1stVO: *Hi, this is . . .*

SFX: *There is a crackling and crunching noise as the machine chews up the tape!*

2ndVO: *John . . . John . . . I have these tickets for . . .*

SFX: *The machine is now starting to squeal.*

2ndVO: *John . . . What the heck, I'll call Jim . . .*

Video: *Machine is going backwards and forwards as it destroys the tape.*

Anncr: *Qwest Voice Messaging. $3.99 a month.*

Anything else isn't worth it.

Title: *Qwest logo . . . "Ride the light."*

All three spots were shot for the same company. Each of the three had a different objective. All three had vastly different production budgets. Yet all the spots did exactly what they were intended to do—and that's the point. It isn't about what it costs to produce your TV commercial; it's about its content. If you really want your TV advertising to work the way it should, it doesn't matter if you have a $1 million or a couple of thousand to spend. Concentrate on getting the message right; make sure it's simple and easy to understand. Above all never forget, you only have 30 seconds.

You should also note that the three spots I have just gone through were presented in the form of written scripts. When it comes to creating your own TV commercials, whether you are doing it personally or working with outside help, a written script should be more than sufficient to get the concept over for production purposes. Remember, if the idea is right, it should come across on the written page without relying on the help of clever visuals. And anyway, the only person you have to convince is the client, and that's you.

A FINAL THOUGHT

Let's assume you've decided as part of your overall advertising program that the development of a TV advertising component makes sense, but you're not too sure about spending that kind of money. You should consider you may be able to use the spots, and the extra footage you shoot to produce them, in other parts of your communications program. They may be helpful on your web site or, depending on the nature of your business, as part of a booth at a trade show, perhaps even as an element of a sales training or promotional film or DVD. There are many ways you can and should make use of this film or video material because in effect, it's free. You've already paid the production company or the station producing the spots for the work it took to produce it. Just make sure that in the contract you negotiated with whoever is shooting the spot that the proprietary ownership of all materials is spelled out in your favor. That way you'll guarantee you've got the freedom to use these materials for other promotional activities.

Always consider television as simply another media option. Too many people, both on the client and ad agency side, and particularly at the ad agency, see the use of TV as some kind of Holy Grail. Years ago, when there were far fewer media options, it could be the silver bullet (particularly if you spent a ton of money) that guaranteed distribution and sales. Now with the hundreds of channels available, the many ways consumers can block or skip through ads, and the growth of online media options, the power of television is rapidly diminishing. Do not waste too much of your budget on it simply because you think being on television will give your company some kind of stature or prestige. The days of the value of such claims as "As seen on TV!" are long gone.

Having said all that, it is a great visual medium, and if you have a product or service that can best be demonstrated visually, and dramatically, in 30 seconds or less, then by all means utilize the power of television. But don't forget to use it as part of your overall program. Support it with your print and radio. Also use it to drive people to your web site so they can get more information than you can possibly deliver in a 30-second commercial.

Television can still be a powerful medium, but only if you use it intelligently and dare I say—sparingly.

CHAPTER EIGHT

Creating radio ads: theatre of the mind, fame, and fortune–all for the price of popcorn

The first and single most important thing you need to realize about radio advertising is that for a relatively small amount of money, it lets you pinpoint your target audience better than virtually any other choice of media out there. It doesn't matter what geographical market you are operating in, I guarantee you'll probably have far more radio stations to choose from than all other media vehicles combined. These stations are also much more segmented and selective in the kinds of audiences they appeal to than most other media choices. OK, there are many periodicals published that deal with specific interests. Remember the bicycle example I gave you in Chapter 3? There are at least a dozen magazines dealing with various aspects of this sport. But all are national, sometimes even international, in their coverage. And so, they are not only expensive to run any kind of meaningful campaign in, but will also engender an enormous amount of waste in terms of what it will cost you to reach any kind of local audience. The beauty of radio, on the other hand, is that you can pinpoint exactly who you want to talk to in terms of interest, income, or age and you can do it in strictly defined areas of coverage so that you get a much higher ROI.

Radio is a medium that's been around longer than TV and is more pervasive. People listen at home—most homes have an average of six radios. In the car—95 percent of cars have radios. Even in the office—nearly two-thirds of people listen to the radio when they are supposedly at work. In fact, radio is probably the most pervasive media there is, impacting people throughout their nonsleeping day and being relied on by a great many as their primary source of music, news, and information. And because radio listeners fall into a routine of regularly listening to the same small group of stations, they become loyal and captive audiences. Unlike print, they don't feel inclined, or indeed able, to turn a page to avoid an ad. And unlike TV, they rarely take a bathroom or coffee break when your high-priced, lovingly crafted spot is on, or even worse, fast forward through the show they recorded last night so they could cut out the annoying commercials.

> Radio has the greatest reach of any media in the United States, with a national average listening audience of 81 percent per day for people of 18 years of age and over.

Radio allows you to capture the audience's attention far more effectively than print or TV. But having said that, be warned that whatever you do, when you succeed in capturing their attention, communicate something of interest, perhaps even humorous. (Humor seems to work better in radio than in all other forms of media.) At least, try to be informative. At all costs, do not be overbearing, repetitive, or attempt to treat your audience like a bunch of morons as so many radio advertisers do. Remember what I said earlier about how to produce great TV advertising? All those principles apply in spades here. And please, if all else fails, get one thing through your head: even though you're dealing with a captive, almost 24/7 audience, if you take them for granted and insult their intelligence, they'll never stop hating you, your company, and whatever it is you're selling.

WHO SAYS RADIO IS RIGHT FOR YOU?

I say radio's right for you. I believe it's right for everyone. There's a common misconception in the ad business that radio is primarily an *immediate* media for people trying to make *immediate* sales. In other words, it's for retailers, car dealers, restaurants, sporting events, malls, concerts and all those businesses that need to whip up immediate enthusiasm to sell tickets, move merchandise, fill seats, get those turnstile clicking, and do all the stuff that reeks of:

*Get your fanny down here . . . now . . . while these incredible values last . . .
'cuz in three days we have to fold up the tent and move on to the next town
on our trek West!*

No wonder so much radio advertising is awful and smacks of turn-of-the-century, county fair, snake oil merchants.

There are three major reasons Madison Avenue's Adverati choose to ignore radio advertising. Firstly, it doesn't generate the kind of license-to-print-money, massive income that national TV campaigns do. Secondly, most people working in the creative departments of big agencies consider it below their station to do something as menial as writing a 30- or 60-second radio commercial. Thirdly, radio is very much a local medium. Apart from the fact that local advertising falls well under the income requirements for the average Madison Avenue account executive to cut short a three-martini lunch, these Godzilla-sized agencies are so removed from the way the rest of the country lives that they don't have anyone on staff capable of creating a radio spot that would make sense to someone living in a city of less than a couple of million inhabitants. Now, don't get me wrong here, I say all this only as a reflection on

> Because most of the BDAs of Madison Avenue rarely think of radio as a meaningful component of a major campaign, they have not driven prices up. Consequently, smart advertisers recognize the inherent value of radio.

the current state of the advertising business. Once upon a time, there used to be lots of people who were not only capable of creating great radio campaigns but also actually enjoyed doing it. Unfortunately, all are either retired, dead, or writing this book.

The reverse of this rather depressing coin is the fact that it leaves the field wide open for you. You, and you alone, can create one of the great radio advertising campaigns of all time, and best of all, you can do it for peanuts.

FORGET THE MONEY, WHAT ABOUT THE RESULTS?

The good news is that the money involved in producing a worthwhile radio advertising campaign is miniscule when you compare it to what it will cost you to produce and run most other forms of advertising. Depending on the size of your market, the number of stations, and the number of times you want to run your ads, you can have a reasonable radio campaign up and running for a few thousand dollars. In a small market area, you can even do it for a few hundred. Another great advantage of radio is that when you need to, you can change your ads very quickly, which is ideal if you have a special promotion or event you need to talk about at the last minute. Because radio production is cheap, and if you have the foresight to write your radio scripts cleverly, you won't need to rewrite and rerecord everything in the spot, simply change the *tags* or *donuts* in your commercials to make them current. (I'll get to the specifics of this and radio production generally later in the chapter.)

> As with your print or TV advertising, your radio commercial will not happen in a vacuum, it will be surrounded by other commercials, probably lots of commercials, most of them bad. Make yours good; that way it will make an unforgettable impression.

Radio is like other forms of media in that if you do your homework and get it right, you can be pretty sure you're buying the audience you want, one you think will deliver the right prospects for what you have to sell. This may sound obvious, but it is surprising how many advertisers look at their media choices merely as buying the cheapest space or time. They think they are being rather clever, because it appears they are getting more for their money. But if all that extra exposure doesn't deliver the audience they need to make a sale, it doesn't matter how little they paid for it; they've wasted their money.

WHO DO I WANT TO TALK TO?

All radio stations deliver what they call a programming format. This is the kind of content they pump out, and who it's primarily aimed at. There are many dozens of variations of programming, but broadly speaking, the majority of them fall into the following categories:

- All talk
- All news
- A combination of news and talk
- Top 40 (current top of the charts hits)
- Classic rock
- Alternative/metal/garage/grunge etc.
- Classical
- Oldies/big band/swing
- Adult contemporary
- Christian/religious/spiritual
- Hispanic
- Urban

A few local radio stations will be affiliated with the major networks, which gives them more credibility on the news front because they can pick up prestigious reports from network correspondents in major places of interest around the nation and the world. Of course, the rub-off of this is that it usually means their rates are more expensive because they can claim to attract a higher quality audience. But the vast majority of local radio stations are independent, even though many are members of regional and national buying groups, which is only an advantage if you are planning on running a national or regional campaign that might necessitate your buying big blocks of time outside your immediate geographical area.

Like TV, commercials on commercial radio are divided into time slots of 15, 30, and 60 seconds. These spots occupy about one third of every programming hour, that is, about 20 minutes or so of commercials. That's a lot of interruption to the programming and that's why there's a natural tendency for listeners to tune out the ads. So, it's important to create commercials capable of breaking through all this clutter and quickly grabbing the listener's attention. Breaking through doesn't mean you have to scream your message to make the audience take notice. There are much more subtle ways to do this, and I'll discuss them later.

The size of the radio listening audience fluctuates throughout the day, with the largest audience occurring during the A.M. drive time—6 A.M. to 10 A.M. and the P.M. drive time—3 P.M. to 7 P.M. Obviously, these are the most expensive time slots to buy, but they do deliver a large, captive audience. Anyone who's ever commuted by car in a major urban area can testify to that. It's least expensive to buy radio in the evening when most people are watching TV. Late night radio is really cheap because of its small audience, but it's also a fanatically loyal audience for people with a favorite station. If you've got something to sell that they might be interested in buying, these people could provide a great return on a very small investment.

The first thing you need to do if you think radio should be a part of your advertising program is try to listen to all the stations that serve your area. Get a feel for who they are and what kind of audience they're aiming at. If you're selling organic, shade-grown coffee from environmentally friendly plantations where part of the profits go to socially responsible programs for the indigenous native population, the last station you want to be on is the one carrying talk show pundits of the ilk of Rush Limbaugh who might be talking about environmental Nazis just a couple of minutes after your commercial has aired. But as I will never stop saying throughout this book, that's all a matter of common sense.

GRABBING THE AUDIENCE'S ATTENTION

In common with all other forms of advertising, the effectiveness of radio advertising depends on two things: reach and frequency. At least, that's what every other book you will ever read on advertising will tell you. But I'm here to tell you that that's wrong—dead wrong. The effectiveness of any form of advertising is based on how strongly the audience you are addressing relates to your message.

In orthodox advertising terms, reach is the total number of listeners who hear your radio spot one time. Frequency, obviously, is the number of times that listener hears your message. The argument most commonly used by the charlatans of Madison Avenue to get their clients to spend buckets of money is that most listeners don't pay attention when they hear your commercial, or that a single exposure doesn't have enough impact to engender a reaction from the listener. To me that implies if the commercial needs to be hammered repetitiously into the skull of the unfortunate listener, like some kind of Chinese water torture, then the commercial is no good in the first place. It's no

> Radio is ubiquitous. It's almost like wallpaper of the ears. Don't let your radio campaign become part of the background mush. Make it stand out. Make it work.

different than going to the doctor because you are suffering severe headaches and on every visit the good doctor amputates another appendage. When she finally gets around to cutting off your head, the problem no longer exists.

If your radio spot is going to be effective, it should be so on the first hearing. That is not to suggest you should only buy a single 30-second spot and wait for the customers to beat down your door. Again, it's all about the simple application of common sense. Far too many advertisers rely on the weight of dollars they can throw at a problem, rather than coming up with a killer campaign that creates word-of-mouth around the watercooler, "Have you heard that great radio spot for Acme Widgets?" This is the kind of advertising that's worth its weight in gold, and it has nothing to do with frequency, it's all about superior content.

So when you've decided which radio stations seem to fit the profile of the audiences you want to address, give 'em a call and ask for their rate card and media kit. Before you've hung up the phone, you'll have station sales reps coming over the transom with all kinds of deals and packages. At this stage, don't commit to anything, just let them know you're considering options, that you're not even sure if radio can do the job for you. Find out if they have first-time advertiser rates, what their contractual obligations are. The rep will always try to get you to sign up for the longest possible term he can. Most flights are 13 weeks. But he will offer all kinds of discounts if you go for 26 weeks or more. Ask what kind of special packages they have. These are combination buys that give you a cross section of various time slots, mixing prime-time and off-peak periods, offering significant discounts if you allow the station a certain amount of flexibility in deciding when your spots will run. These deals make sense on stations that tend to have a steady audience through the day, rather than during the peak drive-time hours.

You can also sponsor certain segments. For example, if you manufacture or sell ski gear, sponsoring the snow report would make sense, as any other news or special interest segments that naturally tie in with your business. The problem is, most of these highly desirable sponsorships have been taken by the same people for years, so you will probably have to wait for someone to give them up or go out of business before you get a chance to take make the buy.

All the station reps will be only too happy to put together a proposal for you that covers the schedule, size of audience, demographics of the audience, total costs of the package, and a variety of things they'll throw in for "free." This often includes their writing the spots for you using their inhouse writer, the production costs for making your commercials, which probably includes the cost of one of the station announcers reading the script, preparation of tapes, etc. All sounds great, right? But, be very careful here. Radio production is usually peanuts compared to TV. So saving yourself a hundred or so dollars by having the station produce your spots could cost you dearly in another way. inhouse writing talent is rarely something to get excited about. Ask yourself why they're working inhouse. And, do you want the same voice reading your stuff that also does the traffic reports, weather, and "what's on at the movies this weekend?" Wouldn't you rather have a distinctive voice that separates your message from all the other stuff that's going on at the station? Don't be penny wise and pound foolish when it comes to radio production.

But before I get to radio production, a final word on radio station reps. Don't let them make you commit to anything at this early stage. Make sure they know you're talking to other stations. And never forget, virtually all these guys work on commission, so they'll do anything to make the sale. Use that to your advantage.

MAKING KILLER RADIO SPOTS

Remember what I said about TV production: how you should always try to produce the least expensive spot possible because that really helps to sharpen the mind?

With radio production, the reverse is true, because radio production is *extremely* cheap compared to TV. You can't go broke doing a great radio spot, and you can do a great deal of good for your bottom line.

Exactly how do you create a great radio spot? Well, you could try to write the script yourself. Who knows, you might have a heretofore undiscovered natural talent. The odds are though, that you don't. Bad local TV spots can be pretty awful, but bad local radio spots can be excruciating. For the sake of spending very little money, you might consider hiring a freelance writer to create the scripts. You can still have the radio station handle the production for free as part of its overall package. I'll be dealing with how to work with consultants and freelancers in a later chapter, but for now we need to concentrate on what should go into the creation of good radio advertising, irrespective of who actually sits down at the keyboard and writes it.

As with all forms of advertising, you can break a radio campaign into two broad categories, *brand* and *response*. Both serve entirely different purposes, and you can rarely expect one campaign to do the job of both. Unfortunately, many advertisers do and are then left scratching their heads wondering why all that expensive advertising isn't working. So that you don't fall into that trap, let's consider the differences and which kind of advertising might do the most good for you.

> Even if your business isn't in immediate response or retail, radio can still work for you, particularly if your competition doesn't use it. This is one of those few times were the medium can be part of the message by helping you become distinctive.

The Brand Radio Campaign

When you run a brand campaign, it's all about creating an image, either a new one or protecting an existing one from competitive threats. Its primary function is to leave the listener with a definite impression of your company and what you stand for. It isn't about selling specific products; that's the job of the response campaign. Having said that, the brand campaign can certainly talk about the range, quality, availability, and value of the products you sell but only to create the perception in the mind of the listener that your company is the very best source he should consider when in the market for these kinds of products.

Don't expect brand campaigns to produce immediate results. By their very nature, they do not make the cash register ring every time a commercial runs; that's the job of the response campaign. To which you may then ask, so what's the point of running a brand campaign at all? If you are a new company with no recognition or awareness in the market you are aiming at, a well thought out and constructed brand campaign can start to build recognition and an image for your company that will work for you for years. It comes down to if you're prepared to look at your advertising as a long-term investment and if you can afford to run it over an extended period. It also comes down to how you want your company to be thought of in the market you are in. Businesses that run nonstop, relentless response advertising incur the risk of being seen as discounters who do anything for the quick sale and pay little attention to the quality of their customers' experience before, during, and after the sale. Need I mention our old friend the car dealership again?

The Response Radio Campaign

Response radio advertising is exactly what it sounds like. If it's done properly. it should make the listener want to drop whatever he is doing and get over to your store, factory, or wherever the wonderful thing is available that you've just told him about. You've made it so enticing that he must have it now. This advertising usually involves making some kind of new product announcement, a price reduction, a sale, a how-to demonstration by a recognized authority on a particular subject, special financing, and so on and so on.

Unlike the brand campaign, everything about the response campaign is purposely short term, very often using "get them now while they last" language. It is designed to elicit an immediate response. An important subset of this advertising which is found primarily in print, TV, and radio, is *direct response*. These are the ads requiring you to call an 800 number or visit a web site so you can order the product being advertised directly from the manufacturer or distributor. Unfortunately, too many of these ads treat the audience like morons, urging people to call now and order the ten-gallon drum of SuperSudso, which is not available in stores, and telling them if they do so in the next ten minutes they'll get a SuperSudso applicator thrown in for free. I discussed this kind of

> Because a response radio campaign requires lots of commercials, which need to be constantly refreshed, it can be very costly in both time and resources. It would make sense to outsource this function to a consultant outside your company.

advertising in the TV chapter, and the principles are the same for direct response radio. Unless you have the kind of business that lends itself to this garage-sale approach, I wouldn't recommend it.

The key to response radio advertising is to keep it fresh and original. You can only run the spots for a limited amount of time before they become dated and devalued. It's like walking past all those big city stores that have had the same "Going Out of Business Sale" posters stuck on the windows year after year. You have to make the spots newsworthy, even to the point where you might have to do new ones every week. But that's the beauty of radio, your production costs are cheap, and you can turn around new material quickly, allowing you to update offers and customer incentives as often as you think is necessary. You can also make more ambitious, 60-second hybrid spots that are semibrand in nature, talking about the company in general and what makes it special for 45 seconds, then using the final 15 seconds to tag on this week's special offer or incentive.

Whoever produces your spots will keep master tapes of everything, allowing you to quickly tag new endings on existing material as you need them. Response radio can generate immediate sales, particularly if you plan and act quickly to get your special offer out there so fast that by the time the competition becomes aware of your program and reacts, you have moved on to your next promotion.

CREATING RADIO THAT WORKS

Whether you decide to go the brand or the response route, there are some things you should consider when writing and producing radio ads, whether you do it yourself or employ someone else to do it for you.

- *Be consistent.* Have a theme. One-off ads certainly don't work in a brand campaign. And it doesn't hurt to have a family resemblance and some kind of continuity from spot to spot, even with response ads. When you develop this theme, do it out of your USP. This will then serve as the platform for all your advertising, and will be particularly important when creating brand ads. Irrespective of whether you're doing a 30- or 60-second spot, write the spot so that you get the listeners' attention in the first five or ten seconds, otherwise you've lost them.

- *It's advertising.* Never forget your ad doesn't simply run in between the programming; it will more than likely be in the middle of a big block of advertising, most of which will be bad. So be sure to make yours stand out from the rubbish surrounding it. You can do this if you keep in mind what I said at the beginning of this chapter about radio being theater of the mind? That means you have to paint a picture in the listener's head. But the good thing about this is that is unlike making TV commercials, you don't have to go on location, you won't have to build sets, you probably won't have to cast and pay for a bunch of actors who are doing this as a stepping stone to a movie career, and you don't have to shell out a fortune for special effects and graphics. All you have to do is come up with the right words. And the only way to do that is by starting off with an idea. I know that sounds like a no-brainer, but as I get older, it seems to me fewer and fewer TV and radio ads are based on any kind of well thought out or original idea. Many are incredibly well made and have obviously had buckets of cash thrown into producing them. Unfortunately, in the immortal words of a long dead writer, "There's no there, there."

- *Consider music.* But only if it's relevant. Someone will try to convince you that what you really need is a jingle. If they do, immediately leave the room, or insist they leave the room. Most jingles, even the ones that cost a fortune to write and produce, are not just pathetic; they usually bring nothing to the table. Like all effects—visual, sound, and music—these are things you should use only to enhance the central message. If music gets in the way or, even worse, overpowers what you are saying, why on earth would you want to use it? The only ad jingles most people remember are the ones they hate.

- *Don't get funny.* You may find that after trying to convince you to use music, this same radio expert suggests you should use humor. After all, there have been some really great humorous radio campaigns in the past, with the great Stan Freeberg being the master of the art. Unfortunately there have also been thousands of clunkers that may have seemed funny to the person writing them, but not to the vast majority of the listening audience. So, the whole exercise was a waste of money. Another thing you should consider is if you begin a campaign based on humor, you're then going to be stuck with humor, and trying to come up with funny stuff week after week is no laughing matter.

- *Time is of the essence.* Think about the length of your commercial. As in TV, 30 or even 60 seconds isn't a great deal of time. OK, with a 60-second radio spot, you've got double the amount of time you have with the average TV commercial. But you don't have the advantage of stressing points you want to make through the use of graphics, titles, or product demos. It's theater of the mind, remember? So, you have to rely on words to paint that picture. The same rule applies in radio as in TV, stick to saying one thing, say it well, ruthlessly edit everything, and stay on message.

- *The importance of pacing.* If you listen to the average radio announcer, usually rattling along at the rate of about 220 words a minute, which is OK if she is doing the traffic report or telling anyone remotely interested exactly what today's school lunches are going to be. She is a familiar voice, one that regular listeners are accustomed to hearing. The voice or voices in your radio spot are not ones listeners will recognize—unless you're using a station announcer, which, is not recommended if you want to stand out from the other programming. So, try to keep your word count down to about 150 for a 60-second spot, and 80 for a 30-second one. Buy yourself a stopwatch. Not a SuperSpeedo fluorescent mini-wrist job, but a big old handheld one. Find a watch just like the monster your track coach in high school used as he screamed at you on your pathetic workouts long before you put on the beer belly and developed cellulite. Time your scripts with the big stopwatch, but do it while you read them aloud. Don't worry what what people around you think. With today's hands-free cell phones, everyone appears to be talking to themselves, anyway. The reason why you need to read your script aloud is because then it's not as easy to cheat on time by squeezing those extra two or three more words into the copy in a pathetic attempt to beat that inexorably sweeping second hand.

- *Be real.* If your spot is based on or supposed to resemble a conversation between two or three people, make it sound like a conversation. In other words, the pacing should be normal and relaxed. Don't make your characters deliver their lines like presenters. At the time I am writing there are currently dozens of spots with pseudo-doctors advertising expensive pharmaceutical products with improbable sounding names. But the people in the commercials don't sound like doctors; they sound like actors pretending to be doctors reading a script. The whole presentation is counterproductive to the idea, because the listener feels, rightly so, that they are being conned, which means the advertiser—and quite probably their agency—is falling into the very common trap of treating the listeners like idiots. That's guaranteed to make them mad and turn them off you and whatever it is you're advertising.

- *Getting started.* Like much TV advertising, many radio ads follow the problem—solution—resolution format. This is a particularly easy format to follow when doing a straightforward announcer presentation script with no actors, music, or added glitz. Here's a for-instance example of what I mean.

Got a situation with gophers digging up your lawn?
Try "Gopher Gone." Gets rid of gophers quickly and easily.
It's the end of all your gopher problems.

Simple, but not very sophisticated. It is also too much like a so many other radio spots out there. The trick is to take the formula, and put a spin on it:

Gophers destroying your lawn?
Try Gopher Gone with Added Dynamite.
SFX: Loud explosion noises.
Works three feet down to get rid of gophers while it aerates your lawn. You
end up with a beautiful lawn and no more gophers.

Slightly over the top, but guaranteed to be more attention getting. I hasten to add though that I'm not suggesting these as actual scripts. I'm merely demonstrating the point that you should always avoid the expected. There's far too much of it out there. You should also try to write the script so that it works within the programming choices you've made for your media schedule. Obviously you wouldn't run a youth-oriented spot on a big band swing program or a spot selling retirement benefits on a heavy metal station. On the other hand, those retirement benefits might be just the ticket for a classic jazz audience reliving their old club-hopping days. So, try to write the spot accordingly, not just in terms of content, but also in the style and presentation that makes the audience most comfortable.

PRODUCING RADIO THAT WORKS

Compared to TV production, radio is relatively simple and far less costly. But because it is less expensive doesn't mean you should try to cut corners. A well-written and well-produced radio campaign will be worth its weight in gold, delivering meaningful response and value for money. There are a number of things you should consider when producing your radio commercials.

Keep in mind that even though the term *production* sounds like some kind of mechanical procedure, it's much more of an art form. High-quality production values can make or break a radio campaign. They can give a good campaign greatness and a turn a mediocre one into a waste of time, money, and effort.

You have three choices when it comes to radio production. You can work with the station that will be running your spots. You can work with a radio/TV production house, or you can hire a freelancer to take care of everything for you. As I discussed earlier in the chapter, working with the radio station has the advantage that it will probably throw in the cost of production as part of the package. If you are in a start-up mode with no experience and a severely limited budget, you can certainly try this route. But remember, the disadvantages will include expected, formulaic writing, same old announcer voices, and less than ambitious production values. After all, you'll be one of hundreds of advertisers it cranks this stuff out for. You always get what you pay for, and in this case you're not paying anything.

Working with a production house will give you a much more professional job because it will have better facilities, as well as access to larger music and sound effects libraries. However, you will have to supply the script and voice talent you intend to use to record the spots, which is why you might want to consider going the third route and using a freelancer. An independent or freelance writer/producer can give you the best of both worlds. Not only will he write the script, he will also handle the talent casting and studio production as well. Most freelancers have a regular number of talent agencies and production houses they work with on a frequent basis, and so they will be able to give you an up-front cost for creating and producing the work. In Chapter 10, I will be talking in greater detail about locating and working with freelancers.

As to costs? That depends on many variables. Firstly, on how ambitious your script is. If it requires specially written music, a cast of thousands, on-location recording, and a celebrity spokesperson, it could cost you a small fortune. On the other hand, if it's a straightforward announcer-read script produced by the station that will be running the spot, it'll cost you next to nothing. The answer is to get quotes on everything first, whether you intend doing the whole thing yourself or through a third party. Don't be shy to ask; everyone who wants your business will be more than happy to give you a quote.

Depending on the nature of your business, with the possible exception of the Yellow Pages, radio is one of the least expensive, yet most effective forms of advertising you can invest your money in. That is why it's also the one media most ad agencies, particularly those on Madison Avenue, are least interested in. Big ad agencies see little return on their investment of time and effort from the creation of radio advertising. The income via fees and commissions is small, the kudos to the creatives are insignificant, and if they were to be totally honest about it, most would have to admit that they don't know very much about it.

It's also the very best media option for a business that's prepared to do most of the work inhouse. As I've discussed earlier you can do the whole thing yourself or hire a freelancer to work with you. But either way means you are in total control. Of all the traditional media, radio is the one you can get up to speed and become proficient in very quickly. (This is also true of some of the so-called new media that I will be dealing with in Chapter 9.)

Radio allows you to identify and target your audience very efficiently. It's very flexible, so you can rapidly change your schedule to meet emerging opportunities in the market. And if you get the elements right, it can be a long-term, extremely valuable component of your marketing and advertising program.

CHAPTER NINE

Creating ads the new fangled way: the internet, web sites, and blogs–everything the average 15-year-old knows and you don't

How can you use the various New Media as a powerful series of communication platforms to help you sell your business to existing and potential customers by providing them with the information they might need to make a purchasing decision, and doing it at a time when they are most inclined to react? And, of course, while never forgetting what it is you need to be saying to all these people through the wonders of the digital age.

At the time of writing, I had just returned from a conference in Silicon Valley on New Communications. It lasted three days and I was one of about 30 speakers. My presentation was "Advertising for Start-Ups." Strangely enough, even though the entire conference was based on better ways to communicate with customers in the electronic age, I was the only speaker who talked about what you might want to say and how best to say it when you managed to get their attention.

The other 29 speakers seemed to be more preoccupied with the mechanics of the process, talking in detail about the wonderful array of technologies and techniques available to advertisers through the use of various forms of New Media and how best to use them as tools. And that's the problem with New Media. There are lots of companies, experts, consultants, gurus, and just general know-it-alls who can wax eloquently about the nuts and bolts of the process, but few seem to be overly concerned about the content.

WHAT IS THE NEW MEDIA?

The catch-all phrase *New Media* covers primarily those electronic-based methods of connecting with customers that have grown tremendously since the launch of the internet. These include web sites, e-mail, blogs, e-retailing, e-commerce, e-banking, and just about anything else you can stick an "e" in front of to make it trendy. Having said that, it's worth pointing out that of these new ways of conducting commerce many are merely electronic versions of traditional bricks-and-mortar businesses.

Even the much-hyped Amazon was simply an electronic version of the Main Street bookstore, albeit on a grander scale. Yet, thanks to a great deal of incredibly successful PR and the ability of its CEO to keep smirking through adversity, not to mention being designated *Time's* Man of the Year in 1999 when the company was already up to its armpits in debt, Amazon became the poster child of the dotcom revolution and developed an uncanny ability to keep the Investerati of Wall Street forever nibbling at the carrot of future profitability. Now, the one time bookseller has expanded into a veritable online Wal-Mart, offering far more choices than any single store could possibly hope to carry in its inventory. But at the end of the day, it is still simply a store that's managed to convince millions of investors it's OK to rack up billions in debt on the promise of way, way in the future profitability. Even after 12 years in business, it is only now starting to show a razor thin EBITA profit, which is today's investor speak for not really much of a profit at all.

The only truly original business model to have grown out of the dotcom boom is eBay, a company prospective MBAs should study tirelessly until they understand exactly how and why this tremendously

Don't confuse New Media with other forms of communication being increasingly thrown about, such as—guerilla, buzz, word-of-mouth, viral, and the like. New media are primarily electronic in nature and rely on the internet for their effect.

successful e-commerce venture, which grew out of an idea someone developed to enable a group of like-minded people to swap, trade, or auction PEZ dispensers, has grown into the world's largest electronic marketplace generating commissions from every single transaction. And unlike Amazon, it carries no inventory and doesn't need to build warehouses and storage facilities, and makes money from every one of the millions of transactions that flow through its web site daily.

Another business model that was originally considered to be a sure-fire dot-com winner yet failed miserably in practice were the numerous B2B, barter web sites that sprang up supposedly to enable businesses to swop excess inventory on a global basis. Within months, most had disappeared without a trace, along with millions of dollars in investor funds. They also left many of Madison Avenue's biggest and dumbest with mountains of unpaid media bills.

One segment of business that has shown success with the explosion of the internet is that of search engines, with Google being far and away the leader in this category. I shall cover search engine advertising and how it can reap benefits for small- to medium-businesses later in this chapter. For now, it's worth remembering that like eBay, Google is not an extension of a traditional bricks-and-mortar business, because without the internet, there would be nothing for Google to search for.

HOW IS THE NEW MEDIA DIFFERENT?

New Media is a series of options that go beyond the traditional ones of print, direct mail, billboards, TV, and radio, options that enable advertisers to communicate with existing and prospective customers through a series of interactive computing vehicles, often across sophisticated, multimedia platforms. OK, enough, already! That may sound like a load of geek-speak to you—and to be honest, it is.

It's the kind of baloney Madison Avenue agencies are now increasingly hitting their clients over the head with to convince them they are now experts in the wonderful new world of New Media, so clients will feel more than comfortable to spend an ever-increasing portion of their humungous ad budgets through the same old agency that previously blew their humungous ad budgets on increasingly ineffectual Old Media.

What it all means in plain English is that you can now talk to your customers through computers, cell phones, VOIP phones, PDAs, games, set-top-box TV devices, even interactive supermarket trolleys. And you can do it in a way that encourages them to talk back to you, take advantage of immediate offers, let you track what their preferences are, and find out why they like some of the things you have to offer and why they dislike others. It's a rapidly changing world. Even with the most sophisticated Old Media, fine tuning your advertising to the point where you had a reasonable idea of how effective it was and what you might be able to do in terms of making it better through refining your language, modifying the presentation, and testing media placement and timing to make it more effective was inevitably a long drawn out and rather costly exercise. With New Media, you can make changes and alterations to any part of your program and see the benefits almost immediately.

A recent British survey showed that only 7.5 percent of clients say their BDAs are more effective at offering integrated communications strategies than small independent firms. (They didn't actually use the word *dumb*.)

However, be aware that many of the so-called New Media are in fact Old Media that are now being punted by the Madison Avenue crowd as newly discovered forms of viral marketing: A wondrous cornucopia of stencils, tattoos, word of mouth, product placement, and guerilla and even Godzilla advertising. Yet, any high school graduate will tell you that the definition of *viral* is some kind of deadly pandemic such as the bubonic plague, which left untreated will spread unchecked throughout the community. But when you consider how bad the majority of the advertising you are subjected to these days is, they may have a point.

For generations, people have corresponded using paper and pen, told others around the water cooler how much they love our new Rambler Rebel, noticed that the little packets of artificial sweetener in the coffee shop were invariably Sweet 'n Low, and as inhabitants of Greater Los Angeles can attest, driven past many 30-foot-high inflatable gorillas outside car dealerships. So even though it's all being presented as something quite new and revolutionary, most of it isn't really new at all. Merely the wrapping of the package it comes in is new. Perhaps it can be best summed up by this recent observation: "Although viral marketing has garnered a great deal of attention in the trade press, almost nothing is known about the motivations, attitudes, and behaviors of the people that constitute the essential component of any such strategy." Still, when you consider that was true of most forms of advertising in the past, we shouldn't be surprised that Madison Avenue is always poised to jump on the next big thing.

But, having said that, if judiciously used, New Media does offer opportunities for small- to medium-businesses to achieve greater results for their advertising dollars than Old Media ever did, but only if you concentrate on those that not only offer the best results, but also give you an opportunity to measure their effectiveness.

These opportunities came in three broad categories worthy of your attention: web sites, e-mail, and blogs. All are delivered over the internet, and all are relatively inexpensive. Having said that, all of these are somewhat high maintenance in terms of their upkeep and management, and will require either you, someone within your company, or an outside consultant to handle the process on at least a daily basis.

WEB SITES

Every company, whether it be B2C or B2B, must maintain a web site. There is no longer any excuse for you not to have one. A web site is now the single most effective way a company can present itself to and communicate with customers, vendors, investors, the press, and even employees. See my web site in Figure 9.1. Think of it as an electronic version of the world's glossiest, most jaw-dropping company

Not having a web site is akin to being in business and not having company stationery, a telephone, lawyer, accountant, or machine that makes very bad coffee. Not having a web site makes you look like a nebbish and is inexcusable.

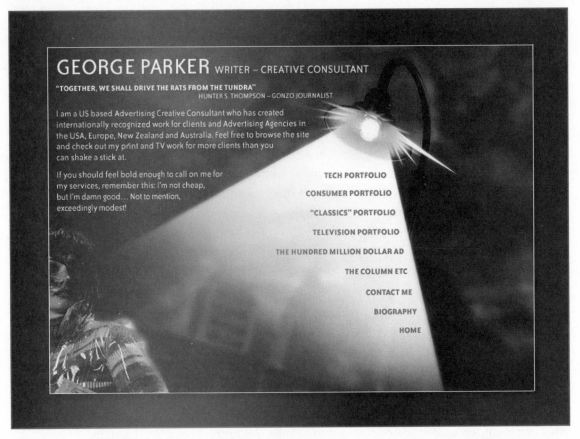

FIGURE 9.1: *My web site, www.parkerads.com, is where I refer prospective clients. They can find in one place samples of my work, my history, my references, and other essential information. It was designed by my mate, Jeff Barker.*

brochure but with a great many **differences** and **advantages** over virtually all other forms of literature.

Once you spent a ton of money to create and print a 16-, 32-, or even a 64-page booklet talking about and showing how great your company and its products were. The publication probably took you and a lot of other people weeks of effort to produce. Yet within days of it being delivered by the printer, it was probably out of date, so the vast majority of booklets ended up collecting dust in storage. You can now have something up and running within days that is not only completely flexible, enabling you to make instant changes but will also allow you to show your company and its products in a more realistic environment than was ever possible on the flat, printed page. Your web site will also be the ultimate information resource for people that you guide to it through all your other forms of advertising.

Is a Web Site Absolutely Necessary?

If you are in business and are committed to reaching and influencing the largest audience you possibly can for the least amount of money, you must have a web site.

- *The purpose of your web site.* Above all else, the prime purpose of a well-designed and well-architected web site is to deliver information. No matter what kind of business you have, the best way to capture and retain customers is to give them every possible piece of information they might find useful to enable them to make a purchasing decision. This can be done intelligently and elegantly for a fraction of the money people have spent on TV and press campaigns. My own web site, Figure 9.2, and that for Oral Fixation Mints, Figure 9.3, are examples of how creative small companies can be with their web sites. Going to the other extreme, IBM has a web site that comprises tens of thousands of pages. The purpose of this 800-pound gorilla is not to bury visitors in unessential information, but to make sure the information a visitor is looking for is accessible to them when they need it, and in a way that makes it easy to readily access.

  A well-architected web site may have hundreds, even thousands of pages, yet is designed in such a way that it does not overwhelm visitors. It simply guarantees them that what they are looking for is available. Think of it as having all 24 Moroccan leather-bound volumes of the Encyclopedia Britannica on your bookshelves. When you need to look something up, you need only reference a single volume, and you can open that volume at exactly the page that has the information you need. And, having said that, it's always reassuring to know you have the other 23 volumes available.

- *Who should your web site appeal to?* It might sound simplistic to say, but your web site should appeal to everyone. And, that's not impossible. The beauty of a web site is that if well designed and architected it can function

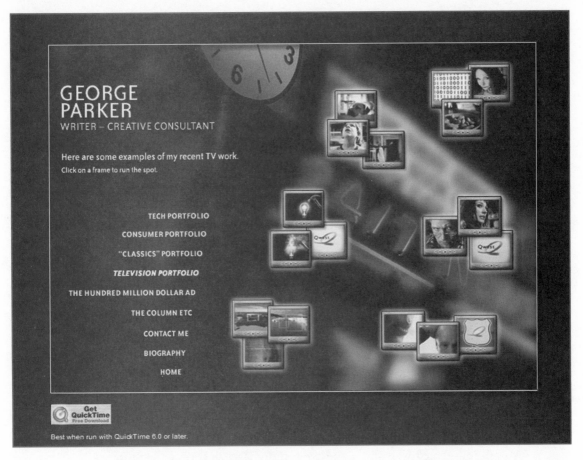

FIGURE 9.2: *Several of the pages on my site show samples of my work. This one covers my television work. By using streaming video, visitors can actually run the TV spots.*

in whatever capacity the visitor wants it to. In the days of Old Media, companies would be continually printing individual brochures and literature for such diverse things as corporate capabilities, standard product lines, new product launches, service, investor relations, and so on and so forth. Today, all these subjects can be accommodated within a single web site, which then becomes a customer resource available 24/7 to provide the latest product

FIGURE 9.3: *A magnificent web site for Oral Fixation Mints, designed by Jonathon J. Harris. It is a perfect example of how a small company can set itself apart from its competition through the use of great creativity and beautiful design.*

details, delivery options, financing, warrantees, and all the other information that provides the reassurance customers might need before committing to an order.

- *Who else will find your web site useful?* Everyone who works with you should find your web site useful—not just your staff but also vendors and suppliers. Through an extranet, which is simply a password-protected web site working over the internet, you, your employees, your contractors, and your vendors can access inventories, orders, delivery schedules, product availabilities, and everything else you might consider necessary for them to know to help in the day-to-day running of your business. Although this is not usually considered as part of your advertising program, it should be borne in mind as an essential function to be built into your web site architecture.

- *How can you make your web site successful?* If the prime purpose of a web site is to deliver information, its second priority is to make that information actionable. This means you must not only make it easy for customers to place orders directly from the web site, you should also incentivise them to do so. You can do this through offers and discounts, even if your merchandise is also available at bricks-and-mortar retail establishments.

Having been somewhat caustic in my comments about Amazon as a dot-com business model at the beginning of this chapter, I have to acknowledge that you might do a great deal worse than study the way Amazon incentivises its customers and keeps them coming back. It's all about maximizing revenue: It does it by cross-selling similar, but different, products in addition to the intended purchase. Whatever book/video/CD a customer intends to buy, Amazon automatically suggests two or three others covering the same subject or from the same author or artist. Then it offers to bundle it with the first book/video/CD at a reduced price for both, which means if it makes the sale, it's increased its revenue by two-thirds. It also offers advance purchases at a discount for not-yet-released items, and free shipping is included for orders over a certain minimum value, which unfailingly encourages customers to top up their order to qualify.

> You've gone to a lot of trouble to get people to your web site. Don't blow them off when they get there. Give them reasons to stay and hunt about for extra stuff they may have not have originally intended to commit to.

Amazon's central strategy is to identify and incentivise people who've built up a track record of buying specific types of merchandise so it may then target them with future offers. Amazon has invested enormous sums of money to build a sophisticated customer database that allows it to track millions of potential buyers in terms of what will probably appeal to them.

You can do the same if you recognize that the third very important function of your web site is to gather customer intelligence. That means you should use every possible opportunity to get as many details as you can about the visitors to your web site. This information will allow you to implement a viable program of relationship building and customer retention: The objective is to give customers a strong incentive to register with your web site and provide you with an opt-in e-mail address. When they do this, you can begin building a customer database that provides you with an invaluable tool you can utilize to communicate with an already loyal audience on a regular basis to sell more products.

For those willing to register on your web site, you are providing something of value, both through specific offers and deals but equally importantly, by demonstrating an understanding of their likes and dislikes. In this way, they become more than just customers, they become confidants. By securing the customer's opt-in e-mail address, you have started on the rewarding road to the development of long-term relationships via periodic e-mail newsletters and other communications.

Depending on the nature of your business, have visitors register for regular updates on product launches or extensions. If you're a technology or manufacturing business, offer white papers or analyses on specific industry developments. Have them sign up for weekly or monthly reports or other added-value items such as DVDs, CDs, or downloadable industry reviews. The prime aim of all this activity is to get their e-mail and personal addresses, phone and fax numbers, and anything else that will enable you to develop and

> Become recognized as the expert on whatever it is you make or do. Let your web site develop as a resource, not just for your company, but also for everything to do with the category of business you are in.

maintain a continuing dialogue with them. In a B2B business, the same applies to any kind of company or corporate information you can acquire.

Making Your Web Site Profitable

Even though virtually all companies now have web sites and some have invested a great deal of money in their development, few have figured out how to make money from them. Obviously, there are exceptions: Amazon, Expedia, Dell, and others. These companies however, are ones whose core business model is selling direct. They do not rely on bricks-and-mortar outposts to initiate or complete the sale. All transactions go through their web sites (and a rapidly declining number over the telephone). The problem is that many other companies regard their web operations as nothing more than another cost of doing business, like a showroom, service depot, or call center, and are consequently prepared to lose money on them.

Try to avoid thinking like this. Otherwise, you will be missing a great opportunity. Do not simply look at your web site only as a source of company and product information and a vehicle that provides customers with an overall positive experience; you should never stop thinking of how you can use it to increase continuing revenue and profitability.

So, how can you apply traditional methodologies of B2C and B2B planning and marketing to the internet in a way that enables you to create a web site capable of generating sales for your business? Even though I have touched on these few rather obvious things to consider when creating a web site before, I believe they are worth stressing again:

- *Make it look appealing.* What does your homepage, as the first page a visitor sees, look like? Is it inviting? Does it immediately inform the visitor who you are, tell them what you do, and spell out exactly what's in it for them if they commit to doing business with you?
- *Make it easy.* Is it full of information, yet easy to use? Is it designed for easy navigation so a visitor can easily drill down for specific product and service information? Is there a search box and a site map?
- *Make it worthwhile.* When you show products or talk about services, do you spell out not just features but also end-user benefits to the customer?
- *Make it reassuring.* Do you back up your quality of merchandise and services with guaranteed after-sales service and consistent customer relations?
- *Make it beneficial.* Do you provide added value through downloadable offers of white papers, how-to guides, industry news, even free DVDs or CDs? Are you doing everything necessary to acquire opt-in e-mail addresses and the customer information that will enable you to maintain an ongoing dialogue with current and potential customers?

- *Make it worthwhile.* Are you offering discounts for multiple purchases and bundled products? Do you cross-sell related products? Do you highlight free shipping and possible seasonal/special occasion gift wrapping?
- *Make it an experience.* Do you do cross merchandising with other companies via their web sites by linking yours to theirs and vice versa? Do you constantly improve the level of your Google ranking through the inclusion of key words?
- *Make it work.* Are you prepared to take the time and effort to update your site regularly?

As a final note, unless you are a genuine propeller head, do not attempt to create your own web site. It will be dysfunctional, look awful, and only end up turning off potential customers. Hire a professional to do it. The money spent will be well worth the effort.

E-MAIL

Although not normally considered to be a form of advertising, e-mail is a useful adjunct tool that can amplify many of your other advertising efforts. It can also be a disaster if abused. The majority of people in business now communicate through e-mail, and there's little doubt that it has increased business productivity. However, in many other ways, it has hampered productivity, particularly in the amount of unnecessary mail people receive every day, simply because they are included on group mailings. And these are merely the semilegitimate mailings. When you also recognize just how much spam people are subjected to on a daily basis, it's important that you think through how to use an e-mail advertising program very carefully.

E-mail must always be *permission-based*. This means no blanket mailings to lists of thousands of prospects who more than likely have no interest in you or what you are selling. Even though a bought-in list may have been cheap, believe me, the odds are it's worthless. Remember, permission-based means people gave you permission to communicate with them. Doing it without permission isn't just rude, it's stupid.

Even with permission-based mailings, an average of over a fifth of the messages either don't get delivered or end up in junk mail folders. B2B e-mail nondelivery rates are higher than B2C e-mail, with nondelivery rates of nearly a third.

The trick is to incentivise recipients into adding your domain name to their address book to ensure they receive e-mail from you. This you can do through the various options discussed in the web site section.

Your e-mail campaign can use specifically written and targeted letters to people who have expressed an interest in a particular product or service. These can be modularized so that you have a growing library of templates to avoid writing each one from scratch. See Figure 9.4 for an example.

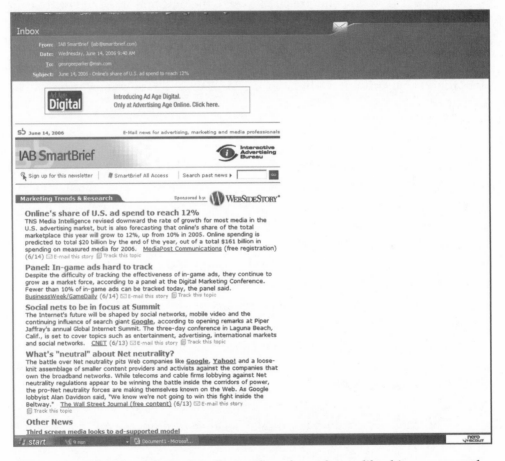

FIGURE 9.4: *Relatively unsophisticated e-mails and newsletters like this are extremely effective for reaching existing and prospective customers with news on new products and services.*

You can have people sign up for a regular e-mail newsletter that, depending on the nature of your business, can cover the entire company offerings and capabilities, or zero capabilities, or zero in on specific segments that are of particular interest to the recipients. All e-mail elements should encourage feedback and extra involvement, such as directing

> Consistency is the key to successful e-mail programs. Subsequent mailings should have continuity with the previous ones. Don't do a series of one-offs.

them to your web site, or to virtual (via the internet) or physical events, such as seminars, conferences, trade shows, exhibitions, and any other occurrences that would be of interest and value to the recipient of the e-mail.

Avoid using e-mail for an obvious advertising purpose. This is acceptable for traditional media and the web site, but e-mail is a form of correspondence; it should have a more personal feel to it. You wouldn't stick an ad inside a letter you wrote to a member of your family. Why would you do it to someone you are attempting to establish a long-term relationship with?

As with every other part of your advertising program, e-mail should be based on your communications plan, through which you are going to fully utilize and leverage your USP. Don't just throw any old mud against a wall and hope some sticks. Research your market and define your target groups, then decide which wall you're going to throw it at and what kind of mud is likely to stick best. Think of the wall as the target groups and the mud as the message.

Look at your e-mail advertising as an ongoing campaign. Plan it out in monthly or quarterly increments. You don't have the time or the patience to reinvent the wheel every time you sit down to write the next e-mail in the program. That's why you should keep records of everything. Where replies are coming from, what are the demographics of the respondents, and the level of response depending on the content of the message. Obviously, offers and promotions pull better than generic messages, but by how much? At what offer value does the response rate level off? What is the lag between sending the message and the response? How is that affected by the value of the offer?

Like everything else discussed in this book, e-mail is just one part of your advertising program. Don't look at it in isolation. Make it work with everything else. Madison Avenue agencies talk up a storm about their integrated communications capabilities and how everything they do works seamlessly together to synergistically (they love that word) empower (they love that word, too) the client's brand. But, that's baloney, because in BDAs, everyone works in silos, so the people creating the print ads don't talk to the people creating the TV and radio, and absolutely no one talks to the people creating interactive (New Media). Consequently, everyone is flying off in a different direction while happily blowing the client's money. You won't have that happening to you because you can't afford a BDA, and even if you could, you're too smart to throw your money away on one.

Finally, don't ever send spam—ever.

BLOGS

Blogs are a relatively new but a rapidly growing medium of communication, so much so that the number of new blogs created every day is reputedly in the thousands. At the time of writing, if you Google the word *blog*, you'll get 2,180,000,000 hits. And by the time you've finished reading this book that number will have probably doubled.

Technorati, a company which monitors blogs through a kind of blog of blogs, currently tracks more than 33.7 million sites and 2.2 billion links. If used in conjunction with your other advertising and communication activities, setting up and maintaining a blog will provide an effective and very inexpensive extra weapon in your marketing arsenal. So what exactly is a blog?

Often described as an online diary, many blogs have grown to be much more than a series of entries dealing with what happened at your weekend barbecue or where you took Rover for a walk this morning. A growing number are now having a tremendous impact on the news media, journalism, politics, the arts, and many other areas of human activity, including business. For example, see Figures 9.5 and 9.6 which show my blogs AdScam and AdHurl. A blog is a web site, but one that can be easily updated as often as you feel you have something worth communicating. Most blogs combine text, images, and links to other blogs and web sites that are relevant to the subject of the blog.

> Be warned, blogs are addictive. Once you start, it will be difficult to stop, particularly as you acquire regular readers and get feedback you'll want to respond to.

Many businesses are now using them to not only inform customers, suppliers, and workers about what they are up to, but also as a means of getting valuable feedback on what customers expect from their company. The major difference between a blog and a web site is this instant interactivity between those hosting the blog and those reading it. Unlike an intranet, which is open only to those authorized to have access, a blog is completely public, and is therefore open to anyone to

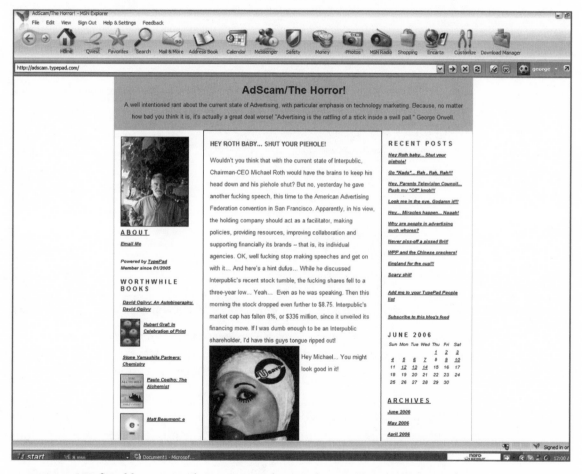

FIGURE 9.5: *My first blog www.adscam.typepad.com where I give my strong uncensored opinions on the current state of the ad business, with particular emphasis on Madison Avenue.*

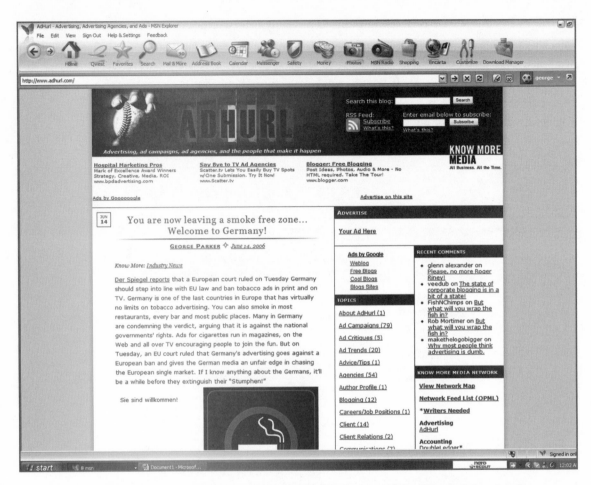

FIGURE 9.6: *My other blog www.adhurl.com is part of the "Know More Media Group," a very powerful syndicate of more than 60 business blogs covering a range of subjects and reaching thousands of readers and potential customers worldwide.*

read and post comments on. The caveat to that is because they are so public they can be vulnerable to abuse by those with an ax to grind. However, there are filters and other safeguards that allow the writer of the blog to screen and only allow posts after they've had a chance to read them. Having said that, you should refrain from merely allowing positive posts that paint you as the greatest thing since sliced bread. This not only devalues the legitimacy of your message, it serves to reinforce the commonly held attitude that most advertising and business communications are self-serving, comprised of nothing more than snake oil.

A true blog is the work of a single individual, reflecting the thoughts and philosophy of that person, even if it's about advanced plumbing techniques. Avoid making your blog collaborative. It shows in the writing to the detriment of the message.

Another great value to creating and maintaining a blog is that you become an instant expert, pundit, champion, sage, and recognized expert. More than your web site, which will be primarily seen as a selling and promotional tool for your company, your blog is much more personal in the subjects you choose to write about and the way you write about them. It then becomes a fountain of information, tips, advice, and techniques, and a resource for all those interested in the particular area of business you are active in.

A blog also allows you to be more direct in the way you speak to your audience. You can express your opinions and points of view in a way that would be difficult in traditional advertising vehicles.

Above all else, successful business blogs draw attention and readership. Even though they are ancillary to your company's mainstream advertising efforts, they provide a unique platform in today's digital age for you to engage in conversations with people you may choose to agree or disagree with, but who are all potential customers.

Considerations When Creating Your Blog

A blog is an online journal. And although yours will be business based, it will still be a reflection of you and your company's character. Because it will be an ongoing conversation with your audience, talk to them as you would if they were sitting across the kitchen table from you—not across the boardroom table. It is also one of the fastest, easiest, and least expensive means of spreading news and information about your business available today. It allows you to build your audience quickly and easily through the use of links, trackbacks, RSL feeds, and live search engines. (See Resources for more information.)

Creating your blog and getting up to speed are easy. There are numerous blog-hosting companies providing simple, intuitive ways to design your site through the use of templates allowing you to start posting content within minutes. For more information, see the Resources section.

As with all your other advertising and communication vehicles, a blog is only as good as its content. If what you post isn't relevant to your audience, it won't read it. If it's boring, it won't read it. If it's badly presented, it won't read it. Write about what you know—your business. Write it with passion, but write it so it has significance to the audience. Your blog should never be about *you*; it should always be about *them*.

When it comes to content, there's always stuff to write about. When you sit down at your keyboard, you aren't about to create another *War and Peace*, you're going to tell readers not just what's new at your company but also what's new in your business category. You might talk about how new government, environmental, legal, or financial regulations could affect how you do business in the future and what impact that may have on your customers. You can throw in independent reviews of your products or services, or general industry trends that will affect what you do and how that might impact your customers. There's tons of stuff out there in the general press, trade press, web sites—even other blogs.

Never forget your blog is a two-way street that not only allows you to talk to customers and feed them information. It also allows them to talk back to you, ask questions, get help with problems, find out about upgrades, and ask about new products and the use of features. Just be careful not to duplicate information that already exists on your web site. For run-of-the-mill questions, direct them to the FAQ (Frequently Asked Questions) section on the web site or to your service hotline. However, if you can answer some specific questions on the blog, it will only serve to reinforce the impression that you are responsive to your customers' needs.

The single most important thing you can do to make your blog effective is to post as often as you possibly can. There is nothing more off-putting than being directed to, or finding through a link or search engine, a blog that is hopelessly out of date. Updating requires discipline. I have two blogs, and I post on each three or four times a day. I make myself do at least one post first thing in the morning, even before I've had my first cup of coffee. Then I know I've at least started, and then I do posts in between doing other work. In the 15 months I've been doing AdScam, my visits have risen to between 1 and 2,000 a day. AdHurl, which I've only had up for three months, is now up to between 200 and 300 visits a day. Not bad, considering they deal with a very specific business segment. Then again, it's logical; the more you post, the more chance people and search engines have of finding you.

To increase your hit rate even more, it's essential that you learn to use what are known as *keywords* in your posts, preferably in the title. Let's go back to our bicycle example. If you are a manufacturer or retailer and you want to talk about the new range of titanium frames you intend to launch in July, don't do a post headed "New Acme Titanium Frames." That will only pull in queries for "Acme" and "Titanium." If you did a post headed "The New Tour de France Acme Titanium Frames" and posted it in June or July, you would have every cyclist in the universe hitting your blog as they search for news and results of the world's biggest bike race. It's all about making it relevant and easy for people to find you. So don't be vague or talk in generalities, particularly in your headlines.

With time and as you develop a personality for your blog, try to extend it out so it becomes more than merely about you and your business. With the right kind of content, you can make it a resource for the industry category that you operate in. This will result in your becoming linked with other blogs dealing with your type of business. As your blog grows, your posts will be archived in a format that makes them easily accessible to your readers. You become a valuable resource for visitors, who then become customers, who then in turn recommend you to others.

> You should list other blogs that you consider relevant to your business on your blog. Then these other blogs will list your blog on theirs. Once you start tracking your traffic you'll find lots of hits coming from these sites.

Do use your blog to drive traffic to your web site. Think of the web site as a big catalogue containing everything you make or sell. It can have hundreds, even thousands, of pages so visitors can drill down into the architecture to find exactly what they are looking for. A blog is normally a quick read designed to impart information or a point of view rapidly. For a more indepth treatment of the subject being talked about, the blog should provide links to your web site, and perhaps other blogs, web sites, or online articles that continue with the theme. As with the web site, you might feature special offers or new products, but do it in such a way that visitors are forced to take the extra step of going to the web site and registering.

That way you've captured their information and are on the way to making them customers.

Remember the communications plan and your USP. These are just as relevant when creating and running your blog as in all your other advertising and communications activities. You should look on your blog as another way of impressing on prospective customers exactly what it is that makes you different from the competition. A blog can be much more than a sales tool; it can also be a very effective branding tool.

NEW MEDIA SUMMARY

Although e-mail, web sites, and blogs have been around for a relatively short time compared to Old Media, there's no question that they're rapidly becoming increasingly important in the advertising plans and strategies of even the largest companies. This is because more and more people are coming to rely on online sources for most of their information and entertainment. In spite of Madison Avenue's protestations to the contrary, the days of blowing most of their client's money on network TV and massive print campaigns are definitely numbered.

New Media allows advertisers to more clearly define and penetrate the audience relevant to their needs. It's also interactive, allowing the target audience to, in effect, have conversations with the advertiser. And because all of this is immediate, or as New Speak proponents love to say, in real time, advertisers can quickly change and fine tune messages, not only to accommodate fluctuations in the market place, but also to drill down through all kinds of socioeconomic divisions to find the marketer's Holy Grail—that audience of one.

Best of all for the small- to medium-sized business, New Media is inexpensive when compared to many others. Properly used it will provide a positive experience for prospective customers while giving you invaluable feedback on your marketing.

As I stress throughout this book, good advertising and communication are all about the application of logic. So, simply changing the media you choose to run your advertising in should not affect the core content of what you have to say. Web sites, e-mails, and blogs are nothing more than different vehicles for your message and should always be easy for your core audience to understand and empathize with.

If properly mastered, these new ways of addressing your audience, used in conjunction with a well-structured and disciplined overall advertising program, can immediately raise awareness and sell more of your goods and services. In the long term, they'll give you an opportunity to look over the horizon to more effectively plan, promote, and grow your business in the future.

CHAPTER TEN

Doing it with help–and how to go about getting it

Let's assume you've gotten big enough to think you might want to get some kind of permanent on-staff or consulting help with your advertising, perhaps even hire an ad agency. In this chapter, I'll discuss the benefits of either forming your own inhouse advertising agency or relying on outside consultants and freelancers for everything from media planning and buying to the creation of all your advertising materials. Obviously which of these options makes the most sense for you depends on what stage of growth your business has reached and the size of your ad budget. Dealing with an ad agency will be covered in Chapter 11.

CREATING AN INHOUSE AGENCY

I can best sum up my advice to you on inhouse ad agencies in one word. Don't. Why would I be that adamant about it? Because over the years I've worked with, and been exposed to, several inhouse advertising agencies. All of them, for various reasons, have been a disaster. On the surface, the idea of having an inhouse agency is very appealing. It makes a great deal of economic sense, and it's definitely one way to avoid falling prey to the Madison Avenue sharks who start circling as soon as word gets out you might be looking for an agency. Having your own inhouse agency was a popular alternative in the days when the majority of independent agencies made their money (and lots of it) via the 15 percent commission they received from the media for booking space or time on their client's behalf. Now, with most ad accounts being handled on a fee basis, that particular argument doesn't make as much sense. However, as your own agency, you would be able to buy your own media and be eligible for the 15 percent commission rebate, so in effect, you would be getting your media for 85 percent of the normal rate card rate. But even that argument is now somewhat weak because most media will do deals for less than rate card, depending on how much money you're prepared to spend with them.

My major reason for disliking this inhouse solution is that without exception, the end results are awful in terms of the quality and effectiveness of the advertising produced. Common sense will tell you why. The majority of people who are prepared to work inhouse are those who can't get a job in a real agency. They also have to be satisfied working on a single account, day in and day out. This is not good for the creative libido. Writers and art directors need the stimulation and cross-fertilization of ideas that come from working on a variety of accounts, meeting diverse challenges across different kinds of product categories, and dealing with different kinds of media. This will inevitably be reflected in the better quality of their work. Plus if you think about it, the guy who signs their paycheck is the guy who runs the company. This is not someone they want mad at them, so are they likely to stick to their guns and argue for their point of view if they should happen to disagree with him on the advertising? Not if they want to stay employed. Inevitably, once the originators of advertising lose their objectivity, the quality of the work undoubtedly suffers.

I think the perfect example of this was the Gateway Computer Company when it was still run by Chairman, CEO, and Founder Ted Waitte. The myth is that he started the company in a cow shed somewhere in South Dakota. Actually, he founded the company on his family's farm in Iowa with a $10,000 loan secured by his grandmother, then moved to South Dakota where the company generated its down-home style of branding, which was even reflected in its packaging with computer boxes patterned in black and white cowhide graphics. Like Dell, Gateway only sold direct; you could not walk into a store and buy a Gateway computer. This required it to run tons of ads in the numerous computer publications (most of which no longer exist) to keep the phones ringing.

Ted realized he could save a ton of money on media commissions and high-priced agency fees if he formed an inhouse agency. This he promptly did, hiring lots of people who were prepared to work for peanuts and live in South Dakota. The end result was a long-running and somewhat notorious campaign that consisted of multipage ads that, while selling various Gateway products, consisted of grandiose tableaux based on famous events through history. Hundreds were produced, covering everything from man's discovery of fire, or the wheel, or whatever. Washington crossing the Delaware. Moses coming down from the mountain with the Ten Commandments. And so on and so on.

All the ads were produced inhouse as Gateway had extensive photography studios, typesetting, and finished art studios as well as just about every other production facility you could think of. The kicker was that everyone in the ads was a Gateway employee. But of course, the central character, whether it was the cave man with the biggest bone in his nose, or Washington, or Moses, was always played by Ted. Can you imagine the chairman's reaction if some bright spark had jumped up one day and suggested maybe Ted wasn't quite right for the part of Alexander the Great in the upcoming ad, that perhaps it was time for someone else to get the starring role? There aren't too many agency jobs around in South Dakota, so I guess that never happened.

And that is my point. With an inhouse agency, objectivity always goes out the window. Yes, I know you're too open minded to act in such a gauche fashion if you should decide to set up an inhouse agency. All I can say is, have you ever heard the phrase "delusions of grandeur"? It's an easy trap to fall into. Don't take the risk.

Also, the money saving argument doesn't hold much water if you consider the overhead involved in bringing everything inhouse. You would have to hire at least half a dozen people to do everything from managing the operation to actually executing the ads.

Unless you have an advertising budget in the millions, rather than the thousands, it's not a very cost-effective way to go, particularly if the quality of the work produced as the end result of all this effort is substandard.

FREELANCERS AND CONSULTANTS

Being a consultant, it goes without saying this is the solution I will unhesitatingly recommend. But let me give you some of the reasons why I truly believe this to be the best direction any small- to medium-sized business can take.

1. If you are a start-up, or a very small operation, your advertising budget is probably quite small, and you'll be forced to do nearly everything yourself. You can get help and guidance from the media outlets for no extra cost if you've committed to a schedule with them. This is particularly true of local radio and TV. Having said that, in terms of the originality and quality of the spots they create for you, you will be more or less stuck with what they offer you, even if you are less than thrilled.

2. Once you've begun advertising and have committed to an ongoing program with high quality content that truly reflects what you need to say, you should then start thinking seriously about getting professional help for planning, buying, and executing future programs. You need to find people within your geographical area who are qualified in media planning and buying, copywriting, and art direction for both print and broadcast advertising. The same

is true for web site design and other online promotional efforts. If you intend to do any volume of print work such as brochures, direct mail, leafleting, and coupons, in addition to writing and design, you need to find someone with print production experience who can liaise with printers to get the best prices, organize the art work, and supervise the process through to delivery of the finished materials.

> Spend your money on the important stuff—the creative. The media you have selected will throw in most of the production costs as part of the package deal you work out with them. The ads are the important thing. Invest in them.

3. Your web design can be done by the company that will actually host your web site. However, if you choose to go that route, you will more than likely end up with a generic-looking site based on one of a half dozen templates the hosting company works with when dealing with low revenue customers, (which at this stage of your company's development will probably apply to you). If, on the other hand, you are prepared to make the worthwhile investment required for a distinctive site, then you need to find an independent web site designer who will give you something out of the ordinary, perhaps even something extraordinary. Never forget that because your web site is often one of the first impressions a prospective customer will get of your company, this is not an exercise you should skimp on.

4. Nor should you skimp on your print work. Even though you could work directly with a printer who might offer to throw in the design as part of the overall cost of printing the job, as with the web site, you are more than likely to end up with undistinguished, me-too materials. Far better to find and work with a freelance art director or designer, even if you write your own copy. And as mentioned earlier, an experienced print production person will bid out your job to a limited number of printers he works with on a regular basis to negotiate the best quote for you. He will also save you money in pre-press preparation and management while maintaining quality control throughout the printing process. Finally, as part of your contract with him, he will make sure the job is done to your satisfaction.

5. Working with freelancers and consultants means you are in total control of everything from establishing the original budget, to the final execution of the creative, to deciding when and where you want to run it. But on the other side of the coin, that means you are totally responsible. If the advertising doesn't work or produce the desired results, you are the person who signed off on everything and approved it to run. Then again, this holds true even if you use a big Madison Avenue or any other advertising agency. You still end up paying the bill, and if you do use a Madison Avenue ad agency, the bill will be significantly higher than if you had used freelancers.

> Hopefully, you will find a small number of freelancers you can work with on a regular basis, but because these people are not on staff, and so not part of your regular overhead, you can change them when necessary.

HOW DO I FIND THESE WONDERFUL FREELANCERS?

Unless you live on a desert island in the middle of the South Pacific, there are bound to be a number of freelance advertising, marketing communications, design, and digital practitioners living in your neck of the woods. All you have to do is root out the best ones. The best way to start is the way people always used to when looking for a local plumber or tree trimmer, check out the Yellow Pages. But if you want to be totally 21st century and up-to-speed about it, why not also do it on the internet? This is where most of the Yellow Pages happen to reside now anyway. All you have to do is type in what kind of help you are looking for, then input your zip code, and voilá. Before you know it, up pops a list of people you might find useful in helping you achieve your objectives.

Then again, if before starting up your own company, you came from one that pursued a similar line of business, you've probably thought about getting in touch with some of the people who provided advertising and marketing services for your old company. However, a word of caution here, you should get guarantees of confidentiality from anyone you contact. You certainly don't want to let your old employers know you're planning on putting them out of business.

It's also worth checking with local newspapers, magazines, and other publications published in your area to find out who they use for their writing and design work if and when their on-staff people are over-loaded. There are also trade groups and dedicated web sites that list art directors, graphic designers, writers, and others by geographic area. I show you how you can find these in the Resources section at the end of the book.

Another option is available if you live in a community large enough to support a university that boasts a business, journalism, or art school—or per-

> Use freelancers initially on a "per-job" basis until you see how they work out. If you are happy with them, you may want to negotiate a retainer based on hours per month. As this is guaranteed income, many freelancers will work out a favorable rate.

haps all three. You can use their senior students as resources, particularly when you want desktop publishing or other computer-generated graphics work done inexpensively. (Never forget, you're giving them on-the-job training for crying out loud.) You can also call on the services of experienced faculty members, who are usually delighted to do some consulting work on the side. Just be careful that you don't end up with some educator with an impressive title who only happens to be beavering away in the halls of academia because he couldn't quite make it in the real world of business.

WORKING WITH FREELANCERS AND CONSULTANTS

So, assume you've found out where all these freelancers and consultants are. Now you have to figure out how you pick the right ones. Here are some suggestions:

First, make a short list of the people with the various skills and experience you need in the areas of media planning and buying, copywriting, art direction and design, print production, and web site and online design and production. Initially, you can make this list based on what it is you like about their respective web sites. But be warned, if they don't have a web site, they are not very professional and probably shouldn't be on your list.

Next, look at what they've done for others. Usually, this will also be on the web site. If there are no examples of their work on their site, it might very well mean they have nothing they consider worth showing. Very suspicious. Don't even waste your time talking to them. If you see examples of their work that you like, call whoever it was done for and ask for references. Isn't that what you would do with any supplier?

Even if you delegate day-to-day contact with freelancers to someone else, make sure you are involved when it comes to decisions on content, execution, and final approval of everything they do. It's your company. The results reflect on you.

If you like the work they've done for others, ask yourself why you like it. Don't just rely on initial or surface impressions. Analyze it. Think about what went into its creation: the positioning, the original concept, its execution in copy and art. Is what you like about it common across all their work, or is it limited to a couple of show pieces? Ask to see samples of work for all their clients. In other words, make sure their work has consistency in both content and execution.

Don't try to find people who can handle all your work all at once. Start with a simple project. Look at it as a test case. For media planning and buying, get one or two of whoever is on your list to come up with a proposal for a limited duration campaign covering a couple of media options. Get them to provide you with the potential cost, frequency, and coverage metrics for the program. But be fair; do not get them working out detailed schedules, putting in a lot of time for what at this time is a basically a speculative presentation. If they are any good, they will have other clients they need to devote their time to.

Use the same strategy when it comes to looking at people for your creative work. Ask for proposals and costs from no more than one or two suppliers for a simple project. This can be a single ad, a thumbnail and copy outline for a brochure, or the home page of a web site. Again, be fair with people. If you want something more ambitious, such as a complete campaign or a fully worked out architecture for your web site, you should pay them a presentation fee, which goes some way toward covering their time and out-of-pocket expenses.

You should discuss with all your prospective freelancer and consultant suppliers how they expect to get paid, and then after you have used them on a trial basis and are satisfied, work out a formal agreement. Most of these arrangements usually work one of three ways.

1. *You can pay them on a project basis.* This is a flat fee for writing or designing to your satisfaction one or more ads, collateral pieces, or online materials. The fee is agreed upon up front between you and the supplier. It can

only be changed if you alter the brief while the job is in progress, such as wanting more pages in a brochure or web site, or a campaign of six ads instead of four. The fee should not be changed by the supplier if after they realize starting the job that they have not budgeted enough time or other resources to complete the job. However, if you feel the supplier has a legitimate reason for asking for changes in the fee, it's at your discretion to renegotiate.

2. *You can pay suppliers at an hourly or daily rate.* Many ad agencies who use freelancers prefer to do this because they want them on site and immediately available for meetings, etc. This is not a good arrangement for you to consider. One of the reasons why Madison Avenue agencies are so outrageously expensive is because they work in a feast or famine mode, with members of staff sitting around with little to do. Strange as it sounds, this is even true of the many occasions they use freelancers. I have personally sat around for days waiting for briefings, meetings, research results, and the thousand and one things agencies find to do to justify their exorbitant fees.

You certainly don't want freelancers hanging around your offices waiting to complete their work. Also, an hourly rate encourages what's known as the New York cab driver syndrome, that's the one where out-of-towners get driven round the same block a dozen times and a $5 cab ride ends up costing you $50. Much better to go with the first option and agree on an up-front fee for a given project.

3. *You can put freelancers you use regularly on a monthly retainer.* This is particularly useful if you like their work and intend to keep using them on an ongoing basis. It also guarantees that if they are in demand by others because of the quality and value of their work, you get first call on their services. The retainer can be based on a specific number of hours or days a month you think you may want to use them. This is a guarantee, and you must pay it on a regular basis, even in those months when you don't use all of the agreed number of hours. On the other hand, if you occasionally use more hours or days in that monthly period (within reason) than the agreed amount, the retainer should stay the same. Over an extended period of time, it usually averages out on both sides.

When using freelancers for jobs that include third-party production fees, such as photography or radio/TV production, have the production houses bill you directly. If you pay through the freelancer, it is normal for them to add a markup.

If you decide to work with freelancers on a by-job, prequoted basis, you should get written estimates and verification before agreeing to the work. Also, in the case of broadcast production, particularly TV, it is normal to pay 50 percent of the production costs up front. This may also apply to work that involves significant outlays on the part of the supplier, such as displays, trade booths and stands, etc.

You should also agree with any freelancers and consultants you use on who will retain ownership of the materials produced. Normally, this is the person who is paying for it, which would be you. Very rarely, some of the rights for original music, illustration, and photography may remain with the originator. This should be discussed and agreed to before committing to work from an outside supplier.

In the final analysis, you will choose freelancers and consultants based on the work they have done for others and whether you think they have an appreciation and understanding of your needs. You should also take into account the personal chemistry between you in any initial meeting. After all, you will be working with and trusting these people to create the essential elements of your overall business communications program. If you don't get a good feeling from them, don't use them; there are plenty more out there.

GUARANTEEING THE BEST RESULTS

As I've stressed throughout this book, good advertising is based on information and the application of a great deal of common sense. Just as you would expect one of your clients to give you the input you need to complete an order, you should do the same when working with outside consultants and freelancers. There are a number of points you should consider in any ongoing relationship with a supplier if you are to reasonably expect high-quality work and value for money.

Depending on the size of your operation and the number of freelancers you intend to use, you should establish a single point of contact for them within your company. It may indeed be you, but unless you're prepared to dedicate sufficient time to do this properly, you may want to delegate this responsibility to someone else. That doesn't mean you should be divorced from the process. It's your company and your money, after all. You will obviously need to have the final say over budgets, strategies, and the execution of whatever materials the freelancers are producing. But as the principal manager of your overall resources, you should never fail to be mindful of the most efficient way to utilize them.

Always understand the difference between giving input or information and giving directives. The CEO of one of America's largest software companies is notorious for this very fault. (Please note, I did not say *the* world's largest, just *one* of the world's largest.) The company I am referring to happens to have a very successful product that is used by virtually every one of the *Fortune* 500. However, this raging, egomaniacal, un-named CEO (although if you'd like a clue, he's rather fond of racing ocean-going yachts) insists on micromanaging all of the company's communications. The result is some of the world's worst advertising, the unreadable and stultifying format of which hasn't changed in more than 20 years because every ad agency (and there have been many) his company has ever used has been browbeaten into doing everything his way. And in the typical spineless fashion of the Madison Avenue Adverati, as long as his company continues to spend millions of dollars on this mindless dreck, the agencies are happy to prostitute themselves producing and running it. Concluding this particular rant, I should say that in spite of my earlier claims to the contrary, this is one of those rare situations where if the client stopped advertising, I doubt very much that it would affect the company's sales one iota.

Show and discuss samples of the kind of advertising and communications you admire with the people you have selected to do your work, particularly that from companies in the same category of business. But, do *not* tell them you want carbon copies of these ads. Instead, explain to them why you admire this particular work, why you think whoever did it did a good job of communicating the advertiser's USP, and how they established a look and character that makes the ads stand out from everything else out there.

> When working with freelancers, remember that even though it's your company, your products, and your money, what you want from them is their ideas and input. Don't dictate; otherwise you may as well do it all yourself.

Ask your freelancers if they agree with your conclusions. Listen very carefully to their responses. Those who immediately go on the offensive and pooh-pooh the idea of being influenced by someone else's work should be regarded with a certain amount of suspicion. These are the same people who loudly proclaim creative integrity yet are not averse to having every copy of every advertising award annual on their bookshelf, handily convenient for a quick reference when stuck for an idea. On the other hand, you should also be somewhat wary of those who slavishly agree with everything you say. Hmmm, am I making this too difficult? Then think of it as having a conversation with someone you meet by chance at a cocktail party or a backyard barbecue. Some people you can talk to for hours, others you can't wait to get away from. As I never fail to stop saying, all of this boils down to using your common sense.

There will be the odd occasion when you instinctively know you've found the right people to help you create kick-ass advertising. If you really feel this very strongly, hire them. OK, I know I said earlier that you may want to check out one or two with a test project after you've boiled your selections down to a short list. But seriously, if based on what they've done for others and how you got along in your initial conversations you feel they are right for the job, then, as I say, hire them. If they screw up after the first project, you can always stop using them.

Once you start working with freelancers, be open minded about what they present to you. Remember, you've hired these people because you don't have the time or expertise to do everything yourself. When they show you initial thoughts or concepts, do not judge them on the basis of how you would have done it. You don't go to the doctor because you have migraine headaches and tell him to amputate your leg. These people are professionals. Believe it or not, they may actually have a few better ideas than you. Give them the opportunity to talk you through the work, explaining why they have done it the way they did and why they think their solution will be the right approach for the job at hand.

If there are definite points of difference between what they present to you and what you think should be done, present your criticism in a constructive way. Obviously, if they have misunderstood the brief or have made factual errors, you should correct them. If, on the other hand, it's a matter of creative interpretation or presentation, try to look at the piece through the eyes of the end reader or viewer who will be seeing it on the page or TV screen. Not everyone out there shares your incredible sense of style or wonderful sense of humor.

When it comes to content, that is, what it is you want prospective customers to know about your company and what it is that makes you so special in comparison to the competition, you have to be the final authority. How it is said and the style in which

> Few members of your staff would have the temerity to offer advice on how you should go about extending your line of credit at the bank. All of them will unhesitatingly bury you with advice on your advertising.

it will be presented will depend on the skills and creativity of the people you are paying to do that job. Allow them to do it to the best of their ability.

It's your business. Ultimately, you are responsible for whether it is a success or failure. Don't fall into the trap of getting numerous opinions from others in your company. Yes, if freelancers are working on materials that your sales force will need to use as part of its selling operation, get its input upfront. If your showroom staff relies on point-of-sale displays or literature to help it function properly, get its input also. But, do not ask for or allow them to pass judgment on such esoteric subjects as the choice of typeface or the color of the paper the piece is printed on. It's a fact of life that most people (except you and I) have notoriously bad taste when it comes to those things. (I shall expect lots of hate mail for that particular comment.)

The same advice applies to wives/husbands/partners/pets and anyone you play golf with on the weekends. Everyone is an expert on advertising. That's why there is so much bad advertising around. You can get opinions from anyone you want on what you should be saying and who you should be saying it to. What you don't need is their input on how you should say it and where and when you should run it. That's what you're hiring all those expensive freelancers for.

Although I am a great believer in getting the legal profession involved in business affairs as infrequently as possible, you may feel it necessary to have your attorney look over a basic contract or letter of agreement between you and whomever you've decided to work with, particularly if you intend to go with them on the basis of a monthly retainer. And depending on the nature of your business, you might also want them to sign a nondisclosure agreement. I've found this to be normal practice when working with technology clients, who seem to share a common paranoia that everyone they deal with is intent on disclosing to the world the secret formula of their crown jewels. When you consider the breakneck pace of technology development these days, it's more than likely the formula will be worthless by the time the company's various internal review and approval committees have signed off on the advertising, let alone run it. But when it comes to deciding how much legal cover you need when dealing with outside suppliers, you and your legal eagle will have to be the judge of what kind and how much proprietary information you are prepared to give them so they can proceed with their work.

If you are retaining freelancers to create and then produce work, apart from their hourly, project, or retainer fees you will also be faced with the production costs for such things as photography, printing, radio, and TV production, etc. If these costs are billed through the freelancer, they will normally have a mark-up added that can be anywhere from 5 to 25 percent. These should be prequoted and agreed to by you before you authorize the supplier to commit to these charges. You are far better off paying these production costs directly yourself. In fact, most free-lancers prefer it this way as they are not then obliged to carry the costs while waiting for you to settle all charges on the completion of the job. Obviously, paying for production directly will also save you the cost of the mark-ups.

TRANSITIONING FROM DO-IT-ALL-YOURSELF

As I stated at the beginning of the chapter, I can honestly offer no arguments in favor of going the inhouse agency route. Using freelancers and consultants pro-vides the ideal solution for small- and medium-sized companies that have arrived at a stage where the principals can no longer devote sufficient time and attention to the creation of their own advertising yet want to keep control over its creation.

Even if you start off in business by doing your own advertising, as you grow you can start to phase in the odd freelancer for specific projects. This particularly applies to those that need good art direction and design. Most business people can write fairly well and lucidly, providing they stay away from PowerPoint and busi-ness speak. Design and layout skills are a much harder commodity to come by. So why not use freelancers who have these skills to augment your own efforts? You will be pleasantly surprised how much your wonderful prose is improved by good design.

You may find all your needs completely covered by a small coterie of regular freelancers you can use cost effectively to produce everything you need. Then again, you may grow to a size where you start considering using a full-service agency but wish to avoid the pitfalls that too often befall those forced to work with the snake and oil merchants of Madison Avenue. The next chapter will spell it all out in sordid detail.

CHAPTER ELEVEN

Doing it with an agency–the plusses and the pitfalls

In the preceding chapters, I've talked about the benefits of doing your own advertising, whether it be by single handedly relying on your own skills, or in conjunction with freelancers and consultants. So, why am I now devoting a chapter to explaining how you can best work with an agency? Because when you grow to a certain size, your choices are to form your own inhouse agency or hire an agency. I have previously explained it is never, ever, smart to create an inhouse agency. That only leaves one choice. There are definite benefits to working with a full-service agency, but only if you know exactly how to make such a relationship work to your advantage. That is what this chapter is all about.

Unless you've grown overnight from a small- or medium-sized business to a General Electric- or Proctor & Gamble-sized behemoth with a multimillion dollar ad budget, you probably won't be interviewing any of the BDAs of Madison Avenue. Not that they'd be inclined to talk to you anyway. With today's slim operating margins, few of the large multinational agencies can make much money from a client spending less than $10 million a year on advertising.

Having said that, all advertising agencies are the same in terms of what they do and how they go about doing it. It's simply a matter of scale. Each and every agency loves to represent itself as being completely different from all the other sleazebags out there. All claim some unique business methodology masquerading under such grandiose titles as "360-Degree Branding" or "Tribal Ethnographic Solutions." There are dozens of these pathetically obtuse slogans pasted over the reception areas of most major ad agencies, the majority of which are based on whatever the leading business schools are currently punting to those dumb enough to pay many thousands of dollars to achieve their Master of Business Administration degree.

Speaking of which, don't you find the word *administration* rather pedestrian? Wouldn't you think these high-priced bastions of academia could come up with something a little more grandiose? My suggestion would be something like *flummery*. After all, the dictionary defines *flummery* as meaningless words, statements, or language. (It's also described as a custard dessert.) But whichever definition you lean toward, both seem to me to sum up perfectly what an MBA degree is all about: flattery or flan. And, Master of Business Flummery has a certain honest ring to it.

Anyway, back to the reception areas of BDAs. If you return to them in a couple of years you'll find new slogans strategically placed above the portrait of the founder, the awards cabinet, or the blow-ups of the one or two recent ads they're not too ashamed to display. Each new slogan will be, without a doubt, as meaningless as the ones they've replaced, and all will be just as irrelevant to the real world of business.

It's a strange anomaly that 99 percent of advertising agencies never advertise themselves. After all, if the primary function of these companies is advertising and communication, why are they not communicating the benefits of working with them to potential clients? Could it be that they don't actually believe in what they do? Yet advertising agencies continue to exist, and the amount of money spent on advertising continues to increase, with the vast majority of that money being spent through ad agencies.

> While historically many have questioned the effectiveness of advertising, advertising revenues continue to increase and are forecast to grow by 7 percent in 2006.

Even though in certain parts of Europe and South America choosing to work in an advertising agency as a profession has acquired a certain cachet (albeit similar to that of being a music producer, drug dealer, or pimp), in the United States this choice of career has always been regarded as a somewhat suspect and a less than noble way for grown people to earn their daily crust. It's also one of the least understood businesses around. Just look at any of the dozens of movies based on advertising Hollywood has foisted on us (with the vast majority seemingly starring those heartthrobs of the 1950s and 1960s, Doris Day and Rock Hudson). Not one of them bears the closest resemblance to what actually goes on in an ad agency.

Advertising people are often viewed in the same light as chiropractors or astrologers. Everyone knows their expertise is mostly based on trickery and fake science. (I'm standing by for the lawsuits.) But people desperately want to believe in what they do, so they pay someone to draw up their chart and advise them not to make investments when Venus is in the ascendant or to jump up and down on their spine until they hear the bones crack and the pain is almost unbearable, because, hey, you never know, all this stuff might just be doing us some good. And, the miracle is that occasionally it does work. There are definitive, provable case studies that show without a shadow of a doubt that advertising has worked for a large number of companies.

Dell Computer became a multi-billion dollar company that kicked the living daylights out of IBM and Compaq, primarily through its in-your-face advertising. I know this for a fact and can shamelessly boast about it, because I created many of those ads for the San Francisco office of Chiat/Day in the mid-to-late 1980s. (See Figure 11.1.) By contrast, far too many companies have been suckered into spending millions on so-called branding or image advertising campaigns that did very

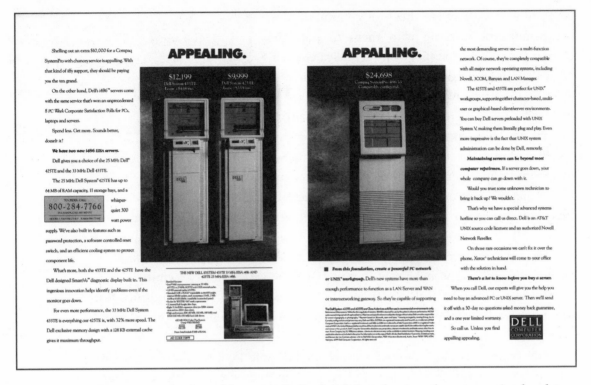

FIGURE 11.1: *Another of the many Dell ads I did at the time they were going head-to-head with Compaq Computer. If the ads hadn't worked, Dell wouldn't be the market leader today!*

little for their business while certainly enhancing the bottom line of the agency responsible. Yet a great many companies keep on doing it.

Why is that? Is it because they have always spent substantial amounts on advertising, particularly if they are in consumer package goods or the pharmaceutical industry, and therefore have some kind of Pavlovian urge that drives them to continue? Or, is it because they simply *hope* it might work, even though deep down inside they doubt its effectiveness. Because, in spite of what their agencies might say and attempt to reassure them to the contrary, no one can guarantee that whatever advertising they produce for them will do the job.

Remember the old adage at the beginning of this book about the various clients' worries that they knew half the money they spent on advertising was wasted but unfortunately, they didn't know which half. This is certainly true when you look at some of today's very large advertisers and ask yourself when was the last time you were influenced by their advertising. Do you actually believe that the next time you fly on Meat Grinder Airlines, you will be sitting in a half-empty first-class section drinking champagne out of a crystal flute, rather than being in the last seat in economy next to the rancid lavatory while you try to catch the attention of the one flight attendant who's looking after 300 other passengers? Of course not. So why do they continue to bombard us with their advertising? Perhaps, as I said, because they simply *hope* it might work.

> In spite of ever increasing ad spending, Sir Martin Sorrell, chairman and CEO of WPP, the world's second largest advertising group with hundreds of agencies in dozens of countries, has stated that in the future less then half the group's revenues would come from advertising-related activities.

OK, enough of the bad publicity, let's look on the bright side. There can be many advantages to working with an agency when you have grown to become a business of a certain size. If properly managed by you and whoever you've appointed to be responsible for the ad program within your company, you should be able to invest your budget wisely and expect to see reasonable results that outweigh those you might get by continuing to handle your advertising yourself. It's all a matter of doing it right. Now it's time to consider how to go about doing this.

FINDING THE RIGHT AGENCY

Finding a decent agency is not as difficult as you may imagine. As I have repeated ad nauseum, simply apply logic and common sense. Ask yourself how you go about finding any kind of resource. You research it. And the first thing you need to research when you start looking for an advertising agency is what advertising have you seen recently that's made an impression on you? It doesn't matter whether you intend to advertise locally, nationally, or internationally; you are constantly exposed to other companies' advertising via everything from newspapers to magazines, television, radio, and the internet. Which are the ads you've seen recently

People are becoming increasingly agitated by the amount of advertising they are exposed to. Don't make yours the straw that breaks the camel's back.

that made an impression on you? They don't necessarily have to be in the same category of business as you, although that might help to clarify your thinking. Simply consider anything that's caught your attention recently.

Think about why you are impressed by these particular ads. Don't be overly persuaded by glossy execution. Lots of money spent on high production values can rarely cover up bad ideas, or the lack of any idea at all. Try to analyze what went into the ad's creation. Remember how earlier in the book I discussed developing a communications plan. Do the ads that impress you look as if they are based on something organized and well structured? Do they have that all important USP? Is there something about them that makes you think, "I need to find out more about this company or these products"? Has the advertising captured your interest enough to make you want to go to the next step of visiting its web site or store, or making a phone call? If it has, then it has performed the first and most important task you can ask of an ad. It's captured your interest and incentivised you to react favorably.

Start with a Shortlist

Let's assume you've made a list of three or four companies that have impressed you with their advertising. You now need to find out who was responsible for it. Get in touch with the companies and ask who manages their advertising and marketing within the organization. I'm sure I don't have to tell you to make it obvious to whomever you initially contact that you're not trying to sell them anything, that you're just very impressed with their advertising and would like some information. I've done this many times and never had a problem finding out everything I need to know. Most people are only too pleased to give this information out, particularly if you've complimented them profusely on the quality of their advertising. If you do manage to talk directly to the marketing or advertising director, he or she will probably give you the rundown on the agency, how long its worked with them, what the people are like, how the chemistry is, and most of everything else you want to know, with the possible exception of the financial basis on which they work with these people.

Do this for all the companies on your list, but keep the list short. Don't waste your time or the prospective agencies' time by talking to too many. A surprising number of companies, particularly the bigger ones, make their agency selection process a long, drawn out, tedious, and expensive procedure. This is one of the things that's always driven me nuts about the agency business. I am constantly reading in the advertising trade press that a client has

> When picking out the advertising you like in order to talk to their agencies, do not go for major multimillion dollar campaigns. You don't have a multimillion dollar budget, so there's no point in talking to that kind of agency.

decided to leave its current agency and is about to conduct a search for a new one. Sometimes the client does this by itself, but increasingly, large clients are starting to use search consultants. The reasoning behind this makes as little sense to me as the need for wardrobe consultants or jury consultants. Still, I suppose as an advertising consultant, I should keep that particular criticism to myself.

The Madison Avenue Way

The way a Big Dumb Client goes about selecting a Big Dumb Agency has changed little in the last 20 or 30 years. The first step taken by whoever will be responsible for the search is to send out an request for proposal (RFP), which is usually a multiple-page questionnaire asking for details of the agency's resources and capabilities. This can go to as many as 20 or 30 agencies. Most of the questions are straightforward. At this stage no one in any of the agencies contacted gets too excited or starts thinking about doing anything other than filling out the RFP.

Once these are returned, the winnowing of the wheat from the chaff begins. A long short list of about a dozen agencies is put together, and members of the client's middle management team visit each agency to see some of the current work and meet a representative sample of its people. After this, a short list of half a dozen agencies is prepared, and they are informed they have made it into the quarter finals. This is where people who should know better start going off the deep end in terms of putting together dedicated teams who will now start spending lots and lots of time and money on the *pitch*.

After more agency visits by more senior management the short list is whittled down to three agencies that become the *finalists*, each of which then proceeds to go

> You don't engage in speculative pitches when selecting your doctor, lawyer, or accountant. Why on earth should you do it for your advertising agency?

ape, particularly if this is a really big or prestigious potential client. The spigot is opened, and money runs out like there's no tomorrow on: lots of research, focus groups, consumer studies, analyst's reports, store visits, finished TV commercials and print ads, online web sites, pop-ups, even book matches and chocolate piñatas if anyone thinks it will turn the trick. No one questions the wisdom of spending all this money when you only have a one in three chance of winning the business. Eventually, the final presentations are made. A winner is selected and appointed the agency of record. The losers go off to lick their wounds and hopefully bury all the money they blew on the pitch into their existing clients' bills. Then more often than not, the whole charade is repeated a year later.

I go through this explanation merely to point out the futility of the entire process, both on the part of the agencies taking part and the client who rarely succeeds in getting the agency it really deserves. I know that at this moment you do not have the kind of multimillion dollar budget that would tempt BDAs to burn money in a futile attempt to win your business, but unless you are careful, you might fall into the trap of engaging in a similarly futile process, which even though it will be on a somewhat reduced scale, will still be a waste of your and the prospective agencies' time.

Meet with Your Choices

Much better to make a list of two or three agencies that you think have done good work for their respective clients, go to meet them or have them come to you, talk about your business, and get some kind of feel about how they react to your problems and aspirations. Then choose one. Don't ask for speculative work, and even if it offers to do it, refuse. It doesn't know enough about your business at this stage to be able to put together a campaign that would make sense. And even if it has worked on a similar account in the past that might possibly be a help to them in terms of its understanding of your market, it still doesn't know enough about your business in particular to be able to realistically come up with the goods.

If your business is B2C you can probably work with any agency that has a reasonable range of experience on a variety of accounts. Just be sure the quality of work is of a consistently high standard across everything they do, irrespective of the nature of the account or the media it runs in. If, however, you are a B2B company, you might be well served to find a B2B specialist agency, or at least one that has a fair proportion of B2B accounts on its roster. The creation of B2B ads and the management of the account require a different mind set than most consumer advertising, and this is a situation where prior experience of B2B accounts can be invaluable.

Anyway, when you do select an agency, have it understand that the first three months will serve as a trial period. If it doesn't work out for you, you can always pull the plug and go talk to one of the other agencies you interviewed. (Don't worry, few agencies will ever walk away from a piece of business.) You should know within the first three months of any client/agency relationship if it's going to work or not.

YOU'VE HIRED AN AGENCY—WHAT NOW?

When you've found what you consider to be the right agency and committed to a relationship, it's time to establish a few rules—both for them, and for you. They don't have to be a list of do's and don'ts written into some kind of contract or agreement. Think of them more as general working principles you should continually consider and perhaps refer to as the association develops and you get used to each other. If you both start off on the right foot, the agency will be able to create much better work for you and you'll be more inclined to give it the freedom a good agency needs to develop that work.

Never hire an agency to tell you only what you *want* to hear. Hire an agency with the moxie to tell you what you *need* to hear. Sometimes there's a big difference, and the difference can be an unpleasant shock. Remember my story at the beginning of the book about the company chairman who refused to believe that his after-sales service was abysmal? Never rely solely on the people who work for you to keep you up to speed on the current state of your business. And never kill the messenger if you don't like the news she brings.

Understanding Your Business

Make sure your agency and the people who will work on your account understand what kind of business you are in. If they haven't had prior experience of your particular category, give them time and encourage them to acquire it. Sometimes it's even better to work with someone who doesn't have that experience; you'll get a fresh perspective and won't be offered the same old clichés that are often used as a crutch to avoid the hard work necessary to come up with original work. You see

Every few months insist on having a joint agency/client competitive review where you lock yourselves away in a conference room and cover the walls with the advertising your competition is producing. Critique it, and see if yours matches up.

that all the time with ads for cars, travel, insurance, health care, you name it. Most of them end up being what I call "Your logo goes here" ads. Anyone could run them; the only difference is the name of the advertiser.

Of all the people who will be working on your account, make sure you get to meet regularly with the writer and art director who are creating your ads. Take the time necessary to get them to under-

stand what your business is all about and what added value, in comparison to your competition, you bring to the marketplace. In other words, make them understand your USP. Encourage them to visit your factory, showroom, or wherever it is you conduct your business.

I believe this approach is of fundamental importance, in spite of the words of a very famous Madison Avenue creative director, who was well known for advising the creative people who worked for him that they should never visit the client's factory, or anywhere else associated with the manufacture, sale or distribution of the client's products, as this would merely serve to cloud their creative judgment. I would like to go on record, here and now, as saying this is the single dumbest thing I ever heard in all my many years in this business.

Great advertising is not created in a vacuum. It can only come about when you've gained sufficient in-depth information and background on the client's business to be able to write and design intelligent, attention-grabbing communications that spell out in reasonable language why the potential customer should patronize it. This guy's words are nothing more than another demonstration of the ivory tower approach far too many Madison Avenue agency people bring to the business of selling and communicating the benefits of their clients' products. If you don't take the time and make the effort to understand completely what it is you're selling to the reader or viewer, how on earth can you possibly hope to do it with any kind of conviction or authority?

> David Ogilvy always took great pride in saying that he always used his client's products: Shopping at Sears, washing with Dove soap, drinking Bacardi rum with Schweppes Tonic, and always driving a Rolls Royce.

Dealing with Suits

Never allow the agency account executive to act as the gatekeeper between you and the creative people who produce your ads. With a few rare exceptions, most account people will try to second-guess what they think the client wants. Even worse, some feel they are blessed with a God-given ability to be able to judge what the client will buy. They are very much like our much-maligned friends the used car salespeople; they can't help themselves because they are cursed with this endemic trait that everything is predicated on *making the sale.* It doesn't matter what they sell, it may be radioactive waste from Chernobyl. The object of the exercise is to *make the sale.* Because *the sale is everything.*

Make it clear to the principals of your new agency that you expect the account manager of your account to manage the account. If he wants to take you for lunch, get you sky box seats for the next Super Bowl, or engage your great aunt's third niece removed as a summer intern next year, fine. Just make it absolutely clear that this will have no effect on the way you judge the quality of the work the agency does for you. He won't believe you of course. But after he has employed your idiot, great niece for a summer and you have to fire the agency because its work sucks, you can always say, "Well, I did tell you it was all about the work."

OK, I'm getting a little carried away here to make a point. But, it's a very important one: you should never judge your agency on anything other than the quality of the work it does for you. Everything else is inconsequential. And, wasn't it the work it had done for others that attracted you to it in the first place?

Begining the Relationship

When it comes time to get started on the work, that is, beginning the planning and writing of the strategy you will jointly use as the foundation upon which to build the advertising, talk to the agency about the principles and methodology of your communications plan (based on what you created in Chapter 3). It may have some proprietary model of its own that basically does the same thing, albeit under a different name. That is fine, because most good agencies should have a system they have perfected over time as the best way for them to produce quality work. Just be sure the end result will be based upon the same application of logic and common sense I've discussed.

If you feel that its method lacks the structured approach of the communications plan, ask it to take you through its method. You may find upon inspection that it has enough similarities to yours that you can be comfortable with it. If, on the other hand, it seems to have an over reliance on a flying-by-the-seat-of-your-pants approach with little reliance on logic and reasoning, tell it so. Then, ask it to consider the way you've been doing your own advertising up until now, using the communication plan methodology. Its reaction to this suggestion will more than likely be a good indication of how the future of your relationship will develop.

> A successful client/agency relationship is built on trust. While you must let the agency get on with its work, you should make it aware that you expect to be involved at various stages before the presentation of finished work.

Tell the agency you want to be involved at all stages with the development of your advertising. This is not to interfere with its thinking or pressure it to do things the way you want them done. Remember the first point on this list, you didn't hire the agency to tell it what you *wanted* but to have it tell you what you *need*. Having said that, you should make it clear you can provide valuable input to help it get to that conclusion.

Make it understood that you want to be presented with a clear strategy and executional timeline you can sign off on before the agency proceeds to execute the creative materials. This is for the benefit of both you and the agency. It will save having to backtrack from bad creative solutions based on an unsound strategy, which is something that happens too often in many client/agency relationships. Involving the agency's creative people in the development of the strategy will also ensure that the work they eventually produce is relevant to and on the strategy.

The Creative

When you have signed off on the strategy, the agency can start developing the creative work. There are two schools of thought here about just how involved the client should be at this stage. The majority of agencies like to go away for a few days or a couple of weeks to work uninterrupted, then present layouts, scripts, or storyboards in a fairly high state of finish for the client's approval. This is known as the *dog and pony show*, meaning parading your wares for judging and quite possibly being at the mercy of the whims, preconceived notions, and sometimes the sheer bloody mindedness of the assembled layers of client management.

A small number of smart agencies do it a different way. One of these is Chiat Day, creators of many famous campaigns for everything from Apple to Nissan cars. At Chiat the idea is to get the client involved while the work is in progress by holding what are known as *tissue sessions*. During these, people from both the agency and client side sit in a room where the walls are covered with all kinds of ideas and concepts that are at a very early and unfinished stage. Everyone pitches in with comments and ideas. Because nothing is finished up to any stage of completeness, it is unthreatening, allowing people to be honest and frank with each other. The layouts are little more than magic marker scribbles, sometimes backed up by what is known in the business as scrap art, which is little more than pictures torn out of magazines or stock photography books. The idea is to give a visual feel for the look and mood of the direction the creatives are exploring for the finished advertising. If television is being discussed, use might be made of film clips or videos and audio tapes.

The whole purpose of these meetings is to give an indication to the client of the agency's thinking at this stage of the process. But besides these tissue sessions being a heads-up for the client, they also get it involved in the process, allowing it to buy into the concept at an early stage and feel as if it is contributing to the advertising in a much more meaningful way than merely approving the finished advertising. See Figure 11.2 for examples of the kind of ads that came out of tissue sessions.

Working this way also would allow you to appreciate the value of the ideas being presented. Just about every agency worth its salt these days can put on a presentation that makes the ads look like dynamite. Equipped with the marvels of

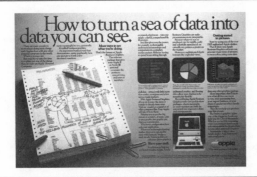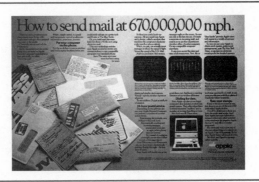

FIGURE 11.2: *Without client input during tissue sessions, creating these impactful ads and many more in a very successful series, would not have been possible.*

current digital technology, scanned-in and clip art, and high-resolution color laser prints, *anyone* can make a silk purse out of a sow's ear. Good art directors and skilled designers can achieve miracles.

So when you consider the ads in your agency's presentation, make sure you go beyond how they *look*. Consider what they *say*. Is there a core idea that makes sense and works against the target groups? Does it excite you? Will the campaign have the legs that will allow you to run it for at least a year or two? Are the ads going to grab and then hold the attention of anyone outside the presentation room? (Remember, people don't read ads, they read what interests them.)

Don't look at the ads hanging on the wall mounted on shiny presentation boards; this isn't an art gallery. Look at the ads the way the consumer will—in a newspaper or magazine, surrounded by dozens of other ads, most of which look the same as each other and are saying the same things about me-too products. Why on earth would you want to throw all your hard earned money away on advertising that looks like everyone else's advertising?

> Great advertising campaigns can run for years with little or no change. Marlboro is probably one of the best examples of a long-running, international campaign, irrespective of your views on the product.

Content

When it comes to content, impress upon your agency that you want your ads to talk to grown-up people in grown-up language. Fight the metaphors, clichés, and puns. Open any newspaper or magazine, watch any television, and you will see the same repetitive visuals and headlines. The mother in the TV ad for paper towels is all smiles when her two-year-old has

covered the kitchen and the dog in chocolate syrup, yet you know she probably wants to kill the little bugger. The same car is going down the same empty road in seemingly the same car commercial. The same health care or local hospital ads talks unceasingly about how they care. I would certainly hope that when I go in for my lobotomy, someone will be caring; they shouldn't have to keep reassuring me of it. In the same way, most B2B advertising uses language that is completely foreign to the way normal people talk, using words like synergy, optimization, empowerment, resonance. Go to their web sites, and they speak the same way. In real life, no one speaks like this, unless they live and work in Silicon Valley.

Consistency Is the Key

Avoid having your agency structure your advertising around a series of one-offs and promotions rather than a consistent campaign that will continually build the value of your brand and its long-term awareness among the people you want to influence. Do not ask it to run ads relying on the borrowed interest of annual events such as Presidents' Day, Halloween, the Super Bowl and worst of all, the Olympics. I am constantly amazed at the number of ads running prior to and during these events. All using the same cliché visuals of high-jumpers, baton-passing relay runners, flaming torches, gold medals, all of which sport soporific headlines talking about teamwork, the pursuit of excellence, and that ceaselessly regurgitated classic, "Going for the gold." As I never fail to keep reminding you, why should you pay good money to run the same ads everyone else is running?

Impress upon your new agency that you are only interested in the quality of what it does for you, rather than the quantity. Without fail, any agency worth its salt will swear to you that its primary reason for existing is to deliver only the very best, brightest, and highest-quality, kick-ass work to you, its favorite client. That is understandable because if you were in its shoes, why would you not promise your clients exactly the same?

Still, you have to understand that in common with the rest of the advertising agency Scamerati, these people would sell their first born into slavery and pimp their wife if it meant making sure you, the client, remained happy. As a consequence, most agencies lack the courage of their convictions. Their convictions can change at the drop of a hat, particularly if it's the client's hat that's dropped. That's why they always show lots and lots of stuff. They think it will impress the client by demonstrating the depth of their thinking. In reality, it merely shows the shallowness of it.

Approving the Work

When your agency shows you the work it thinks is right for you and you haven't gone through the tissue session routine described earlier (although you really should insist on that), you will very probably be seeing all of its work for the first time. Make a mental note of how many different solutions it comes up with. If you agreed on the communications plan or something close to it before it started to work on the creative, there should ideally only be a single solution.

Unfortunately, very few agencies have the courage of their convictions, let alone the guts to present a single recommended campaign. Instead, your agency will show you lots of stuff. Sometimes, lot and lots of stuff. And to compound the felony, often they will not even make a recommendation. Like our old friend the used car salesman, its primary objective is to make the sale.

It may even stoop to offering what I call the Chinese menu option. That's the one where if you like the headline from this campaign, the visual from this one, and the copy from this one, no problem. It can meld them together into a homogeneous, totally ineffective piece of noncommunication. But as far as the agency is concerned, that's OK, because it just made a sale. You should avoid these situations at all costs.

AGAIN, WHY SHOULD YOU HIRE AN AGENCY?

So now you are wondering why I've even suggested you consider putting your ad account with a potentially scrofulous bunch of Ad-whores. I do it only on the basis that it will make sense when you have arrived at a certain size and have sufficient revenues and turnover to justify it. And also, to be honest, there are some amazingly bright and clever advertising people out there who can help you build a successful business through the judicious application of kick-ass advertising. However, many of the very best exist in advertising agencies because that's the pond they like to swim in, and if you wish to benefit from their expertise, that's the pond you'll have to dip your toes in.

If you have arrived at the stage in the growth of your company where you think you can benefit from the employment of an advertising agency, congratulations. It's an indication of your success. But I repeat, you must be careful how you approach both the selection of the agency and your working relationship. If you do both right, you will benefit from its expertise and enthusiasm in helping you build your company and your brand.

Just as you have to look at the money you spend on advertising as an investment rather than an expense, so too your work with an agency. You must approach it as a long-term commitment, and you must regard it as an investment, not just in money but equally in terms of time and how you intend to work with the agency. Will it be as partners, vendors, or people who merely execute your great idea of the day?

Finally, however you do your advertising—by yourself, with the help of freelancers and consultants, or even swimming in the scary currents of Madison Avenue replete with its sharks—making good advertising isn't brain surgery. And it certainly isn't great art or literature. It's mostly common sense and logic, albeit with a generous sprinkling of flair, chutzpah, moxie, or whatever you want to call it.

Never forget that to make good or even great advertising you only need three things. In order of importance, these are information, time, and money. You can create great ads on tiny budgets. But it gets real tough on tight deadlines, and it gets close to impossible with no information. That's why the anonymous creative director who advised his writers and art directors to avoid factory visits and anything else that might have provided them with the information to create a great campaign was an unmitigated idiot!

Steve Jobs told his agency over 20 years ago, "I want insanely great advertising." The agency was Chiat Day. When Steve was forced out of Apple, corporate management moved the account to another agency. When Steve returned to Apple, he moved the account back to Chiat Day. It's still there, and the agency is still producing "insanely great advertising." A no-compromise, committed client working with an enthusiastic, talented, and enthusiastic agency will always create great advertising.

CHAPTER TWELVE

Measuring the results and planning for the future

You've figured out how to create kick-ass advertising, whether it be done on your own or with the help of others. Now it's time to decide where you go from here. The best way to begin thinking about this is by finding out if what you've done so far is actually working. Meaning, does it get the interest of potential customers and make them anxious to spend their hard-earned money with you? More importantly, does it provide a worthwhile return on all the hard-earned money you've put into it?

ADVERTISING EFFECTIVENESS

It's an unfortunate fact of life that while the volume of advertising produced in both the United States and worldwide is increasing annually, the cost of creating and running it is also increasing year after year.

In contrast, the cost to consumers of most products and services is declining. Look at everything from travel to food to electronics. When I bought my first computer in the early 1980s it cost nearly $5,000 and had less power than a modern digital wristwatch. Now I can buy a top-of-the-line laptop for less than $1,000, and yet it packs more power and features than a 1970s Cray Supercomputer!

> While most print and broadcast audiences are shrinking, the costs of buying space and time are increasing. Print and broadcast production costs are also going through the roof. The average cost to make a 30-second TV spot suitable for network airing is now in excess of $400,000.

Yet the ultimate effect of costly traditional advertising is declining. Advertising is less effective through a combination of overexposure and the increasing numbers of people who are finding their news, entertainment, social interaction, and general information in the proliferation of noncommercial media and online environments. Because of all these other nontraditional opportunities for people to access and interact with each other, you must be absolutely sure the money you're spending on advertising is being spent in the most cost-efficient and effective way.

Despite what most of the people who make a living creating advertising tell you, advertising's effectiveness is pretty well near impossible to measure accurately, with one major exception: direct marketing. Direct marketing is an activity that absolutely relies on selling products as a result of customers responding to specific advertising messages, all of which contain a traceable call to action or some other identifying trigger that allows the advertiser to track with great accuracy exactly which ads and media are generating the most sales. Dell, the single largest manufacturer of PCs and small business servers in the world, and Amazon.com, which although starting with books, is now selling everything from gourmet foods to garage tools, are perhaps the best examples of the ultimate direct marketing business model. Hundreds of other successful, but lesser known companies have relied on this form of advertising, using every media vehicle imaginable, from TV to print to catalogues to windshield leaflets! And the single largest factor contributing to their success has been their ability to continuously develop and fine-tune their advertising. Skillful direct marketers are masters at knowing

> In 2005, the crossover between the numbers of hours Americans under the age of 40 watched TV versus being online occurred. Consequently, as they age, an increasing number of Americans will get their entertainment, information, and news online, not from the TV. Little wonder traditional media is worried.

exactly what messages work on specific target groups and are constantly experimenting with new forms of media and communications to make their ROI even more impressive.

Unless you are selling direct, you will have to rely on less precise methods to evaluate the effectiveness of your advertising. And the key word here is *effectiveness*. It's relatively easy to find out such standard media metrics as frequency, reach, and to a lesser extent, penetration, all of which can be obtained through all the various media channels. But never forget all these guys will be delighted to bury you in information and statistics that invariably show their respective publications or radio and TV stations in the most favorable light. However, finding out whether or not the advertising you run with these various media is actually working will always be a much tougher nut to crack.

GAUGING EFFECTIVENESS

The single best way to measure the effectiveness of your advertising efforts is to get as close to the methodology of the direct marketers as possible. Always put some kind of incentive or call to action in your advertising. Don't fall into the trap of thinking you can afford to run ads that merely improve your image rather than your sales. I don't mean you should only produce schlocky hard-sell stuff like the old "anvils in the head" or "flaming stomachs" so beloved by many of the OTC drug companies during the 1950s and 1960s or, sad to say, is still being thrust upon

> Your audience is you. Even better, she's your mother! You wouldn't bullshit yourself, let alone your mother, so don't do it to your prospective customer.

us by some die-hards today. Remember what I've stressed throughout this book: Treat your customers with the respect they deserve; don't talk down to them because if you do, they'll only end up despising you for it.

If your advertising is designed and written to generate inquiries via the phone or the internet, then it must be tagged or coded in such a way that you will always know exactly which ads and which media the ads are running in are generating the most interest and response. OK, unlike the pure direct marketing model, this will only translate into sales through the effectiveness of the next link in the chain, that is, the people handling the inquiry, either via the internet, the phone, or in person at your salesroom or warehouse.

Just be sure that the people handling the inquiry always find out where the prospective customer first heard about you. Then, as you discover which advertising and media is actually working best in driving the customer to the next stage in the transaction cycle, you'll be able to concentrate a more significant portion of your adverting dollars on these messages and media, while eliminating those you realize you're wasting money on because they aren't delivering the best results.

Another thing to consider when evaluating the effectiveness of your advertising is that this is an exercise that always has to be done in retrospect. The ads must run before you can attempt to find out whether or not they've worked. The media you are considering running your ads in will, if it's print, bombard you with all kinds of favorable circulation figures, market penetration, and readership studies up front. (Never forget, readership and circulation are significantly different.) But, there will be no way they can tell, let alone guarantee if your campaign will actually fulfill its objectives. And if the media of your choice is radio or TV, each and every one of them will do the same with nonstop audience viewing and listening figures, particularly if they can skew them in their favor. So whether you are considering print, radio, TV, or even book match covers, never forget that the sole purpose off all these various studies, overviews, reviews, analyses, or any other kind of data is to make sure the media company paying for them is put in the best possible light.

Let's be honest, they're only doing what you would in their place, trying to give their advertisers some kind of half-way believable proof they can deliver on all of their grandiose promises. Simply remember that none of this is any kind of guarantee as to the numbers of people who'll actually see your advertising, let alone be affected or influenced by it. You, and only you, will be evaluating its effectiveness after the ad has run, so it is imperative you gather all the information possible regarding any inquiry the ad drives as quickly as possible.

> The CEOs of most large companies rarely get involved in the creation of their advertising. There are exceptions. Steve Jobs at Apple does and that's why Apple's advertising is great. Larry Ellison at Oracle does and that's why Oracle's sucks. It depends on the CEO. So make sure you're the Steve Jobs kind of CEO.

Effectively gathering information requires establishing a system, albeit a relatively simple one, that allows the person handling the inquiry or sale to input the data regarding what exactly it was that incentivised the customer to make an inquiry or place the order in the first place. Far too often this is a salesperson saying, assuming they remember to do so, something as simple as "Where did you hear about us?" This is usually answered by the customer's blank stare or a moment of silence if this is a telephone inquiry, then a mumbled comment about seeing an ad in the *Big Butt Bugle*, or whatever the local newspaper is.

Interestingly, a surprising number of people will say "The Yellow Pages" even when this is a patent lie because you know for a fact you've never advertised in the local Yellow Pages. That only serves to reinforce the power of long-running, well-recognized campaigns, even when they are less than inspiring from a creative point of view, in which clients are smart enough to have stuck to their guns year after year.

So you must train your salespeople to get as many advertising-related specifics as possible, such as which particular ad drove them to make the purchase, what periodical the ad ran in, and when it ran. This is a tough row to plow, because most people don't remember stuff like that. That is why you have to do what I discussed earlier, give them a trigger or code within the body of the ad that delivers an added value when they get to the next stage of the transaction cycle. It can be a discount, two-for-one, bundling, free delivery or shipping, even a free Pilate's workout video. It doesn't matter, as long as it gives you the information you need to measure the ads effectiveness.

Supplying a trigger or code means more work for your sales and marketing people, but if you do it right and do it consistently, you'll start to build up a database of what kind of ad content and which media choices are delivering the best results. Long term, it will only help make your advertising decisions that much smarter, not to mention save you money.

There are a couple of formulas and methodologies some companies rely on to measure the effectiveness and value they get from their advertising budgets. The first is *advertising payback*, a calculation based on an analysis of a year's sales returns. It is supposedly a rough indication of the advertising's ROI and is achieved by deducting the costs of what has been spent on advertising from the sales generated by that advertising. Sounds pretty straightforward, but unless you are selling direct, it's very hard to identify what sales came as a result of the advertising and were not influenced by other factors. The second is *media productivity*, a calculation similar to the one above, but applied to specific media vehicles so you may supposedly evaluate the ROI of each.

> When all the measurements and focus groups are chucked out the window, it all comes down to gut feel. Bill Bernbach presented the Avis "When you're #2 you try harder" campaign to the CEO of Avis after research indicated it would be a disaster, the CEO said, "Well, you're the expert, let's run it." Ah, the good old days.

Personally, I find both methods of little use, particularly if you aren't P&G or General Foods or some other major packaged-goods company and can rely on massive amounts of data input from store groups to evaluate exactly what lines are selling as a result of your massive advertising campaigns. No, you aren't quite at that stage yet.

Another method of measuring advertising effectiveness that's been getting a great deal of hype in the last few years is the pseudo-science of *econometrics*. The Big Dumb Agencies of Madison Avenue love to lay this on their clients. It gives them a veneer of respectability in as much it partially removes the commonly held perception that most advertising is based on blind guesswork rather than a defined methodology. Econometrics relies on lots and lots of computer calculations designed to distinguish between independent variables (stuff that causes sales) and dependant variables (the value of the sales). It goes on and on, and to be honest, I don't really understand it. Come to think of it, I don't think the people who promote it really understand it either. After all, after spending inordinate amounts of time and money, they usually come up with such blindingly obvious conclusions as the one stating that the largest single influence on a brand's sales is how well the brand is known, and how well the brand is actually known is determined by how much advertising has been put behind it. As Bart Simpson would say, "Duh."

Many BDAs actually charge their clients hundreds of thousands of dollars to come up with these jaw-dropping conclusions. But, as I've pointed out earlier, the client's middle management is happy to go along with these scams (others include lots of research and ad testing) because it serves to cover their rear ends if the advertising should ever be perceived by senior management as a load of old tripe. Those responsible for it can always claim to their boss that it tested like gangbusters in Boise, and the econometrics were enough to make Einstein weep.

TRUST YOUR GUT

At the end of the day most of it does come down to flying-by-the-seat-of-your-pants. But the essential thing to remember is that what we're talking about *your* pants. Remember the definition of an entrepreneur as a risk taker? There's more than an element of truth in that description when it comes to advertising. The best example I can give you is Steve Jobs, co-founder and CEO of Apple Computer. This is a guy who has consistently told his ad agencies in the past, "I want insanely great advertising." And unlike many other CEO's who asked for "breakthrough" work, he hasn't backed off when they present it to him. I personally have had numerous situations where a full-of-piss-and-vinegar client has insisted, "I want really edgy advertising." But when the requested "really edgy advertising" is presented to him, he says, "I didn't mean *that* edgy." Every client wants an Apple 1984 TV spot. Unfortunately, few would sign off on it.

What I'm saying here is that if you want to play it safe and somehow or other hope that the money you are spending on advertising isn't being wasted, you have two options. You can do the same boring, repetitious stuff everyone else does, which will ensure you don't ever annoy or offend anyone, and also won't excite or grab anyone's attention. Or you can decide not to advertise at all and put your money into a savings and loan CD that returns 2 percent after taxes. Either way, depending on what kind of business you're in, you'll eventually go out of business.

But if you'd already decided advertising was a load of old tripe and a complete waste of money, you wouldn't be reading this book, would you? No one knows your business better than you do. You started it. You sweated bullets building it, so you know what it is that makes you different from everyone else out there. And most importantly, no one knows better than you how it should be reflected in your advertising. When you see that difference, you'll recognize it, whether you produced it by yourself or with the help of others. So when you do, trust your instincts and have the courage of your convictions to go with it. The worse thing that can happen is it might not be as effective as you thought it would be.

So, you lick your wounds and try something else. And if you've followed the advice throughout this book, you shouldn't have spent an arm and a leg to create and run it. Don't worry, you won't be the first to have made the odd wrong call, but at least you'll be doing what *you* want to do. It won't be what some jumped-up, MBA-flaunting marketing genius or Zegna-wearing Madison Avenue bullshit artist says you should do in order for them to suck at your company teat. Wow, I feel better for getting that off my chest.

> Many entrepreneurs have built successful companies with limited advertising budgets by creating a contrarian image when compared to their competition. This is what appeals to their initial audience. When the company is bought out by a larger company, the original image disappears. Many times, so does the original company.

Apart from Steve Jobs, there are many other visionaries who've built successful companies because they were determined to create a different kind of business. Not just in the kind of products they made or how they ran their companies, but also in the way they would *advertise* in comparison to their competition. Think of examples such as Ben & Jerry, Starbucks, Virgin, even J. Peterman who built a giant direct sales company off the back of tiny ads in the back pages of the *New Yorker*. (He blew it when he went into retail stores and expanded too rapidly, but now he's on his way back with the catalog plus a line of very expensive furniture. A true entrepreneur.) These companies and the CEOs who ran them didn't rely on market research or audience studies to decide what would be the safest kind of advertising to run and how quickly they could expect to begin seeing a payoff. They chose to go with what they instinctively sensed was right for their companies, they stuck with it, and more often than not it turned out to be the right thing.

Patience Pays

You can only really know if and when your advertising is delivering a healthy ROI after it's been running for some time. This requires patience and a belief in what you have committed yourself to. The majority of businesses change their advertising far too quickly. That's because the people responsible for it see it all the time and so they assume everyone else does. The general public is exposed to several thousand advertising messages a day. But when you talk in terms of the entire population, you're including everyone, even babies in strollers and guys doing time in Sing Sing. So if you only consider the people you've defined as your target audience, they're more than likely seeing hundreds of advertising messages a day.

What you need to do is make sure yours is sufficiently unique and well targeted to stand out from all the rubbish out there, then give it time to work. I'm not attempting to spout the usual lame arguments Madison Avenue and the media invariably trot out about impact being dependant on high frequency and how advertising needs to be repeated over and over to get through to people. By saying that, they are implying you should treat your audience as idiots, which makes it necessary to hit them over the head repeatedly with a two by four to make an impression. I guarantee if you do do that, you'll have a lot of very pissed-off people who are never going to think about doing business with you.

The Fallacy of Frequency

There have been many studies on how the effectiveness of advertising is governed by the frequency you run it. Yet surprisingly, after three insertions of the same ad over a seven-day period, its impact on the reader is extremely small; over a longer period of time, it has no effect at all! So, you have to ask yourself why many advertisers persist in running very concentrated bursts of the same advertising over a limited period in the belief they are having a more pronounced impact on the reader. Obviously, the media encourages this belief and offers discounts to persuade advertisers they are getting a better deal by running so many ads in such a short period of time. In reality, far too often, all the advertiser is doing is wasting money.

Contrary to what the Madison Avenue Adverati would have you believe, a single ad can have a very dramatic effect on either a brand's image or the sales of products and services. Occasionally but rarely, it can have an effect on both. Remember the Apple 1984 TV spot I discussed earlier. It ran once. In fact, to have run it more than once would have been counterproductive, because it would have been perceived as merely another Super Bowl ad rather than as an event in its own right. In the opinion of a great many people, it is the most famous TV spot ever produced. And considering it only ran once and that was more than 20 years ago, even today an amazing number of people can give you a fairly accurate description of it. Of course, the fact that for months after it ran it received a tremendous amount of PR and news coverage certainly helped.

It's also worth considering that if a big package goods or pharmaceutical products company had produced a TV commercial that received the acclaim the 1984 spot did on its initial showing, it would still be running it today. Because big dumb companies are like big dumb ad agencies, they underestimate the sophistication, and indeed the tolerance of the audience they are addressing. Howard Gossage was a great believer in producing advertising so different, so intriguing, and so targeted that you only needed to run it once. And if you think about it, there is a wonderful element of logic to this argument. If a member of your target audience reads your ad and the ad is well done, then it should perform its function perfectly, moving the reader or viewer to take the next step in the sales cycle.

> When was the last time you were driven by an ad to take some action? Did you take that action after seeing the ad 20 times or after you'd seen it the first time?

Repeated exposure to the message will only result in annoyance, not to mention a waste of your money. However, there is obviously one proviso to this argument. You have to consider what will be the chances of the reader coming across your ad if it only runs once. This depends both on the media you choose to run it in and how well the ad is targeted to your audience. What I'm saying here is that in an imperfect world, you have to strike a balance among the quality of the content of your advertising, where you choose to run it, and how often. (Not to mention how much money you are prepared to spend.)

My advice? Apply maximum time and money to getting the content right, research, define and select the media choices, then finally work out what the minimum frequency needs to be to achieve a reasonable exposure to your target audience. In the final analysis and without the benefit of hindsight, the single most effective measure of how well your advertising is working will be based on your gut feeling.

Evaluating Effectiveness

Yes, as I've said earlier, you can and should track where new business is coming from based on the response to the built-in indicators in your ads. You must also constantly monitor the reaction of your customers to your advertising and promotional programs via e-mail and limited telephone surveys. All of this will certainly give you a good indication of how your advertising is working. You should be able to work out a sales-to-expenditure matrix where you plug in the numbers and track the results. That's the way the package goods companies and big box stores do it. But remember, these guys are dealing in very large numbers of both products and sales, not to mention huge ad budgets. They are also running their ads in many different kinds of media with great frequency. You can't afford the luxury of any of these choices. And you certainly can't afford to waste even the smallest percentage of your investment.

That's why you have to avoid spending money on me-too advertising or on media that doesn't zero in on your prime customers. Don't fall for special media offers or deals that may at first glance look like inexpensive opportunities, but in reality aren't going to reach the people you should be talking to.

SO WHERE DO YOU GO FROM HERE?

You have to consider your advertising as an ongoing, never ceasing program. No, not like you're a caged mouse on a treadmill destined to spin in perpetuity, but as a long-term investment in the health and prosperity of your company. And hey, compared to buying office supplies or liability insurance, it's a heck of a lot more fun.

You should also never forget what I talked about at the very beginning of this book. The best advertising in the world won't do a thing for you if you haven't got everything else in place. Your advertising is just one cog in the entire company machine. If you're a retailer, running a dynamite ad campaign that gets people knocking down the doors of your store won't do you any good if the sales staff isn't up to snuff. If you make products and the products you make don't work the way they are supposed to, advertising isn't going to help you either.

What you have to understand is that every single function of your company communicates to your customers exactly what kind of company you are. I'm sure you've heard the story of the guy that goes into a Nordstrom store and puts down a couple of auto tires on the counter in the men's wear department. He tells the sales assistant that they are the wrong size for his car and he would like his money back. The sales guy asks him how much he paid for them. When the customer tells him, the salesman goes to the cash register, takes out the money, and hands it to the man, while apologizing to him for the inconvenience. Of course, the punch line is that Nordstrom's doesn't sell car tires. True or not, you get the point.

You could run ads for the rest of your life claiming "Customer satisfaction guaranteed." But fail to give that absolute satisfaction to one or two irate customers and pretty soon it will be all over town or, even worse today, all over the internet. Cyberspace is crawling with people who take great delight in hammering companies that fail to live up to their promises. Many companies, big and small—and more often than not arrogant—have discovered this to their sorrow.

Be prepared to be flexible in the way you run the business if the advertising is particularly successful. If you are a manufacturer, can you meet increased demand, will you have to employ more people, and do you have the raw materials and components necessary to fill extra orders? If you are a retailer, is your staff up to speed on any special promotions or sales you are featuring in the ads; are they schooled in finding out what parts of the advertising program drove the customer to the store?

As you track sales and relate them to the coded triggers in your advertising, you should be able to determine not only which offers are generating the best results, but over time you also will be able to schedule your advertising peaks against projected sales targets, evaluating the effectiveness of the advertising in achieving the projected sales.

Your advertising should always be an integral part of your overall marketing program. In earlier chapters I have been somewhat disparaging about the claims of BDAs when they promise their clients "totally integrated communications." This is not because I am against what is basically a very good idea, just the way Madison Avenue executes it. In most big agencies, there is a never-ending turf war between the departments that create traditional media advertising, direct marketing, and online advertising. Not only is each usually run as a separate profit center, but all the creative work invariably starts with, and is dictated by, the TV campaign the agency creative director sees as his personal fiefdom. (Ninety percent of the time, it's a "he.") Consequently, there is very little "integration" and the lack of "communication" is best expressed in the way the nontraditional components are shoehorned into an agonizing fit with the mainstream television campaign. Consequently, everything suffers, particularly the client's budget.

Fortunately, you don't have this problem, because whether you are doing it yourself or with the limited help of others, you are in total control of the content of your communications and how you execute them. Whether it be the advertising, literature, packaging, web sites, blogs, even the signage on the building, you can make absolutely sure your company is perceived by existing and future customers as one with that USP that makes it stand apart from the competition.

Even if you should eventually get to a size that might make you consider having someone else take on the task of running the advertising, be careful not to step away from the decision-making part of the process. It's your company; you started it from nothing. The advertising you were responsible for helped to get you to where you are today. When you delegate the entire advertising program to someone else, you're in danger of losing the entrepreneurial spirit that helped you build the company being reflected in your advertising. You are no longer building a company; you're creating a bureaucracy.

If and when you do decide to hand off the day-to-day management of your advertising to someone else, you must be extremely careful who you choose to undertake this function. You can either delegate this responsibility to an existing member of staff or bring in someone new from outside the company. Personally, I would recommend going with the devil you know, rather than someone new. Apart from the fact that an existing employee will understand the company and your own philosophy and traditions, the chances of finding someone from outside who is not only a good advertising person but will fit with your philosophy are pretty slim. Even worse is when a company gets to a certain size and decides it's time to hire an "advertising professional." These are people who may understand the mechanics of the advertising business, but rarely feel the passion necessary to produce great advertising. That will be your responsibility.

At this stage of your growth, you are in a unique position to establish a character for your company by creating advertising that not only works for you now, but will also provide a solid foundation you can build on for years to come. Lucky you!

Resources

Now is the time to point you in the right direction for all the supplementary information you might need in order to create the various components of your communication and advertising program. I list some books and organization you might find it useful, but in this day and age the vast majority of what you need to access is online. And as I said, a great deal of this information is free; it's simply a matter of having the patience and determination to keep digging until you find what you are looking for. Admittedly, there might be certain studies and references that you end up having to pay for, but it's worth persevering in your initial searches until you've exhausted all possibilities before committing to a paid service.

The most useful section is that dealing with the various search engines. The first part is about general search engines, the second, metasearch engines that agglomerate the work of the individual search engines, and the third, industry-specific information, background, and research details.

Finally, there is a section on blogs. This rapidly growing and increasingly influential subsection of the online universe deserves special consideration. I firmly believe it will have an increasingly dramatic impact on the ways companies, particularly small- and medium-sized ones, address their markets in the future.

BOOKS

The last thing you need are more how-to-make-great-advertising books. You only need one, which is why you bought *MadScam*. The ones I'm listing here are more in the area of background reading. They will give you useful guidance and information to help you better understand how to produce more effective advertising.

Beaumont, Mathew. "*e.*" Penguin Group, 2000. This is not a how-to-make-great-ads tome, a memoir on 50 years in the Madison Avenue trenches, or even a textbook. It's a hilarious novel written entirely in e-mails between people working and generally screwing around within the hallowed halls of the ad agency Miller Shanks as they pitch the Coca-Cola account. A must read for anyone contemplating putting their account with a Big Dumb Agency.

The Book of Gossage. Out of print, although used copies are available through Amazon and other dealers in out-of-print and hard-to-find books. Unfortunately they sell at outrageous prices. Nevertheless, worth every penny. This is a book about one of the greatest minds ever to influence American advertising. Howard Gossage, a legendary San Francisco ad man who died of cancer far before his time. He showed the world it wasn't necessary to spend a fortune to influence people. Just make sure that you spend whatever you have intelligently and with good humor.

Fugere, Brian, Chelsea Hardaway, and Jon Warshawsky. *Why Business People Speak Like Idiots*. Free Press. 2005. Required reading for anyone in business who's ever been tempted to talk bullshit, geekspeak, or the drivel that sounds as if you're reading from a PowerPoint slide. If you buy nothing else on this list, buy this book.

Jones, John Philip. *Fables, Fashions, and Facts About Advertising.* Sage Publications, 2004. Although Mr. Jones's books are primarily text books written for academic courses in marketing and advertising, they are a good read, full of useful information and insights into how the business of advertising works, and far too often how it doesn't.

Ogilvy, David. *Confessions of an Advertising Man.* Dell Publishing, 1964. Quite possibly one of the most amusing and self-aggrandizing books about advertising ever written, although, after reading *MadScam* there may be some doubts about that. Written in 1963 long before you, but not I, were born, David's book has a great deal of sound advice about how you should address audiences without taking them for granted or insulting their intelligence.

————. *Ogilvy on Advertising.* Crown Publishing, 1983. Written 20 years later, this really is much more of a hands-on, how-to book. Even though by today's standards, there is what some may consider to be too much emphasis on the print medium, I share David's point of view that if you can write well for print, you can probably bloody well write for anything.

Rothenberg, Randall. *Where the Suckers Moon.* Random House, 1995. One of the best written and funniest books on advertising ever produced. Living proof that Big Dumb Agencies will forever be big and dumb—until the day they finally become extinct.

Twitchell, James B. *Adcult USA.* Columbia University Press. 1996. Makes a well-reasoned and well-written argument that advertising has become an indispensable part of modern American culture. Although written in 1996 and so doesn't cover the rise of online advertising, the rest of it is still a useful guide to the effect advertising has had, and will continue to have, on society.

Zyman, Sergio with Armin Brott. *The End of Advertising as We Know It.* Wiley Publishing, 2002. The former chief marketing director of Coca-Cola points out the obvious, that Madison Avenue advertising agencies as we know and hate them are doomed if they don't mend their ways. Only worth reading when your advertising budget tops $100 million a year.

WEB SITES

These web sites might be useful to you as you work your way through the book. A few are inspirational and may encourage you to do good work. The majority, though, will be valuable as starting-off points when you do the necessary research for the development of your communications plan. Don't be surprised if some of them no longer exist. They will have been replaced by a multitude of others. After all, that's the nature of the online universe.

General Business

www.parkerads.com. Obviously, I have to put my own web site first. On it you can read my background and see some of the work I've done over the years. Use it more as a representation of what a good freelancer's web site should be like. This will be useful as a comparison tool when you are in the market for outside assistance.

www.entrepreneur.com. The well-known magazine that is part of the group that published *MadScam.* This web site is packed with information on all aspects of starting and running a business. There are many archived articles on different facets of marketing and advertising.

www.bizmove.org. The small business knowledge base. A range of completely free information featuring guides, templates, tools, and techniques. There is a subsection devoted to marketing and advertising.

www.allaboutbranding.com. A vast compilation of articles on all aspects of branding, with particular emphasis on what it takes to create and maintain a brand. Register for free e-mail updates on content that are published on a regular basis.

www.knowthis.com. This web site for the Marketing Virtual Library has links to various resources for product management and branding, with particular emphasis on market research. Has a range of free in-depth tutorials on many aspects of marketing.

Advertising

www.adage.com. The largest of the two general advertising weeklies. Covering agencies, clients, and the media, it is the more substantive of the two.

www.adweek.com. The second of the general advertising weeklies. More agency and advertising personalities focused.

www.commarts.com. The web site of *Communications Arts* magazine. Although primarily aimed at the art direction and graphic arts communities, it has useful articles and reviews of good advertising and web site design.

Freelancers and Consultants

www.guru.com. A free service listing thousands of freelancers in hundreds of skill areas. You can search via competency, experience, and location, then ask for a quote on the job.

www.hotgigs.com. Similar to Guru.com with an emphasis on web site and other forms of online media design and production.

www.ifreelance.com. Writers and designers, some production people.

SEARCH TOOLS

A small selection of search engines you will find useful as you research information for writing your communications plan. If you are not familiar with how these work, the one thing to remember as you use them is you must try to define your search as accurately as possible; otherwise, you will end up with thousands of hits. If, for instance, you are looking for information on atomic widgets, entering just the word *widget* will get you a ton of hits, most of which you don't want. Obviously "atomic widgets" will get you more of what you are looking for. Inserting a + sign between words will then treat them as a phrase. You can also use an asterisk (*) as a wildcard character at the end of the word you are searching, this will give you multiple variations on the original word. Each search engine has different rules, but a quick glance at the help files will point you in the right direction. At the time of writing, Microsoft has indicated that it will be including its search engine as a default in the next iteration, Visa, of its Windows operating system. This will no doubt become a major competitor to Google.

www.google.com. The current 800-pound gorilla of search engines, with literally billions of pages. Pages are ranked by relevance, and the page design is uncluttered and easy to use. Its rapidly expanding menu goes far beyond simple word searches and includes everything from images to maps to video to books. A useful feature is its "Are you feeling lucky?" on its opening page. This brings up what they consider to be the single most relevant answer to your query. And it's usually pretty accurate.

www.altavista.com. One of the original search engines, AltaVista uses the same data base as Yahoo, but gives more flexibility than its parent company. You can do searches by word, phrase, keyword, and case-sensitive. You can also limit searches by headline or book and document title.

www.ask.com. This used to be AskJeeves.com, which then purchased Teoma.com and has finally emerged as Ask.com. Its single best feature is that instead of merely entering search parameters, you can actually ask it questions and it will point you in the right direction for the answer.

www.yahoo.com. As mentioned above. Same database as altavista.com.

www.search.msn.com. At the time of writing, too early to make a judgment on the future of this, but based on Microsoft's determination to dominate every category it commits to, this will be worth watching.

Meta Search Tools

Basically, these are search engines that don't compile their own databases; they search those of other search engines. So in one operation you can look across many search engines. Sounds like this saves you a lot of time and effort, and for shallow searches, it does. However, the results are less precise and often do not allow you to refine your search to acquire more precise information. But they are useful as a starting point, particularly if you have a lot of digging to do.

www.dogpile.com. This combines Yahoo!, Google, MSN, and Ask into one easy reference point. A great starting point if you're not quite sure where to begin a search.

www.vivisimo.com. Useful in that it brings up the results in clusters. This helps to refine your search as each cluster is specific to the search topic but is broken down by different areas of interest.

www.hotbot.com. For a long time, this was the numero-uno search engine. Now it has reinvented itself as a metasearch engine. Unfortunately, it merely gives you a meta-search choice of MSN, Ask, and Google. To which you have to ask yourself, why bother?

Fee-Based Search Tools

The three major fee-based search tools are listed below. But even though they all have a wealth of information, they are not cheap. On the other hand, your local public library probably has free online access to all of them.

www.dialog.com. Part of the Thompson group, it archives content from more than 8,000 publications stored in hundreds of databases worldwide.

www.factiva.com. The online crown jewel of the *Wall Street Journal* group. This is a news and business information service with powerful tools that allow you to monitor competitors, customers, and your industry; you can conduct indepth research, gather company financial data, and more. Accesses all Dow Jones and Reuters databases.

www.lexisnexis.com. Primarily financial, legal, executive profiles, and records abstracted from the public archives.

Any one of the above are only worth subscribing to if you absolutely must have the particular information they have. Believe me, there are less expensive ways to access that information without getting locked into an annual subscription.

What and Who Search Tools

Let's assume that even though you don't know exactly what you are looking for, you can boil it down to one or two specific areas you feel you need to explore in depth. Here are some suggestions on where you should go to start looking.

www.anywho.com. AT&T's web site that allows you to find almost anyone's phone number and address throughout the United States, and it is also rapidly growing internationally.

www.yellowpages.com. Just what you would expect, with a reverse number look-up.

www.sec.gov. This is where you begin when you need information about specific companies or current trends in your market. Every public company and some of the larger private companies must disclose all the information you are dying to know about to the SEC—and you can access it all here for free.

THE NITTY GRITTY RESEARCH WEB SITES

There are literally hundreds of web sites providing information on businesses and the markets they operate in. So many in fact, it would need another book to cover them all. So, I will only give you a representative sample here. To find the ones that might be specific to your business, go back to the beginning of this chapter and use one of the regular or metasearch tools to explore the internet.

www.zapdata.com. Dunn & Bradstreet's online company database. All the basic information you need to know about your competition. But you have to pay for it.

www.bizjournals.com. The free web site for the 41 local business publications that are published by the American City Business Journals. If you are located in one of the cities they cover, it will provide valuable local market information. It also publishes their "book of lists" covering all the various local business categories.

www.dialog.com. A subscription service from one of the world's largest business publishers, using over 600 databases. Very detailed, but expensive. As with all these fee based services, try and access through your public library.

www.reportgalley.com. A free service that allows you to download annual reports from most companies in the United States and worldwide.

MARKET RESEARCH CONSULTANTS

www.bluebook.org. The web site for the U.S. Market Research Organization. Lists members by geography and specialty. Useful if you decide to hire a research consultant for a specific project.

www.guideline.com. A large market research organization offering on-demand research reports tailored to your business and market. Good, but expensive.

MAILING LISTS

Indiscriminately buying mailing lists is not something I would recommend. Very often they are out of date and include people that no longer exist. That's why you get credit cards in the name of your dog. If, however, you feel it might be something you want to try, here are a couple of the most reputable list brokers and managers.

www.directchannel.com

www.directmedia.com

OTHER USEFUL SITES

http://iws.ohiolink.edu/companies/index.htm. This web site was designed as a course aid at Youngstown State and Bowling Green State Universities and is a very useful research guide with tons of links to many other resources. And, it's free.

www.smartbiz.com/sbs/cats/family.htm. Start-up and small business web site.

www.firstgov.gov. Lots of good stuff from the government, including market and statistical research data. You paid for it, why not use it?

www.industrylink.com. Very comprehensive listing of industry web sites.

www.techsavvy.com. If you are in manufacturing, this web site offers a directory of many thousands of companies and millions of products.

www.irin.com. Free annual reports, press releases, and corporate documents.

www.planetbiz.com. If you intend doing business overseas, this is a valuable site that links to tens of thousands of companies in hundreds of countries.

www.prweb.com. Just about every PR release ever written. But searchable. Can be a treasure trove for finding out what others in your business are up to.

BLOGS

Many web-hosting companies and most portals offer blog tools and templates that enable you to get your blog up and running, literally within minutes. Obviously, I will recommend the one that hosts both my blogs.

www.sixapart.com/movabletype. Lots of options and pricing structures. Not expensive, simple to use with preformatted templates. Recommended.

Blogrolls

Put simply, these are listings, or blogs of blogs. Constantly changing, always in turmoil. They are useful if you are looking for interest- and industry-specific blogs.

www.blogarama.com. Useful links and resources to tens of thousands of blogs. Also archived articles and book recommendations about blogging and how to do it right.

www.bloglines.com. A free online service for searching, subscribing, creating and sharing news feeds, blogs, and rich web content. There's no software to download or install. Simply register and you can begin accessing your account.

http://del.icio.us. This site enables you to create and manage collections of links, yours and everyone else's. You can use it to keep links to your favorite articles, blogs, business, research, vendor and customer sites, and a great deal more.

http://top500.feedster.com. Lists the top 500 blogs on a monthly basis. Useful to see what is actually drawing the traffic out there.

www.technorati.com. Huge. Tracking more than 45 million sites and 2.5 billion links. You have to sign up, but it's free. If you can't find it here, it doesn't exist.

SUMMARY

With the amazing growth of online, searchable data resources, there is really no excuse for not being able to access the information you need to make intelligent forecasts and plans about how to best develop your business. Even if you have neither time nor inclination to do it yourself, I have listed where you can find freelancers and consultants who you can hire to do the job for you. It's all out there; you just have to find it. What you then do with it is up to you.

Glossary

AdScam.com. One of two of the world's greatest advertising blogs, www.adscam.typepad.com.

AdHurl.com. The other one.

Above and below the line. Although becoming increasingly blurred, "Above the Line" describes traditional media advertising such as TV, radio, print, billboards, and now cinema. "Below the Line" means direct marketing, sales promotion, sampling, etc. Now with the growth of online, guerilla, viral, word-of-mouth, and other forms of nontraditional advertising, there is really an ever-expanding third category.

Account group. A subset of the agency. The people actually assigned to work on your business. Primarily driven by the same motives (greed) as the larger group, with the exception of the creatives who's driving motivation is to get you to run award-winning work that will guarantee them their next high-paying job.

Added value. Those things you can bring to the table that will differentiate you from the competition. Can be either product or company driven. Avoid smoke and mirrors.

Advertising agency. Whether B2C or B2B focused, this is a collection of people whose primary function in life is to liposuction money out of its clients.

Advertising awards. Although they would vehemently deny it, something most agencies are obsessed with, to the point where many large Madison Avenue agencies employ dozens of people whose sole function is sending stuff to award shows.

Animatic. A rough approximation of what a finished TV spot might look like; used in research; consists of a video of badly drawn visuals and a ripped-off ABBA sound track.

Artwork. The compilation of all the pieces that go into a print ad: Type, photography, logo, etc. This is what they use to make the plates (although they no longer actually make plates, as everything is now digital) that they print from. Don't even think about doing this yourself. Pay through the nose for a specialist.

Audience measurement. Indecipherable stuff the media loves to throw at potential advertisers in an endeavor to prove that the entire universe watches/reads/listens to its media to the exclusion of all others. Approach this hogwash with caution.

Benchmarking. Supposedly identifies how you stand in comparison to your competition. Requires gathering the information necessary to create the communications plan, then being brutally honest with yourself when evaluating it. If it shows you are behind your competition, don't play catch-up, go in a different direction.

Big Dumb Agencies (BDAs). The leviathans of Madison Avenue, who may no longer actually reside on Madison Avenue. Blissfully unaware that "The times, they are a changing." Somewhat akin to the dinosaurs up to their armpits in the primordial swamp as they gaze admiringly at the meteor hurtling toward them.

Brand. Ah, that much loved and abused word, particularly by the Adverati of Madison Avenue who love to bandy it around as the unanswerable reason why clients should unhesitatingly invest millions in "me-too" advertising campaigns that are intrinsically useless and incapable of measurement as to their effectiveness

Brand manager. The poor unfortunate on the client side responsible for a particular line of products who takes lots of stick from her management if sales aren't soaring and lots of aggravation from the agency if she doesn't spend a ton of money and approve imbecilic ad campaigns; a thankless job.

Category. A grouping of similar products aimed at a well-defined market, i.e., hair pieces for geriatric members of Hells Angel chapters.

Change. The most dangerous word in business. Normal people hate change. Business consultants love it. They make money making changes; they make money correcting the foul ups their changes caused. If you're just starting out, change is not a problem because everything is new. If you're trying to turn around an existing business, be careful, very careful, particularly if you run an ad campaign with a promise you can't deliver on.

Circulation. A subset of *audience measurement*. It relates to print media and is based on the sales rather than the number of people actually reading it. Either way, these figures are to be taken with a pinch of salt.

Collateral. No, not the stuff you have to put up to get that loan for the new Ferrari. This is the catchall phrase used in the ad biz for what used to be called in your Granddad's days "ephemera," stuff like brochures, instore displays, ticketing, stationery, even your business cards. It's important because it reflects your company's character; and if it's nice, intelligent, and tasteful, people will be more inclined to do business with you.

Communication. Apart from my emphasis on the development of a communication plan, communication is the single most important thing you can devote your time to if you desire to be successful in your business. It will be the core component of everything you do from advertising to stationery to the signage on your trucks. Fail to communicate, fail in business.

Comparison advertising. Much abused form of TV advertising that is invariably my Oxy-Serbo-Brand versus Brand X. Something rarely indulged in by leading brands, mostly by those playing catch-up. The execution of these spots smacks of desperation and is usually right in the unfortunate viewer's face.

Concept board. Used by most agencies to help sell bad TV ideas to clients. Then used in focus group research to invariably unsell really bad TV ideas to people with nothing better to do than spend hours in a mall sub-basement eating cold pizza and drinking warm soda as a failed psychology major asks them stupid questions about nasal sprays.

Consumer panel. A form of quantitative research that requires you to sign up a bunch of losers, who for less than the price of a warm six-pack of Duff's Brew, will provide you with a nonstop barrage of information on their purchasing patterns. Do you really, truly, cross-your-heart-and-hope-to-die want "insight" from these kinds of people?

Contact report. If and when you work with an agency, this will be a fairly useless piece of paper (or an electronic file) summarizing actions and decisions taken as a result of any meeting (or phone conversation) between the agency and the client. If it is to be of any use, you should receive it within 24 hours of the meeting/conversation. Otherwise, certain overloaded ships will already be heading at full speed towards the rocks.

Cost-per-thousand (CPM). A statistic that has been beaten to death and overly used by BDAs to justify their profligate spending on all kinds of media. Usually punted to clients as the reason why they need to cough up massive amounts of money to be on national TV rather than on match book covers, even though, as the client is the world's number-one manufacturer of giant, evil-smelling stogies, book matches would make far more sense than blowing everything on a couple of episodes of *As the World Turns*.

Direct response (direct marketing). The only form of advertising that is completely accountable, in as much as if the advertising doesn't work the advertiser goes out of business. As I have mentioned throughout the book, Dell is a prime example of how to successfully operate within the constraints of this business model. If you should choose to go this route, be sure to get it right; 'cuz if you don't, there'll be no one else to blame.

Econometrics. At the time of writing, very much a mot du jour in the ad biz. By the time you read this it will no doubt be passé! It means little more than its dictionary definition: "The use of high-order mathematics to establish the existence of statistical relationships between variables." As is usual in higher mathematics, each side of the argument, agency versus client, uses it to kick the crap out of each other. At the end of the day, it's all about creating better advertising.

Flights. Those periods of advertising, irrespective of media, where you concentrate your exposure. Usually three or four weeks on, followed by a few weeks off. I have no idea who first came up with this idea. I also have no idea whether it actually works or not. But as is usual in such a ridiculously capricious business as advertising, it's an accepted practice, because this is what people have always done.

Frequency. Sometime referred to as Opportunities-to-See (OTC.) This is supposedly the number of times that your target audience will be exposed to your advertising. This is fine, until you realize there is no way it can guarantee they will actually see it, let alone be affected by it. As is common with all of advertising's numerous and sometimes baffling metrics, you can play with the various mathematical permutations, but if you aren't saying anything of any interest to your audience, it's an exercise in futility.

Integrated marketing communications (IMC). Ahhh, the much flaunted Holy Grail of every Madison Avenue agency worth its salt. What it is supposed to mean is that all your communication activities—advertising, direct marketing, promotions, online, Web, blog—should have a common theme (something I have hammered away at as a rock solid principle of your ad program throughout this book). Unfortunately, because of the way agencies are structured and the way they measure their incomes, you are much better off making sure that any form of IMC is a result of your efforts.

Market research. There are two kinds of market research: qualitative and quantitative. Qualitative deals with the reasons why people are influenced by advertising and why they prefer certain products and brands. The information is gathered by interviews, either in one-on-one situations or in groups. It is expensive, and in spite of what its proponents would tell you, it is highly unreliable. That's why over 80 percent of new product launches, which have been extensively tested through qualitative research, fail. Quantitative research is simply a formulaic method of collecting data that gives marketers an indication of what consumers' overall preferences for particular categories of products are.

Media. Obviously, these are the choices you have as to where your advertising is going to run. Covered in depth in preceding chapters. Suffice it to say that the traditional media vehicles are rapidly breaking down and you should make yourself constantly aware of new opportunities that will continue to present themselves as better, more effective, and more cost-efficient ways to address your target audience.

Online advertising. This covers everything you do via the internet: web sites, e-mail, blogs, etc. As with everything else you do, it should be integrated into your overall communications plan. Unless you are an expert at writing code, get help with the design side of this; content you can take care of yourself.

Pretesting. Another branch of that all-encompassing, all-smothering discipline known as research. The sole purpose of pretesting advertising is to guarantee that any spark of originality is beaten out of it. As another famous, long dead ad man Bill Bernbach once said, "Anything that is unusual or out of the ordinary will test badly, because the people it is exposed to will have no frame of reference to measure it against."

Production values. This is the reason why the average cost of making a TV commercial fit to be shown on national network television is now in excess of $600,000. Even with relatively simple print ads, it is possible for BDAs to spend tens of thousands of dollars on photography and art work. Good production values can increase the effectiveness of the ad, but it should always be in proportion to the overall budget.

Reach. Also known as Coverage, this is a figure used as part of the justification for a particular media plan. It represents the number of households and individuals reached at least one time during the duration of the program. It does not indicate effectiveness, merely exposure, or Opportunities to See (OTS). The content of the advertising is what will determine its success.

Research. Many books have been written on the subject of advertising research, and many millions of dollars have been spent on it by multinational corporations in an endeavor to gain those unique insights that will give them an advantage over their competition. Most of that money is wasted, which is why, as I've said earlier, 80 percent of new products fail after having passed through lots of research with flying colors. Basically most advertising research falls into two categories: pre and post. Pre can be useful to gather the information that will enable you to create the communications plan and the advertising that flows from it. Testing that advertising via focus groups or interviews is much less useful and often counter productive because of the dangers outlined earlier here. That's why I don't recommend it, plus you can't afford it. Go with your gut. It got you were you are today! Post research is useful because it allows you to not only measure the effectiveness of what you are doing but also to modify and fine tune the program for maximum efficiency. As I have said previously, take a leaf out of the direct marketers' book.

Search engine advertising. If you intend to do a major amount of selling through your web site, it may be worth investing in an optimization program via a search engine. At this stage, you should investigate Google and its AdWords program in which you pay for click-through every time someone comes onto your site via its engine. At the time of writing, some of these programs are starting to get adverse publicity because of dodgy record-keeping. I would advise talking to a consultant before committing to anything.

Share of market. Although usually referring to the big brands found in supermarkets, drug stores, etc., it can also be relevant to your business within your geographic market or within the particular niche you are aiming at. Many advertisers equate their share of market with the amount of money they spend on advertising. This has some validity, but never forget to factor in all the other things that may be influencing your effectiveness in reaching your target audience.

Television ratings. More often known as Gross Rating Points (GRPs). These are what an agency or media buying service will use to justify a particular TV media schedule. A single GRP means a single percent of all homes have their TVs tuned to a particular program. Programs such as *American Idol, Wrestlemania,* and NASCAR racing have very high rating points, which goes to prove something, but I'd rather not get into that right now. To further confuse you, homes that watch multiple programs are counted multiple times. If you get to the stage where you are considering substantial TV advertising, have a media consultant explain it to you.

Writing. The single most important skill to develop if you wish to achieve a successful communications plan and advertising program. Don't write for yourself; write for the person who will be reading it. Be interesting and present the information necessary to make your argument convincing. Keep it concise, which doesn't necessarily mean short, or long. Don't be passive, don't be aggressive, and above all, don't be dumb. Don't bs.

Index